A SNOWBALL'S CHANCE

Philly Fires Back Against The National Media

A SNOWBALL'S CHANCE

From The Writers of

Joe Vallee

Dennis Bakay

Ryan Downs

Matthew J. Goldberg

Billy Vargus

Handbook and Chapter Introductions: Matthew J. Goldberg
All photos by Joe Vallee Sr.
To inquire about or purchase any book photos, contact JosephV985@aol.com
All illustrations by Kaitlin Victoria Brown
kaitlin.victoria.art@gmail.com
www.facebook.com/KaitlinVictoriaArt
Philly2Philly.com has become one of the most personalized sites in the Philadelphia area.
In just 18 months, the site surpassed over 1 million page views.
Visit Philly2Philly.com at: www.philly2philly.com
Facebook: https://www.facebook.com/philly2philly
Twitter: @philly2philly
Philly2Philly.com is a Game Time Media, LLC owned company.

ISBN: 1480100412

ISBN 13: 9781480100411

TABLE OF CONTENTS

ACKNOWLEDGEMENTS

JOE:

Ellen Barkann (Score Marketing & Entertainment), Rob Brooks (Philadelphia Phillies), Rex Gary (Turner-Gary Sports), Jon Evoy, Rich Westcott, Kathi Gillin (Philadelphia Flyers Alumni Association), Cindy Webster (CBS Radio), Rob Kuestner (Comcast SportsNet), ALL of my friends too numerous to mention who encouraged me to see this through, Scott Scioli, Dan Baker, Darren Baker, Billy Staples, Steve Olenski, Greg Olenski, Matt Babiarz and Earl Myers for their contributions, Kaitlin Brown for her amazing sketches, and Frank Olivo, who unknowingly inspired a tale people are STILL talking about all these years later.

The Philadelphia fans- You sometimes set yourself up for those national media guys, but the punishment never truly fits the crime. Keep on keepin' it real, but don't be stupid. We probably don't have enough for another book!

The national media pundits- You all have given me more inspiration than you could have ever imagined.

All of the athletes and broadcasters featured in this book who shared their thoughts and opinions of the greatest sports city in the world with us. Your time and generosity will never be forgotten.

The 2008 Phillies- When times are tough, all I have to do is watch Game 5: Part II of the World Series and all is well with the world, at least for a little while. What you did for an entire city made you eternal legends in this town. Nobody in the Tri-State area will ever forget October 29th 2008 and the greatest Halloween parade ever that followed! (Sorry to rub it in, Nick!)

Brad Lidge, you threw the final pitch which validated most of the sports lives of an entire generation of Philly fans. I've thanked you before, and I'm going to do it again. For you to contribute your thoughts in this book was the icing on the cake for me. You're one of the game's true good guys. Thank you, thank you, thank you!

My fellow co-authors: Downsy, Matt, Billy V and Dennis. It was a crazy, fun, and sometimes tense ride, but it was all for the greater good and I wouldn't trade it for anything. We did it!

My sister Nicky, the REAL writer in the family, whom I constantly bugged at all hours just to get her opinion on how certain chapters were coming together. Not once did you complain. You were always gracious. Thank You!

The best parents in the entire universe: Joe Sr. and Shirley, who continue to encourage me to reach for the golden ring, even in the darkest of times.

DENNIS:

Joe Vallee, for coming up with the awesome idea of "A Snowball's Chance" and for your undying dedication and hard work to a great project.

Ryan Downs, Matt Goldberg, and Billy Vargus for your hard work, attention to detail, and time put into this project.

Everyone from Howard Eskin to Merrill Reese and Dan Baker for their willingness to be so friendly, approachable, and willing to answer our questions for the project. And every single former player, coach, announcer, and local personality who was willing to speak with us, and take part in a wonderful book.

RYAN:

To my late father Larry for watching, playing, and teaching sports to me. You showed me how to enjoy sports and instilled a passion in me that lasts to this day. To my late mother Susan for her strength, courage, and heart of gold. And for not getting too mad when I would throw things at the TV. I miss you both and certainly could never thank you enough.

To my beautiful wife Maria for her constant love and support, specifically during the life of this project while having an infant daughter at home. To my pride and joy Allison; daddy loves you more than you could ever know. To all my family and friends for all of the support through the years.

To my friend Joe for a very inspired and compelling idea. I have enjoyed this journey every step of the way. To Bill, Matt, and Dennis; I truly have enjoyed working with you all on this project, and the finished product is a result of the hard work of each person involved.

To the Reading Phillies for hiring me and giving a teenage kid a taste of daily life at the ballpark; it is still the best job I've ever had. To the 2008 Philadelphia Phillies- you seized the opportunity given and finally ended our misery. In the process, you've managed to keep us all a little more sane. And last, but not least, I thank the Philadelphia sports fans. Often criticized, sometimes misinterpreted, always knowledgeable and passionate. I proudly call myself one. This book's for you…

MATT:

My co-authors Joe, Billy V, Ryan and Dennis for a terrific collaboration; the broadcasters and athletes who made our questions come alive with their great takes; the Philly fans for being so knowledgeable, passionate and never, ever dull and…last but never least…my wife Ruby and son Benny for their love, support and understanding of my great passion for both sports and writing.

BILLY:

I'd like to thank my wife, Sue Serio (weather anchor on Fox 29's "Good Day Philadelphia") for keeping food on the table while I've pursued the enjoyable, but not always profitable ventures of acting and writing.

I'd also like to thank my hands for being so great. I mean, I'd like to thank Freddie Mitchell's hands- as well as all the other hands of the athletes who've provided me and the rest of Philly's fans so many wonderful moments over the years.

PREFACE

I can tell you the exact moment that inspired me to put this book together.

Perhaps all of this was building in my subconscious for quite some time. Nonetheless, all it took was one final moment to put me over the edge, and then it all became so clear. I was surfing the internet like I normally do at night to get material for Philly2Philly.com when this headline caught my eye:

"PHILADELPHIA FLYERS FANS BOO DURING ANTI-CANCER PSA"

Yep, that's all it took. The general premise for this book was a headline I stumbled upon on the internet during one of my legendary all-nighters. In the small crevice of my world, it was the equivalent to Paul McCartney waking up one morning with the words and music to 'Yesterday' already in his head. Now before you think I actually have the audacity to liken myself to one of the Beatles, notice how I said *"small crevice of my world."*

Yes, we threw snowballs at Santa Claus (more on that later), two idiots threw batteries at J.D. Drew (more on that later, too), and have scrapped with opposing players (don't worry, we discuss that as well), but implying that Philadelphia fans booed an announcement speaking out against cancer is downright unacceptable and a new low for sports journalism. I think I can speak for the other guys writing this book and say that we are absolutely offended and disgusted at this notion. Completely below the belt—even for us cold-hearted, barbaric Philly sports fans......

1

Everyone reading this book in some way or another has been affected by this disease. Philly sports fans are no angels, but we do have souls. First off, if you were watching the PSA at the always packed Wells Fargo Center that night in late 2011, you may have been able to hear Sidney Crosby introduce himself before there was any inkling of a cancer PSA. It's been rumored that the Philadelphia National Airport has boos looped into their speaker system the moment he lands in this city (I kid). All jokes aside, it was Crosby who killed the Flyers' Stanley Cup hopes two years in a row back in 2008 and 2009. And oh yeah, Jonathan Toews, who won a Stanley Cup in the very same arena the PSA was being played, was featured in that video, too. Then again, forgive me if the irrational Philly sports fan in me starts making sense.

To know a Philly sports fan is to love a Philly sports fan. It's true that we often take on the personality of our sports teams. If the Phillies win, the sun is shining even on the darkest of days. If the Eagles win on Sunday, it's a very good week. But on the flip side, we've been booing for a long time, because, to be blunt, we've been losing for a long time. Very rarely have we been left as the last ones standing with the championship in our grasp. Then there's the joke that beating a Philly sports team for a championship is like shacking up with the town tramp: Everybody's done it (rim shot!).

1964? Black Friday? Several 3-1 leads the Sixers have blown to the Celtics? Our quarterback throwing up (or not?) in the Super Bowl? The "offsides" call against the Islanders? Claude Lemieux's 40-footer? Johnny Damon stealing two bases on one play? Juan Uribe? The 15-14 game? Joe Carter? The Flyers trading their captain and leading goal scorer to two different teams, only to see them reunite and win the Stanley Cup the following season? Our star first baseman making the last out of the playoffs for two consecutive years and rupturing his achilles in the process? Come on, you can't script this stuff. Even our local competitive thoroughbreds (Smarty Jones) come up short when it matters! Meanwhile, the inventors of these respective sports are scratching their collective heads in utter amazement from the heavens above as to how this is even possible. At times, Philadelphia redefines the impossible, and not in a good way. If there is a way to collapse, our teams usually find a way to do it in excruciating fashion that haunts us for years, or sometimes even half a century.

We are bitter, angry, and passionate all rolled into one. We've earned it, and sometimes actually embrace it. Those boos are from years of anger and frustration. It's our birthright. If you aren't from here, you just don't understand, and chances are you never will. But if you aren't giving it everything you've got while playing in this town, you will be called out for it. We don't take too kindly to slackers around here. In saying that, this is no excuse for ignorance (which sometimes rears its ugly head here and immediately finds a place on ESPN or on blogs across North America).

In Boston, it was the "Curse of the Bambino." In Chicago, it's the "Curse of the Billy Goat." In Philadelphia, there's no love for us: we just lose. There was talk of the Curse of Billy Penn, but we promptly lost two titles in consecutive years despite the fact that the Comcast Building put a statue of Philadelphia's founding father on top of the structure just prior to the Phillies breaking the city's 25-year championship drought. You would think that this city would at least stumble upon a championship before waiting 25 years to get one, but I digress. Sure, maybe the Red Sox did have a curse. In the meantime, their basketball team was beating the crap out of the Sixers almost every year in the 1960's and to a lesser degree in the early 80's, eventually coming home with 17 titles.

At this stage, it doesn't look like we'll ever see the Cubs win a World Series, but Chicago sports fans are at least able to ease the pain with their six NBA titles, a Super Bowl trophy, a World Series trophy from the south side (depending on what kind of Chicago fan you are), and their Stanley Cup, which they won on OUR home ice. Back in 2010, San Francisco Giants' fans were venting how their city was suffering for a title, but they obviously forgot about the Niners' five Super Bowl wins.

What have we (and yes, in Philly we refer to our teams as "we") won since 1983? A World Series title in 2008, and all of the Eagles' yearly salary cap titles. And while we're at it, it took three days to play that damn World Series game for God's sake! Talk about testing somebody's sanity. Were YOU one of the ones at the bar that Monday night crying in your beer that the universe didn't want us to win a title? Were you looking out your window the next day staring at that monsoon wondering when that game was ever going to be played? When in the entire history of sports has **THAT** happened?! Never! And before you New Yorkers go popping off about your championships, if we had almost double the sports teams like you do, we would have won a few more over the years just like you guys. I know, I know, Buffalo and Cleveland haven't won anything since forever, but Philadelphia IS one of the biggest sports markets in the country!

Don't get me wrong, we aren't writing this book claiming that Philly sports fans should be canonized for sainthood in any way. Just as every circus has a clown, every crowd has a few jerks. Whether it's deserved or not (and yes, at times it IS deserved) Philadelphia has always been an easy target for the national media. You know, the guys (and girls) who come into our stadiums once or twice a year and have their finger on the pulse of the city? So much to the point where they just lie in the weeds for one of us to do something stupid and they prance on it like one of Santa's reindeer (You know, Santa, the guy they write about every time they mention a Philly fan?)

Sometimes there's a story behind a story, sometimes they've got it all wrong, and sometimes it's really made out to be a whole lot worse than it is. Any decent, upstanding fan does not condone or tolerate such nonsense on behalf of a few bad apples, and we're here to set the record straight.

Nonetheless, we're not here to declare innocence, but rather to show everybody an exaggerated view from a national media's sports room, followed by our unique perspectives on some of the biggest misconceptions the national media has about Philly sports fans. To support some of our viewpoints, we've recruited the best of the best: Philadelphia athletes, broadcasters, and in one particular example, someone who was actually on the field as one of these incidents was taking place. And it's not like these guys are apologists and homers, either. They call it as they see it.

If you're from the Tri-State Area, this is something you will almost certainly appreciate. If you're an out-of- towner.....well, maybe you'll understand us a little bit better at the end. If you're the national media, well, we really don't care what you guys think. Because someway, somehow, you will twist all of this in the wrong direction and still manage to get Santa Claus thrown into the mix.

So stick around, everybody.

If you leave, you know we're gonna boo.........

Joe Vallee
October 2012

PREMISE FOR THE SECRET HANDBOOK

For quite some time, we have witnessed the type of coverage that Philadelphia teams—and especially us rabid, long-suffering Philly fans—have been treated to (or should we say, subjected to?) by the national media.

We readily acknowledge that we're no angels, but why is it that every instance of fan rowdiness seems to make national headlines if it happens in Philly and barely sees the light of day if it happens elsewhere?

Why are we portrayed as the only fan base who boos its own players mercilessly when our own eyes and ears detect the same type of behavior by fans in other cities? Now, we may boo a little *better*, but even so.

Why is it that media members from Boston to Honolulu paint Philly as the worst town for fans of other teams to visit and the worst place for professional athletes to play and reside in?

And why is it that all media members from Florida to Alaska still resurrect the memory of a day in 1968—44 years ago, and counting—when we had the nerve to boo Santa Claus and pelt him with snowballs? And why is this episode mindlessly revisited as if we do this every single year as some kind of bizarre, pagan Philly Christmas tradition?

WHY? It's as if everybody who covers sports—and news reporters, too—outside of the Delaware Valley received some kind of secret memo requiring them to rip Philly fans. Perhaps, there is even a handbook that is circulated to all media members—print, electronic and bloggers alike—that they must follow in order to keep their jobs. This may sound ridiculous, but how ridiculous is it that 44 years later we are still being lambasted for supposedly running Santa Claus out of town with boos and snowballs?

With this premise in mind, within these pages is what the memos from such a secret handbook to national media members would look like. And as true Philly guys, we offer our own rather spirited rebuttals to all of the myths and misconceptions that have been perpetuated at our expense.

For quite some time, we have taken our share of abuse from the national media. And, there's only a snowball's chance in hell that we will continue to take it without firing back.

Matt Goldberg
October 2012

INTRODUCTION TO THE SECRET HANDBOOK

CONGRATULATIONS!

You have embarked upon an exciting career in the national sports media. You are now a member of *the fourth estate*, if you will, and with that position of influence comes a boatload of responsibility.

As a member of the national media, you have the responsibility to be impartial, fair, balanced and objective. All those good things. That is your sacred oath. At the same time, you have a responsibility to those for whom you work to bring in good ratings. High ratings lead to revenue and in this push for ratings, sometimes objectivity must give way to accepted conventions and stereotypes.

So, which master will you serve: fairness and objectivity or pandering to the lowest common denominator for easy ratings?

In answering this question, we invite you to consider the following guiding principles of this handbook:

1. It is not wise to overestimate the intelligence of your readers and viewers. If in doubt on this important point, just look at the successful Presidential candidates of the last 50 years or so.

2. Taking the time to actually think outside the box about a given event may hinder your ability to be the first and the loudest to report on it. It is also not wise to assume this risk by overthinking. Or thinking at all.

In this handbook, we wish to apply these two principles to the coverage of Philadelphia sports fans. As you may know, Philadelphia is the fourth largest media market in the country. When it comes to sports, Philadelphians are well known to be the loudest, most obnoxious, most dangerous fans in the nation. We would say *in the world*, but there *is* World Cup soccer. Well, it's close.

With our two guiding principles in mind, it is vital that you preserve this image whenever and wherever you can. How can you manage this?

Do not worry. This handbook will give you the tools to do exactly that, on a point by point basis.

Once again, congratulations on your new position with the national sports media, and let the ripping of Philadelphia continue.

1

REMEMBER, PHILLY FANS BOOED AND PELTED SANTA CLAUS WITH SNOWBALLS

Jolly Old Saint Nick. Kris Kringle. Father Christmas.

By any of these names, Santa Claus is one of the most beloved characters worldwide. Santa is always greeted with joy; he is the embodiment of selfless giving—the spirit of the holidays.

Did Philadelphia ever get the memo?

Only in Philly can this virtuous icon of pure goodness be lustily booed by tens of thousands of mean-spirited fans. It happened at a Philadelphia Eagles game in the 1960s right at historic Franklin Field. Not only that, but they pelted this poor man with snowballs.

Media members: It is important to refer to this incident as if it happened every single year in Philadelphia. Poor Santa; I still can't believe it.

"Those famously churlish Philly fans can't hide behind the urban legends. The truth is out there: They simply booed Santa Claus."

-ASSOCIATED PRESS, 2005

RESPONSE: JOE VALLEE

And in the beginning...........Philly fans threw snowballs at Santa Claus.

Yes, if there was ever a biblical passage which involved ripping Philadelphia sports fans, that is exactly how Genesis 1:1 would begin.

It's as sure as trick-or-treating on Halloween and Fourth of July fireworks. Every time our fan base is portrayed in a less than flattering manner by the national media, we hear the same old song and dance time and time again.

Did you ever break a window or drop one of your mom's plants as a kid? Sure you did, but have you been constantly reminded of it decades after the fact? And if you were, you would probably think somebody needs to let it go and get over it, wouldn't you?

Exactly.

You can find any article online that references one of the following incidents we will discuss in this book. If you happen to scroll down to the comments section afterwards, you can bank on a Santa reference almost 100% of the time, often from some uninformed fan who has never even set foot in the state of Pennsylvania let alone one of Philadelphia's sports arenas. It never fails.

In fact, it almost seems if you asked someone who lived outside of Philadelphia in 1968 what some of the top news stories were that year, it's almost a sure bet that one of them would be sports related—and I'm not referring to *The Year of the Pitcher* if you catch my drift.

I pride myself on keeping an open mind and being able to observe the opinions of other people from an unbiased standpoint. In saying that, the Santa reference is so played out that I can no longer take anyone seriously who uses it. From a sportswriter's perspective, it's the laziest form of journalism you can find. They never get tired of writing about this, but they can't find something new to rip us about.

So in a way, I guess you could say this story kind of........snowballed.

Frankly, we are beyond fed up of hearing about this in our city and it needs to be buried and put to rest once and for all. There's a story behind every story, and Philly fans pelting snowballs at Santa Claus is no exception.

So that's why we sought out the one man on this planet who was behind the beard for the single most overblown incident of sports fandom in history: Santa Claus himself, Mr. Frank Olivo.

Yes, we know this story has been told in other publications, but we got down to the nitty gritty with Olivo, a lifelong resident of the Tri-State area. The good-natured Olivo clearly remembers the mitigating circumstances of December 15th, 1968. In fact, you could even argue he was almost Santa-like when recalling the event. Hey, Santa doesn't lie. He knows when you've been bad or good!

"It was something I did every year for the last game of the year," says Olivo, in regards to donning the colors of Mr. Kringle. *"There were eight of us in the family and we were season ticket holders. Our family had them all the way back from the early, early days. My two uncles were there in 1948 when the Eagles won the championship. That was at Connie Mack Stadium, and the fans came on the field to help shovel the snow to get the game started."*

The fact is that Olivo could have streaked naked across the field for all that mattered on that winter day in 1968. Either way, Philadelphia sports and its fans would have come out on the wrong side of a lucky penny.

One of the reasons why old Kris Kringle got pelted was because, to put it mildly, the Eagles absolutely stunk in 1968—except for when they really needed to stink. A two-game winning streak late in the season saw them blow any chance they had at landing the number one pick in the

NFL Draft. The Eagles eventually picked third and landed Leroy Keyes, a solid college player from Purdue who finished second in the Heisman Trophy voting that season. However, Keyes only played a handful of seasons in the NFL. The number one pick went to the Buffalo Bills, who picked the actual winner of the Heisman Trophy, running back O.J. Simpson from USC. You couldn't even count on the Eagles to lose when they should have lost!!

"That was a big part of it," says Olivo, in response to the fans extra surly demeanor during that fateful day at Franklin Field. *"The other was the fact that Joe Kuharich was the head coach, and at that time he was given an unprecedented 15-year contract. He was a terrible head coach and people didn't like him. Because of the weather and all the other things that happened that year, it all seemed to come to a head that day."*

Olivo wasn't joking about Kuharich. After a respectable head coaching career at Notre Dame, Kuharich joined the Birds in 1964 and immediately traded future Hall of Famers Sonny Jurgensen and Tommy McDonald. In eleven seasons as an NFL coach, Kuharich only had two winning seasons (one where he was oddly enough named "Coach of the Year" with the Redskins in 1955) and one .500 season for an overall record of 58-81-3.[1] Ironically, Kuharich passed away on January 25th, 1981: the day the Eagles lost Super Bowl XV to the Oakland Raiders.

So when you factor in both Simpson and Kuharich, Philly sports fans would have taken the heat for years no matter what happened during that game—and I think you all know what I'm referring to here. Chances are we'd have to find a whole new title for this book. I'll leave it at that.

We didn't even get into the fact that Olivo technically wasn't even supposed to be on the field that day. A massive snowstorm (hence, the snowballs) that weekend prevented the Eagles' usual Santa from participating in the *festivities.*

"The Santa they hired used to come on a float. I believe he was from the Atlantic City area and came from Zaberer's restaurant (a popular restaurant with multiple locations near the Jersey shore for decades). Because of the snowstorm, he couldn't get there and he cancelled. The entertainment director named Bill Mullen saw me in the stands with

the Santa suit because we used to get there real early. He came up and asked me if I could help them out and fill in and be their half time Santa Claus. I said 'sure I'll do it.' I told them I didn't have a bag, just a suit, but they said they would take care of that and would be delighted if I would do it. They told me to come down onto the field two minutes before the end of the first half and they would be waiting for me on the track. When I got there, he told me what they wanted me to do."

"The first sign of a hostile environment was when the gun sounded, the team ran off the field and the snowballs started coming at them. Joe Kuharich was covered in snow. I realized the fans were just showing their disgust, but I didn't expect it to carry over to me. The Eagles had a 50-piece band back then. They told me the band and cheerleaders were going to form a column from one goal post to the other goal post."

"When they played 'Here comes Santa Claus,' that was my cue to walk down the center of the column and wave to both sides of the stadium, go down to the other end zone and get back on the field so you don't interfere with the band. As soon as I started walking, the booing started. The snowballs didn't start until I hit the end zone and got off the field, so I was in range."

And contrary to worldwide belief, it was not the entire stadium throwing snowballs at good ol' Saint Nick.

"The snowballs were from the people in the lower levels," recalls Olivo. *"They were low enough to reach the field. I had fake eyebrows and they were knocked off. I couldn't tell from how far they were coming from, but I got hit pretty good."*

Despite the unruly fan behavior displayed in those brief moments that seem to have eternally defined the Philly fan base, it's not like Olivo was permanently scarred, emotionally or physically. In fact, it was just the opposite. Not only did he return to his seat without further incident, but Olivo insists the entire event was not taken seriously whatsoever. By the Philadelphia fans, or by local news outlets.

"No, not at all!," swears Olivo. *"It was all in good fun when it was happening! I was playing along to the crowd and the fans when I was on the crowd. I was making motions with my fist. I told one guy he wasn't*

going to get anything for Christmas, but it was all in good fun. I 'got it.' I understood. It was a small story locally. They played it on the news that night, but that's all. It didn't come to the forefront until Howard Cosell showed it, and then with each next big incident, it blossomed from there."

Until that day in December 1968, Olivo had never recalled the Philadelphia fans being portrayed in a negative light by the media. And if you really break things down after all these years, it's possible that if a journalist less prominent than Cosell reported this story, then maybe this whole ordeal doesn't still have legs almost half a century later. In fact, Olivo contends there were fans in attendance that day who committed crazier acts than throwing snowballs, which people fail to remember or discuss.

"Of course, I was only 20 years old at the time, but there were never any incidents. This (the Santa Claus incident) was not a vicious incident, it was a funny thing while it was done. People did crazy things that day. One guy climbed a flag pole and put the flag upside down. Another got someone to fly a plane with a banner flying over the stadium that said "Joe must go" (in reference to Eagles coach Joe Kuharich). *The Philadelphia Eagles fans were part of a very loyal football crowd. They were frustrated from putting up with a bad coach and bad players."*

Furthermore, Olivo, who is still a diehard Philly sports fan, laughs at the notion that his opinion about the nature of Philly sports fans changed after that day at Franklin Field.

"Are you kidding?! I AM a Philly sports fan. That's what I am!" exclaims Olivo. *"I understood what was going on. I had the passion."*

There are other rumors associated with Olivo that day, including 1) He had a horrible Santa outfit and 2) he was intoxicated.

"Not true," insists Olivo on both accounts. *"They've said that I was a bad Santa Claus, the outfit was bad, I was drunk. All lies. For everything that went with it, that was a very good top notch Santa outfit. As far as the drinking, I went to the games with my aunts and uncles. I was 20 years old. There were no drinkers. You went from church on Sunday morning to my grandmother's house where we all*

met, and from there we would go to Franklin Field. We never even drank beer during the games. That was very rare. I didn't at all. They wouldn't let me. I was underage. Like I said, I was 20. You had respect for your elders back then and you didn't even ask for it. The people that say this are the people who weren't even there. Some of these people weren't even born in 1968. They go by these stories that they hear."

"I got a letter from the Eagles organization thanking me for being Santa. They asked me if I would be interested in doing it again. I told them no, because it there wasn't snow, they would throw beer bottles! I may have looked scrawny, but I was 20. I had to wear a pillow back then for the stomach. I don't need it now! Naturally, I didn't go there prepared to be on stage. I went there to sit in the stands and have fun."

As fate would have it, one of the spectators in attendance was a future Eagle and the inspiration for the Walt Disney Pictures' film *Invincible*: 22-year old Vince Papale. Papale, who is still an Eagles season ticket holder, concurs with Olivo.

"I saw this skinny guy go out there. He claims to the media that he wasn't intoxicated, and I believe him," says Papale of Olivo. *"However, he wasn't what the fans had expected Santa Claus to be like, nor was the team out there expected to be the team that they wanted. It was a cold and bitter day, and I'm sure a lot of people were using 'something' to take away the cold, so the fans took their wrath out on old Santa. The stadium was full, but just a few knuckleheads do something really dumb and stupid, and forty years later you still hear 'Remember, they're the fans who threw snowballs at Santa Claus.'"*

As much as this story has helped national journalists support their families for decades, the first time Olivo even discussed what happened was years later in a random conversation.

"After I got married, I was talking with my next door neighbor during football season and that moment came up. When I told him that I was the guy in the Santa outfit, he was in shock. I had known him for about five years, and he couldn't believe it. He said 'I have to tell my friends at work I live next door to you. You're a celebrity!' I would hear things like that."

Unfortunately, just like many of history's greatest moments, the event itself is left to the memory of the people who were there to witness it firsthand. There is very little if any footage of Olivo dodging those soft wet ice projectiles.

"I used to cut hair for a living, and one of the clients named John Heinz (not to be confused with the late US Senator from Pennsylvania) *who came into the shop was a guy who worked in production at NFL films. This is before it became such a big production. He was getting a trim, and he found out through a conversation in the shop that I had been Santa Claus. At this point it had been about ten years later, so when John sees me, he says 'When things are slow, we run that film just for laughs. I'm going to get a copy of that film and give it to you.' I told him I would love to have a film clip of that. Unfortunately, we never saw him again after that day. The following week, I'm watching Monday Night Football, and Howard Cosell made an announcement that John passed away of a heart attack. I never got the film, and now it's lost. There's just a ten second clip of me just walking on the field with no snowballs being thrown."*

Despite the fact that Philly fans have been raked over the coals for over the last 40-plus years, Olivo never thought that something as simple as wearing a Santa outfit to an Eagles game would stay with him the rest of his life. But when all is said and done, he would do it all over again.

"In a heartbeat," says Olivo. *"Because it was snow. I don't know if I'd do it now because they might throw bottles,"* Olivo laughs. *"Back then, it was no big deal. The day it happened, it wasn't that big of a deal at the stadium. It became a big deal that night because of Howard Cosell and his national show. When it came to the Eagles game, he showed the highlights of Santa Claus and it became a national story. It really wasn't that big of a deal here. Because of other incidents that took place with the national media over the years, the story never died. 'Well what do you expect from Philly fans, they even threw snowballs at Santa.' I think that's what gave the Philly fans their reputation."*

"I'm one of the most famous people in the country from that reference and nobody knows my name! I'm half a comedian anyway. I always wanted to be the entertainer. Even now, I get a kick out of it. I enjoy it.

How many people can have something like this happen to them in their lifetime? They'll be talking about this even long after I'm dead!"

When you really think about it, Philly sports fans and Santa Claus are literally on opposite ends of the likability spectrum. Santa is universally loved, while Philadelphia sports fans aren't exactly known for their sunny demeanor.

"Santa Claus is an icon for giving, greatness, and joy. Now, the 10 or 15 people who were acting like children forever became the face of all the fans of Philadelphia, and that's how people perceive us," says Papale. *"A few knuckleheads do something really dumb and stupid, and forty years later you still hear 'Remember, they're the fans who threw snowballs at Santa Claus.'"*

Papale hit the nail on the head. Usually it's a single individual or a small group of idiots who do something stupid. However, this small number of fans doesn't define the entire fan base, but those two to ten always happen to be some of the dumbest human beings to ever be allowed to attend a sporting event and it gives everybody a bad name. We are a target, and the fans (95% of them being upstanding, hard-working individuals) cringe every time a handful of boneheads do something that is going to make the papers, ESPN, or some national forum.

Eytan Shander has a unique perspective. As a former talk show host in Philadelphia and current host on Sirius' MAD DOG Radio, he interacts with fans in the City of Brotherly Love as well as those from around the country. It was while working in this capacity that Shander heard yet another example of the lame comments from national known broadcasters. This time, it was while watching the San Diego feed of a Phillies-Padres game with longtime nationally respected veteran announcer Dick Enberg doing the play by play:

"I'm working in the newsroom, we've got about eight or nine TVs. The Padres series was in Philly, and there was some (reaction from) the crowd and something happened, and it wasn't anything major. Might've been a strikeout or not running a ball out..not something that would even be talked about in a game recap. I was amazed that the color analyst brought it up. Immediately Enberg references 'You know this is the same crowd that booed Santa Claus.' And I thought 'How lazy can

you be?' Especially a guy who is so well traveled and covered so many things. This was on the Padres TV broadcast. If it's some 25 year-old kid who's just been called up from Triple-A and he's just nervously laughing it off, I may be able to understand, but a guy like Enberg?"

"When people in the newsroom were laughing, I asked them, 'Do you know when it actually happened?' They had no idea it was so long ago, and it's a continued stereotype and imposition that's continually placed on Philadelphia. It's just lazy. In every city in the country we give the national media something here or there, so why do you need to go back to that?'"

As a local talk show host in Philadelphia, 94 WIP's Marc Farzetta always interacts with Philly fans. Farzetta also works behind the scenes for NBC TV, and gets exposed and often subjected to many Santa Claus references.

"I was in Baltimore over the weekend of the Preakness, hanging out with the NBC crew. We were just hanging out, drinking beers and eating pizza and one guy said, 'Oh you're from Philadelphia, your fans are assholes,' mentions Farzetta. "Anyway, he said 'Your fans are assholes, they booed Santa Claus.' My response was, 'That was forty years ago.' And he said, 'No, it was five years ago.' He was confusing that with the batteries and J.D. Drew."

To this day, Olivo can't conceive why nobody has been able to stop talking about this, despite the fact that the event happened almost half a century ago!

"It hasn't died and that's what's amazing after all these years," says Olivo. *"That's because of the national media bringing it up every time something happens here. We used to belong to the Eagles Booster Club, and every year we would go on a trip, maybe to New York or Washington. The New York crowd was always more vile than here."*

So the moral of the story is, if Frank Olivo—the prime target of the most infamous snowball assault in sports history—thought all of this was a good-natured joke, then why won't the national media just leave it alone and move on?

The next time someone mentions this, and it's winter time, they'd better duck.

2

PHILLY FANS NEVER APPRECIATED THE BRILLIANCE OF ANDY REID

Can you believe these Philadelphia Eagles fans?

They had the good fortune to have Andy Reid as their head coach for 14 years, and all he ever did was win, win, win. They were contenders every single year and won countless playoff games. On top of that, they appeared in five championship games.

Not only is Reid one of the greatest winners in the game, but he is also a downright charming man who loved these ingrates with a passion all these years. Now that the fans have gotten their wish and run him out of town, will they treat his new successor, Chip Kelly, any better? Think again. These fans were the same ones that underestimated the genius that was Rich Kotite, and sent him packing.

None of this should surprise you, national media members. Eagles fans even tried to run Santa Claus out of town.

"Fire Andy. It's not a new mindset in Philadelphia, by any means. People have wanted Reid fired since 2005, the year after Philadelphia lost the Super Bowl. Heck, some people in Philadelphia wanted Reid fired right after he lost the Super Bowl, and many of those fans haven't stopped hoping for it to happen since then."

-DAN LEVY (NATIONAL LEAD WRITER) BLEACHER REPORT
NOVEMBER 29TH, 2011

RESPONSE: BILLY VARGUS

There is actually one partially true point in all of that. Andy Reid is a good and decent man. That is, if you're fortunate enough to get to know him a little, as I have. He is a class act, and when his 29-year-old son died during training camp in 2012, Reid decided to go ahead and coach the team's first preseason game less than a week later; during the game, he put a message on the scoreboard in which he thanked "Eagles fans and our Philadelphia community" for their outpouring of support. The fans responded by chanting *"Andy! Andy! Andy!"* in unison. So Andy is a good man, the Philadelphia fans can be very gracious at times, and the criticisms that come his way are all about football, and not personal or vindictive.

But on December 31st, 2012, it was shown, once again, that Philly fans know more about their team than the so-called experts in the national media. That's the day Reid was fired, less than 24 hours after his team had concluded a 4-12 season in which Reid's years of bad decision making completely caught up with him. But anyone paying close attention could have seen the gradual demise of his team over the last several years. (That, of course, precludes most of the national media, whose "expert" analysis consists mostly of looking at win-loss records, oblivious to the downward trend that had been going on for years.) Certainly, many Eagles fans had been calling for Reid's firing the last few years, but the collective outcry became strongest in November of 2011, when the fans screamed *"Fire Andy"* in unison after a poorly managed loss to New England. The national media puffed up its collective chest and announced that Eagles fans didn't know what they were talking about, proclaiming Reid a great coach and insisting he should be brought back in 2012. And when the team's dismal performance in 2012 proved the fans right, the national media guys suddenly became invisible, neither talking about the Eagles on their national shows or coming on local Philly stations to explain how such a "great coach" could have put together a team that not only lost games, but in the process showed no heart, no tenacity and no clue.

As for the network announcers covering the games, they recited each week the same mantra that "if Andy gets fired, he'll quickly get a job somewhere else," without ever attempting to explain how his team became so bad that he would have to be fired in the first place. Only Cris Collinsworth, doing the color commentary during a Sunday night game against Dallas, made an attempt, stating that it was "just one of those years." He made the statement during a soliloquy in which he praised Reid, even as the final seconds were ticking off in the Eagles' eighth straight defeat. At that point, the Eagles record was 3-9, but the previous season they had been 4-8 at the same juncture, so how could anyone possibly say it was "one" of those seasons?

But most folks in Philly knew they were watching the steady demise of the franchise. For 14 years, Philly fans watched Reid make constant coaching mistakes, including never-ending issues with clock management and wasted timeouts, an inability to make in-game adjustments, a refusal to run the ball no matter how advantageous it might be, and a defensive philosophy that caused him to prefer small, undersized performers who cannot stop the run.

And there was nothing more frustrating than watching him do it for 14 years and seeing how he refused to learn from those mistakes, repeating them time and again, year in and year out. Actually, there was one thing more frustrating, and that was listening to Andy's news conferences after the game, and hearing him say, for the ten-thousandth time, *"It's my responsibility. I've gotta do a better job. I've gotta do better at putting my players in position to make plays."* And everyone listening knew that he would come out in the ensuing game and do exactly the same things that helped him get beat in this one.

It's for that reason that Philly fans considered Reid "arrogant." It's not about his personal "charm," but his utter refusal to change or adjust. Maybe a better word would be "stubborn." To win NFC Championship games and Super Bowls, you've got to be a very good coach in all phases of the game. During his 14 years as head coach of the Eagles, Reid did well enough to get to several championship games, (and one Super Bowl), but not well enough to actually *win* them. His teams were 1-5 in NFC Championship Games and Super Bowls combined.

And then, in his final few seasons, things really began to unravel. The Eagles didn't win a playoff game from 2008 to 2012. Reid had "jumped the shark" because of his refusal or inability to change and adapt after the rest of the league caught up to him.

The consistent theme throughout is that Reid undermined his own teams by being unwilling to run the ball, and always relying too heavily on the passing game. Meanwhile, Reid's lack of respect for the importance of the run game also infused his approach to defense. The result was other teams usually ran at will against the Eagles. It's a combination that cost his teams dearly throughout the years.

In today's world, NFL teams often crunch all sorts of numbers, trying to find any key statistic that will help them win games. But no team will ever find a stat more compelling than this: when LeSean McCoy carried the ball 20 times or more in a game in 2012, the Eagles won 100% of the time. When McCoy did not carry 20 times or more, they lost 100% of the time. They were 3-0 when he did, 0-9 when he didn't. (He missed 4 games with an injury.) The most shocking thing about these numbers is that Reid chose the losing option—not giving McCoy 20 carries—three times as often as he chose the winning option, 9-3.

But it gets even more mind-boggling: The Eagles actually started the season by winning three of their first four games, and their running game was a big part of that. In their first four games, they were 3-0 when McCoy carried 20 times and lost the only time he didn't. But did Reid sit down, look at the numbers and say, "Hey, from now on, we have to try to get McCoy at least 20 carries every game?" No, he chose to go the other way, and lost the next game. And the next. And the next. And the next. And the next. And the next. Six straight losses trying to do things his way, and at no point did he ever learn and resolve to go back to running the ball more. And his team went from being 3-1 to being 3-7 (with McCoy in the lineup), and their season was over.

And while the national media was unable to explain the Eagles sudden drop-off, the local media questioned Reid after every game about his lack of running the ball. So if Reid was somehow unaware that he was neglecting the run game, he had no one to blame but himself.

And remember, we're talking about number of carries here, not total yards. The coach may not be able to control how effective the running game is, but he can be disciplined enough to stick with it even if it's not working early on, knowing that he is dominating the time of possession, keeping the ball out of the hands of opposing offenses, and waiting for that moment when McCoy, one of the shiftiest backs in the entire NFL, will eventually explode with a big run.

I realize, of course, that I am oversimplifying things a little. There were occasional games where Reid did try to run early, fell behind by a significant margin and then went into pass-pass-pass mode. One such game came against New Orleans, when McCoy rolled up 101 yards *in the first half;* unfortunately, the Eagles defense allowed the Saints to run even more rampant, as no-names Chris McCoy, Pierre Thomas and Mark Ingram ran around and through them for 106 yards on only 10 carries, helping the Saints build a big lead. But the inability of the Eagles to *stop the run* is also a result of Reid's disdain for the importance of the ground game, as we shall discuss later.

Making the situation even more difficult to stomach is that this was a classic case of *same stuff, different day,* as Reid's failure to run the ball was an Achilles heel that never healed.

The previous year, in 2011, he probably cost his team four wins. Week 2 vs. Atlanta, when McCoy carried only 18 times and the Eagles lost by four points; Week 4, when McCoy had nine carries and they lost to San Francisco by one point, 23-24; the next week, when McCoy carried 11 times and they lost to Buffalo by seven; Week 9, when McCoy carried 16 times and they lost to Chicago by six; and Week 10, when McCoy carried 14 times and they lost to Arizona 17-21. We're not even including an 18-point loss to New England when McCoy carried only 10 times, because it could be argued that the Eagles abandoned the run because they were way behind. (Although the fact is, Reid started that game in his usual pass-happy way, throwing on 11 of his first 14 plays. And that was with his backup QB, Vince Young.)

The five games we cite here were all decided by less than a touchdown; they were eminently winnable games if Reid had made better use of his star running back. And here again, there's a statistical probability to back up that claim: When McCoy carried less than 20 times, the Eagles were 3-7. When he carried 20 or more, they were 4-1. They were 5-1 in games when the running backs (as a group) had 25 or more carries. So if Reid had run more in each of those games, it's statistically viable to suggest they could have won all five, in which case they would've finished 13-3. If the Eagles had won four of those five, they'd have been 12-4. Even winning just three of the five, the team would have finished 11-5. Instead, they were 8-8.

I'm sure some Reid supporters will point out that he ran the ball more than ever in 2011, but there were still too many times when he simply failed to utilize the running game. It reached rock-bottom in Week 4 against San Francisco when McCoy ended up with just nine carries in the entire game, while the 49ers gashed the Eagles defense, rolling up 164 yards on the ground. The Eagles lost the game, prompting fans (and the local media) to begin screaming for Reid to wake up and make better use of his best player, but the following week McCoy carried just 11 times.

Naturally, the Eagles lost that game, too. With the whole town now writing to websites and newspapers (in addition to bombarding the radio talk show airwaves), screaming at Reid (and offensive coordinator Marty Mornhinweg) to run the ball, the Eagles gave it to McCoy 28 times in Week 6—and they won. The following game, they gave McCoy the rock 30 times—and they won again. So did Reid finally "get it?" Of course not. Even when Reid made an adjustment, his heart wasn't in it, and he couldn't keep doing it for long before he reverted back. The next week he went back to his pass-happy ways, giving McCoy just 16 carries—and lost. The following week? Just 14 carries, as they lost yet again.

The worst part is, Eagles fans all knew it was coming. We *knew* Andy Reid would revert back, that he would not continue to run the ball, no matter how much success he had. It's become abundantly clear over the years—it seemed like he would rather lose than change.

Again, the 2011 failure makes it more unbelievable that he did not learn his lesson in 2012. Over the two seasons, the Eagles were 7-1 (an .875 win percentage) when McCoy carried 20 times, and 3-16 when he didn't (a .158 win percentage). Those numbers are too consistent to be a fluke. And again, Reid chose the losing option more than two-thirds of the time.

Of course, I can almost hear the Reid supporters echoing what's become a catch-phrase around the NFL: "But it's a passing league, now!" Yes, passing totals continue to rise, but the correlation between passing and winning does not. In 2011, the NFL set a record for most 400-yard passing performances; 16 different QBs threw for 400 or better. Their team's record in those games? Just 6-10.

But as we've seen, the correlation between running and winning is, and always has been, a strong one. In fact, Reid proved it himself during the one season that he actually was willing to change. It was 2003, and after the Eagles started out by losing three of their first five games, Reid began to emphasize the running game with the three-headed monster of Duce Staley, Brian Westbrook and Correll Buckhalter. The team ripped off nine straight wins. They finished the regular season with a record of 12-1 in games where the backs carried at least 20 times, while they were 0-3 in games when the backs carried fewer than 20. The Eagles ended up in the 2003 NFC Championship Game. In that game, Reid was willing to run, as his backs carried 26 times. However, the Panthers were even more willing, running the ball *40* times themselves in defeating the Birds, 14-3.

Otherwise, the former Eagles coach never strayed too far from his pass-happy ways. Many times over the years, after yet another Eagles loss that could have and should have been a win, I would ask Andy, *"You had success when you ran the ball. Why didn't you keep running it?"*

And he would always answer, *"Well, in hindsight I probably should've run it more."* And then he'd go out the following week and run it *even less.* And the same question would beget the same answer, proving that *"those who cannot learn from history are doomed to repeat it."* (This quote apparently was first uttered by George Santayana, although it's sometimes attributed to Winston Churchill or Ben Franklin. Certainly it wasn't coined by Andy Reid.)

After I departed as sports anchor on Fox 29, I was no longer in a position to ask the coach about his refusal to run the ball, but others did, and received the same-ol' lame-ol' response. I heard a clip of Mike Missanelli of Philly radio station 97.5 FM The Fanatic asking Reid why he hadn't run the ball more after an Eagles loss, and Reid giving the exact same answer: *"Well, in hindsight, I probably should've."* Tired of Reid's admissions of failure that never resulted in change, the station turned the quote into a drop (a quick, taped sound bite that can be dropped into any conversation).

This raises another question that continually befuddles Eagles fans: How can a coach admit, time after time, that he failed—yet retain his job? Over the years, it became laughably routine to hear Reid say after every loss, *"I've got to do a better job."* Or *"I've got to do better at putting my players in position to make plays."* Or, *"In hindsight, I probably should have."* We all wondered how long we'd keep our jobs if we so constantly acknowledged that we had screwed up.

Those failures not only hurt the Eagles in numerous games each season, but cost them playoff wins and potential Super Bowl appearances. We saw him blow a sure shot at the Super Bowl in January, 2003. That year, everything seemed to favor the Eagles as they prepared for the NFC Championship Game against Tampa Bay; the Bucs were 0-6 lifetime in playoff games on the road, and the game was being played in Philly. The forecast called for a cold day, and Tampa's record was 1-21 when the temperature was under 40 degrees.

Then, on the second play from scrimmage, Eagles running back Duce Staley took the ball 20 yards to the house, the Eagles had a lead, and the crowd was in an absolute frenzy. So what did Reid do? Come back and keep pounding the rock with Staley until the Bucs proved they could stop it? No, as always, Reid stopped himself. He seemed to forget that Staley was even on the field. The Eagles failed to score another touchdown the entire game, as Reid called his usual pass-happy offense, throwing 49 times, despite the fact that QB Donovan McNabb was still somewhat gimpy as he continued his recovery from a broken ankle earlier in the season. What made it even more galling is that the passing game just wasn't working. But as Eagles fans have seen so many times, when the passing game isn't working, Reid called passes all the more, hoping to get into a rhythm. This means that even though the running game was working, he abandoned it.

On the other hand, if the running game didn't work early on, he abandoned it. So either way, Reid usually ended up throwing the ball too much and into the teeth of the opposing defense, which knew he was going to throw too much. Such was the case in that fateful NFC Championship game. McNabb ended up completing 26 of 49 for 243 yards, an average of 4.96 yards per play.

Meanwhile, the Eagles running game managed *the incredibly high average* of 7.6 yards per rush. Problem is, Staley only got to run the ball 13 times, and his backups, Brian Westbrook and Dorsey Levens, had a total of five carries. What kind of coach calls twice as many passes as running plays, when his quarterback is being hounded and harassed by the pass rush, and his running game is magnificent? And what better way to slow down the pass rush of Simeon Rice and the other guys who were pinning their ears back and going after the QB, than to gash them a few times with some running plays and make them think twice?

You'd think maybe Reid would have learned something from the team's loss in the previous NFC Championship Game in January of 2002. The Eagles were facing the Rams, whose coach, Mike Martz, is the only play-caller in the NFL who is as remotely pass-happy as Reid. Even though Martz had "The Greatest Show on Turf," one of the most prolific passing offenses in NFL history, he was willing to make the adjustment when he went head-to-head with the Eagles and Reid. The Eagles led 17-13 at the half, but then in the second half, Martz came out and handed the ball off to his running back Marshall Faulk for *seven straight plays.* Martz completely changed his style, and in doing so changed the game, as Faulk ended up carrying 31 times for 159 yards, leading the Rams to a come-from-behind win and a berth in the Super Bowl, while Reid and the Eagles went home. So that makes two times in two years that Reid got outcoached with a chance to go to the Super Bowl on the line.

Then there is the time he actually made it to the Super Bowl, only to have his philosophy betray him again. In Super Bowl XXXIX, Reid called only 16 running plays, while throwing 51 times, more than a 3:1 ratio. The Patriots, meanwhile, had the NFL's most feared big-game quarterback, but still managed a nice balance between Tom Brady's passing and Corey Dillon's running, as Brady threw 33 times while his running backs carried 26 times for 113 yards. The result: Patriots 24, Eagles 21.

(In sharp contrast to Reid, Bill Belichick has always been able to remain ahead of the curve, and to change his approach when necessary. Just when you thought the Patriots had become almost exclusively a passing team, Belichick changed it up and his quartet of running backs rushed for 2089 yards and 21 touchdowns in 2012. Their 523 rushing attempts was the second highest in the NFL.)

As for the national media, they should stop trying to put Andy Reid on Mount Rushmore until he learns to, well, rush more.

Reid's lack of adjustments didn't only relate to the issue of run-pass ratio. There have been many other situations in which he seemed unable to observe what was going on out on the field and make in-game adjustments. Reid often didn't make in-game adjustments, which is something every coach should do. The NFL record book stands as testimony to that fact: In late September 2007, the New York Giants tied a record against Reid's Eagles with 12 sacks in one game. Going into that game, the Giants had managed just four sacks in three games. But Eagles left tackle Tra Thomas was out with an injury, and Reid didn't come up with any special plan to give his replacement, Winston Justice, any help against the Giants' Osi Umenyiora. No matter how many times Umenyiora went through Justice like the average New Yorker going through a subway turnstile, Reid made no changes to give the struggling offensive tackle any help. By the end of the game, Umenyiora had six sacks, as many as he'd had *the entire previous season*, and just one fewer than the all-time single-game record of seven (held by the late Derrick Thomas, of the Kansas City Chiefs).

It wasn't just Eagles fans or Reid haters who jumped up and screamed about his stubborn refusal to make adjustments. Giants' defensive end Michael Strahan (who was "limited" to one sack on the other side of the defensive line) felt compelled to comment:

"That poor kid that they had over there. Why didn't they help him?" asked Strahan. *"I felt, in an odd way, you could ruin the guy. It's his first start and that's what he gets. It's not a good thing."* [1]

Not only did Reid fail to adjust during the game, but he didn't adjust based on his own personnel, which is another thing any good coach will do. For example, 2011 was the year of Tebowmania. When Denver Broncos coach John Fox made Tim Tebow his starting quarterback, he knew that the popular Florida grad had the worst delivery in the NFL, so he was careful not to have him throw too much. As a starter, Tebow averaged 23.7 passes a game. That's a major adjustment, because previously, when Kyle Orton was starting, the Broncos threw 31 times a game. But about the same time, an injury to Michael Vick forced Andy Reid to start Vince Young—who has the second-worst delivery in the NFL—and he had Young throwing almost 38 passes per game (37.6). *That's actually more* than the regular QB, as Vick averaged 33 passes. The results were predictably disastrous, as Young not only threw more interceptions than touchdowns, but his INTs actually *doubled* his TDs (4 TD, 8 INT in his three starts).

Having Young throw 48 times in a game (as he did against New England) is just mind-bogglingly bad. It becomes even more stupefying when you realize that starting wide receiver Jeremy Maclin missed that game with an injury. So with Vince Young throwing to Riley Cooper, Reid still called for 48 passes in a game! Meanwhile, LeSean McCoy (did I mention he's the team's best player?) carried just 10 times in the entire game. No wonder this was the game that had Eagles fans chanting *"Fire Andy."*

Unfortunately, Eagles owner Jeffrey Lurie didn't take their advice; even though he summarized the 2011 season by using all of the following words—*"disappointing, unacceptable, incredibly, incredibly disappointing, unfathomable, terrible"*—he then announced that he would be bringing back the coach next season. And when a reporter asked him about Reid being arrogant, Lurie responded, *"There's very little rigidity in the Andy Reid that we all work with. If I felt there was too much rigidity, arrogance and a sense of separateness, I'd be changing coaches."* [2]

Would someone please explain the meaning of the word "rigidity" to Jeffrey Lurie?

It's spelled R-E-I-D.

Since he was so enamored with his coach, Lurie couldn't figure out why the Eagles underperformed so badly after an offseason in which he spent incredible amounts of money to upgrade the talent. The Eagles signed mega-star free agent Nnamdi Asomugha to a five-year deal for 60 million dollars. They had already traded their "quarterback of the future," Kevin Kolb, to acquire another cornerback, Dominique Rogers-Cromartie, a few days earlier. And they already had Asante Samuel, another premier cornerback. As it turned out, this was a mistake on the part of the coach, because the three couldn't play together: Asomugha is best at press coverage, Samuel at playing off the ball, and DRC was terrible in the slot. But more important than that miscalculation is the fact that Reid's pass-happy approach to offense is also the hallmark of his defensive philosophy. In his mind, you can't have too many good cornerbacks, but as for linebackers, who cares? And so as the offseason spending spree continued (geared almost exclusively toward improving the pass offense and the pass defense), one of the team's signees, backup quarterback Vince Young, declared that the Eagles were "The Dream Team."

But while the national media joined in on the hype, Philly folks were more perceptive, as many questioned how the Eagles defense, comprised entirely of small pass-rusher types, would be able to stop the run. We wondered how having three star cornerbacks would help if the other team came out and ran the ball down the throats of the Eagles small and inexperienced linebacking corps.

If Reid wants to be pass-happy on offense and waste the skills of his star running back, that's one thing, but he can't prevent the other team's coaches from calling running plays. He's coaching against guys who (unlike Reid himself) understand the importance of a balanced offense, guys who (unlike Reid) don't always call for a pass on 3rd-and-1, guys who (unlike Reid) study the weaknesses in the opposing defense and then build their game plan around that, instead of having only one style of play.

And sure enough, the 2011 season began with St. Louis Rams running back Steven Jackson going right up the middle against the Eagles defense on the very first play, galloping 47 yards, untouched, for a touchdown. The die was cast, the trend was set. Thankfully for the Eagles, Jackson pulled a quad muscle, and after gaining nine yards on his second carry, came out of the game for good. It was a huge break for the Eagles since Jackson, at 240-pounds, would have undoubtedly continued to run over and through their small defensive line and linebackers.

But the following week, they faced another big back in Atlanta's Michael Turner, who plowed through their defense for 114 yards on 21 carries to lead the Falcons to victory. In fact, the Eagles were ahead midway through the 4th quarter, until the Falcons handed the ball off to Turner on 1st and 17, and he ran right through the middle for a 61-yard gain. The Eagles did stop him short of the end zone, but he carried it in a few plays later to give Atlanta the victory.

What was really disconcerting is that it wasn't only big backs who had great success against the Eagles rush defense. In Week 4, San Francisco's Frank Gore shredded them for 127 yards—on just 15 carries. The week after that, Buffalo's Fred Jackson totaled 111 yards rushing. Suddenly, the Eagles were 1-4. And by the time Seattle's Marshawn Lynch rampaged through the Birds defense for 148 yards on 22 carries (his second best day ever as a pro), the Eagles were 4-8, and their season was as good as done. Meanwhile, the national media, which had seized upon Young's "Dream Team" proclamation, couldn't figure out why things had gone so badly.

I'm not sure if Andy Reid, himself, ever figured it out, but even if he did it wouldn't matter; Reid likes to play finesse football, and when size and strength became critical, he didn't have the personnel to make a change. His entire defense was comprised of little guys because Reid refuses to compromise, change, or understand that there are times when football is a game of power.

But the media and fans in Philly had known all along that the linebacking corps was going to turn the "Dream Team's" season into a nightmare.

From the beginning, we wondered aloud about Reid's decision to make 4th round draft pick Casey Matthews his starting middle linebacker. Reason number one for this concern is that Matthews weighs just 232 pounds. Reason number two, which is related, is that Matthews played outside linebacker in college, but Reid moved him into the middle for the Eagles. Usually, it works the other way around, as a college middle linebacker may prove too small for the pros and will be moved to the outside. But Reid likes tiny linebackers, and tends to work the opposite way. So the Eagles found the middle of their defense manned by Matthews, a rookie who was undersized, inexperienced, and playing out of position, all while trying to take on the mantle of calling the plays.

This lasted for all of three games before a change was made. But this was simply a carryover of the same failed approach that Reid has used for more than a decade. In 14 years, he never drafted a linebacker who's made a long-term impact. He was fortunate in that he inherited a great linebacker in Jeremiah Trotter, who had been drafted during the Ray Rhodes regime. Trotter made the Pro Bowl four times before retiring in 2007. (He came out of retirement in 2009, but was no longer an impact player.) Reid's attempts to replace the 262-pound Trotter with 235-pound Omar Gaither didn't work. Likewise for Mark Simoneau, an undersized MLB who also proved to be a liability in the run game during his time with the team from 2003-05. Reid also signed free agent Dhani Jones and tried him in the middle, despite the fact that Dhani was only 240 pounds. The results were disastrous.

Really, the only effective linebacker Reid ever brought in was Carlos Emmons, who came over from the Steelers and played for the Eagles for four years. Emmons was a big, physical guy who could be counted on to shut down opposing tight ends. But the Eagles let him walk as a free agent after the 2003 season, and they've had a terrible time trying to contain opposing tight ends ever since.

Many people criticized Reid because they believe he hadn't tried to improve the line backing corps, but that's not true; he just failed miserably trying to do so. Everyone remembers that the first draft pick Reid ever made was Donovan McNabb in 1999, but not too many people remember that his next pick was linebacker Barry Gardner, who never lived up to the expectations associated with being a second round pick.

Quinton Caver, also a second round pick in the 2001 draft, was a bust as well. Matt McCoy, a second rounder in 2005, was another bust. McCoy was a classic Andy Reid undersized linebacker, weighing in at 231 pounds and getting consistently run over by bigger, stronger blockers. At one point in 2005, Reid's starting outside linebackers were McCoy and Keith Adams, who weighed 225. Adams had been a fearless special teams player, but like McCoy, was always giving away a huge weight advantage to the blockers.

The following year, in 2006, Reid seemed to finally realize he had to bulk up and get bigger linebackers, and he used a third-round pick on Chris Gocong, a 260-pound defensive end in college, and moved him to linebacker. And in 2007, they also used a third round pick on Stewart Bradley, a 250-pound middle linebacker who made the Sports Illustrated All-Pro team in his second season. But Bradley suffered an injury in 2009 and was never the same. Meanwhile, Gocong never quite mastered the linebacker position, and when the Eagles let him go, they also let go of the idea of using bigger linebackers. They reverted back to the little guys, with a 2011 roster that included Matthews (232 pounds), Moise Fokou (236), Akeem Jordan (230), Brian Rolle (229) and Keenan Clayton (220).

Almost as if he's not content to mess up by having too many small linebackers, Reid exacerbated the problem with two moves he made between the 2010 and 2011 seasons. He fired defensive line coach Rory Segrest and replaced him with Jim Washburn in January, 2011. The idea was to have Washburn bring his Wide Nine defense to Philly. Washburn's defense spreads the defensive ends further outside to give them better pass rush opportunities, but it also leaves wider lanes for opponents to run through. Wider lanes and undersized linebackers are a really bad combination.

But more incredibly, Reid did this even though he had fired his defensive coordinator, Sean McDermott, a few days before. Why would he hire Washburn before hiring a D-coordinator? What if the new coordinator didn't want to play a Wide Nine?

That may, in fact, explain why some of the prospective defensive coordinators Reid had targeted decided they didn't want to come here. Finally, having put himself in something of a desperate situation, Reid ended up hiring *his offensive line coach,* Juan Castillo, as his new defensive coordinator. I can attest that Castillo is a bright, hard-working guy who was much beloved by the vast majority of offensive lineman he had coached during his prior 12 years with the team. But in addition to having to learn everything from the other side of the ball—Castillo had no prior experience coaching defense in the pros—he was stuck with the Wide Nine, whether he liked it or not.

Reid's hiring of assistant coaches is another area where he seemed to have the Midas touch early on, but lost it as the years went by. Half a dozen of Reid's original group of assistants went on to become head coaches for other teams: Special teams coordinator John Harbaugh, offensive coordinator Brad Childress, linebackers coach Ron Rivera, defensive assistant for quality control Steve Spagnuolo, defensive backs coach Leslie Frazier and quarterbacks coach Pat Shurmer each graduated to head coaching positions. That group, along with defensive coordinator Jim Johnson, who could've become a head coach elsewhere if he'd so chosen, made for an amazing staff.

But it was a different story with many of Reid's later hires. Castillo and Washburn suffered the same fates as their predecessors, McDermott and Segrest. Castillo was fired in October of 2012, and Washburn got the axe a month and a half later.

And while it was quickly revealed that Reid and some of the players may have had problems with Washburn's attitude, the real problem was Reid's idea of defense—get a newbie coordinator and tie his hands with a system he may or may not like, give him 230-pound rookie linebackers along with defensive backs who go out of their way *not* to hit anyone, and then wonder why teams run through your defense with the greatest of ease.

Still, members of the national media, such as AJ Perez of FoxSports. com, try to turn Reid's mistakes around and actually make it sound as though he was the victim in all this:

"Reid is more a victim of what he can't manage (expectations) than what he can (odd play calls in the red zone)," [3] Perez wrote after the Eagles loss to New England in Week 12 of the 2011 season.

"Injuries, dropped passes and the complete inability to tackle anybody in a Patriots uniform won't immediately be solved if Bill Cowher, Jon Gruden, Tony Dungy or anybody else on that oft-cited list of accomplished and available coaches is on the sideline against the Seattle Seahawks this Thursday," Perez argued.

But I would counter by pointing out that it was Reid himself who assembled this group of non-tacklers. I would add that it is inconceivable that Cowher, the complete opposite of Reid when it comes to assembling a hard-hitting linebacker corps, would ever allow his team to be soft.

If Reid was willing to put big defensive lineman in front of his small linebackers, it might not be too bad. But he wanted little lineman who can rush the passer, and to hell with stopping the run. Take the position of defensive end, which Reid paid more attention to over the years than any other. Hoping to replace the departed Hugh Douglas, whom Reid had inherited from Ray Rhodes, Andy drafted Jerome McDougle in the first round in 2003, but he was never much of a contributor. Victor Abiamiri, a second round pick in 2007, was another guy who never made an impact.

And then there was the third round pick the Eagles wasted on a defensive end named Bryan Smith in 2008. Though McDougle and Abiamiri seemed a little undersized at 260 pounds, they were huge compared to Smith, who weighed all of 231. I remember a draft day TV segment in which I debated Dave Spadaro, from the Eagles own website (philadelphiaeagles.com) in which he gave the classic Andy Reid argument that Smith's speed would overcome his lack of size. Needless to say, it didn't. The guy never played a single down for the Eagles.

In 2010, Reid used his first round pick on Brandon Graham, and even traded up to get him. Not content to have taken one undersized defensive end, Reid used his third-round pick in the same draft on Daniel Te'o-Nesheim. DT-N was a bust and was cut by the team the following season. If Reid had taken a superior DE in that draft by the name of Jason Pierre-Paul, he would've shut my mouth regarding the value of these guys. But he passed over Pierre-Paul (who's had 27 ½ sacks in his first three years in the league) in order to take Graham (who's had 8 ½)

In fairness, I'll acknowledge that most of these guys battled injuries that slowed their careers. But when that happens to one guy after another—and each one usually had multiple injuries—you have to question whether it could all be coincidence? What was that Albert Einstein definition of insanity—doing the same thing over and over and expecting different results? Maybe these small-framed defensive ends that Reid loved just weren't built to take the pounding of NFL life. In McDougle's case, his career was derailed by a shooting during a robbery attempt, which obviously has nothing to do with his small stature. But even before that, he battled injuries that caused him to miss eight games during his rookie season, and four games in his second year.

These were all high draft picks that didn't work out. Granted, Reid did manage a great sleeper pick in 2005 when he took Trent Cole in the fifth round. Cole has gone on to become one of the Eagles all-time sacks leaders, although being another relatively small player, he has shown a tendency to get worn down during the course of a season.

Before the 2011 season, in addition to hiring a D-line coach who runs the Wide Nine, Reid also hired an offensive line coach, Howard Mudd, who likes small quick guys on the O-line. So once again, Reid went way overboard with his favorite style, and wouldn't compromise by having a few situational big guys on the roster. And this is, after all, the NFL; there are going to be times when you need to play with power, especially in short-yardage, goal line and red zone situations.

In fact, NFL Network analyst Mike Mayock hit the nail on the head during an interview on 97.5 FM The Fanatic when he said, *"Let's face it, short yardage and goal line has not been good to the Eagles the last couple of years. If it's 4th and 1, sometimes you've got to be able to put your hand in the dirt, get lower than the guy across from you, root him out and get the yard. And they haven't been able to do that. And they end up in the shotgun too often, they end up throwing the ball a lot."* [4]

Mayock, who has equipment in his own house to break down films, is that rarest of national media guys who actually does really have an in-depth knowledge of what is going on with each team in the league.

In addition to having more size on the O-line for such situations, it would help to have a big back who specializes in short yardage. But

Reid almost never had such a player on his roster. To the contrary, he loves having a bench full of little guys at running back; over the years he's had Reno Mahe, Bruce Perry, Lorenzo Booker, Ryan Moats, and most recently Dion Lewis, who is 5'7" and 193 pounds. To his credit, Reid managed to draft some very good starting running backs, notably Brian Westbrook (a small guy himself) and LeSean McCoy, but then he underutilizes them, as we've already discussed.

Unfortunately, there was no one in the entire organization who could stand up to Reid or provide an opposing viewpoint. When Andy was hired in 1999, the Eagles had a solid football man, Tom Modrak, serving as General Manager. But in 2001, Modrak was mysteriously let go, and Reid, now given the title of Executive Vice President of Football Operations, was in complete control. He had GMs Tom Heckert and Howie Roseman, but it was Reid calling the shots. In fact, when Reid was finally fired, owner Jeff Lurie made it a point to imply that Roseman was a better talent evaluator than Reid, but that he had often been overruled by Andy.

Reid's bad drafting began to take its toll in the later years of his administration. During the earlier years, carryovers from the Ray Rhodes era helped to fuel Reid's success with their skills and tenacity, most notably Brian Dawkins, Jeremiah Trotter, Hugh Douglas, Duce Staley, Hollis Thomas and Tra Thomas. Reid was able to draft Trent Cole and Brian Westbrook to replace Douglas and Staley, and eventually signed Jason Peters to take over for Tra Thomas. But Reid never seemed to understand the importance of tenacity, and without Dawkins and Trotter, Reid's defenses lacked identity and toughness. And he never found a solid run-stuffer to replace Hollis Thomas in the middle of the line, if indeed he even looked for one.

The crowning blow for the defense was the death of Jim Johnson, who really deserves a great deal of the credit for the success of Reid's teams. Reid's Eagles would never win another playoff game after Johnson succumbed to cancer.

Put all of these things together—the departure of his best assistants and several of Ray Rhodes' players, the poor drafting, the pass-happy play calling, the lack of respect for the value of size and power, the inability to make adjustments, especially after the rest of the league had adjusted to him—and you see why Reid's tenure, which started out so brilliantly, began going south midway through.

But even as the franchise was going into a downward spiral, the national media guys remained oblivious. Their "analysis" of the situation often consisted of nothing more than glancing at Reid's win-loss record, and his impressive career win percentage of .609. (That was prior to the 2012 season, which dropped the number to .585) But even those numbers were misleading. Cody Swartz of Rantsports.com went deeper into the numbers and found that Reid's percentage against teams with winning records is only .394:

"I went back and looked at the Eagles under Reid in four separate categories: against winning teams, against playoff teams, against teams with a playoff win, and against Super Bowl teams." [5]

Winning Teams:	**37-57 (.394)**
Playoff Teams:	**36-55 (.396)**
Teams With Playoff Wins:	**15-40 (.273)**
Super Bowl Teams:	**5-19 (.208)**
Losing Record:	**100-33-1 (.743)**

More insightful research by other members of the Philadelphia media helped spotlight additional flaws in Reid's coaching repertoire. One such flaw, well-known to Eagles' fans, was the issue of clock management. The national analysts, trying to keep up with 32 different teams, may look at a highlight package and think they understand. But Philly fans who watch every play of every game and seem to live and die with every bad decision, know how many times Reid had to burn timeouts in the third quarter because his disorganized team had too many men on the field, or his coaching staff didn't relay the play call in time—leaving the team with no timeouts when they needed to stop the clock at the end of the game.

"In games decided by just one possession, coaching decisions are magnified," [6] points out Ron Pasceri, a featured columnist for Bleacher Report. So Pasceri did some *real* research, finding that Reid's winning percentage in games decided by 7 points or fewer is only .445, compared to that overall percentage of .609. *"That is a serious drop in performance,"* Pasceri notes.

Here are some more interesting numbers, based on solid research, concerning the inability of many of Reid's teams to play well in the red zone. Philadelphia Inquirer columnist Jeff McLane crunched the numbers and found that in 2011 *"the Eagles' starting 11 is the shortest in the NFL, and only two other defenses are lighter."* [7] McLane's research showed that the average weight per defensive player for NFL teams is 246 pounds. The Eagles checked in at only 240. McLane then did some further digging and uncovered why the Eagles defense was only ranked 29th in the red-zone.

"There was a connection between size and red-zone performance, where the field contracts and speed doesn't matter as much as having big and tall defenders," [7] McLane said. He found that five of the top six teams in red-zone defense were taller and/or heavier than average, and that all of the bottom six teams in red-zone defense were either average or below average size-wise.

What's more, the Eagles' red-zone woes in 2011 were not an aberration. The previous year, the team finished *dead last* in the red zone. And not by a little, but by a wide margin, having allowed 33 TD's in 43 red-zone possessions—and that was under a different coordinator, Sean McDermott. So if the D-coordinator changes, but the problems remain the same, isn't it fair to conclude that the problem is with the head coach? And it cuts both ways, as the Eagles offense also has a history of problems scoring inside the red-zone.

Since his small O-lineman can't be counted on to simply push back opposing players a couple of feet, the coach tries to trick the defense, and in the game against the 49ers in 2011, actually called a play in which running back Ronnie Brown was supposed to run, but also had the option to throw—from the one-yard line! Brown started to run, got hit, tossed the ball away, and turned it over. It was one of the most bizarre plays ever. In looking back over the 2011 season, Brian Baldinger, a former Eagle turned NFL Network color analyst, pinpointed that game as one of the most critical losses of the season, and suggested that run-pass option play *"should've been ripped out of the playbook."*

Baldinger has a national presence, but he is a Philly guy, and has a radio show here, so he knows what's going on—unlike most of the pretentious national media members. And Baldy's stablemate on 97.5 FM The Fanatic, Mike Missanelli, has made it a crusade to try to straighten out some of these national pundits who twist themselves into knots trying to defend everything Reid did. In 2011, Missanelli debated Colin Cowherd of ESPN, pointing out that Reid had lost two NFC Championship games when his team was at home *and* was considered the favorite. He challenged Cowherd to name another head coach who had done that, to which Cowherd replied *"Tony Dungy lost at home to the Steelers as a favorite, lost at home to the Patriots as a favorite. I'm not sure if he was a favorite in New England three years ago. He lost two and was fired in Tampa. They won the next year."* [8]

Duh, Colin. You're arguing that the Eagles shouldn't fire Reid, then you compare it to a situation in which a coach (Dungy) *was* fired *and his replacement (Jon Gruden) won a Super Bowl the very next year.* (Gruden's Bucs were virtually the same team as Dungy's. The coaching change was the difference they needed to put them over the top. Not that Dungy wasn't a good coach; he proved his mettle when he won a Super Bowl later in Indianapolis. It's just that sometimes a change is needed.)

But Cowherd's contradictions didn't end there. He finished the statement by trying to say that Reid's many near-misses were accomplished despite a lack of talent on his teams: *"Outside of McNabb and Westbrook, who did they have?"* [8] he asked.

But when Missanelli pointed out to him that Reid is the guy in charge of personnel, and he had failed to bring in other quality skill position players, Cowherd said, *"But they've also had great depth at other spots. They've spent money in other places. They've always had an above average pass rush (and) offensive line. They've been above average in the secondary. So they've chosen to spend money in other places."* [8]

So like most national media people, Cowherd speaks out of both sides of his mouth, claiming that Andy Reid, Vice-President of Football

Operations, has done a good job of *assembling talent*, while also arguing that Andy Reid, coach, has done a good job while working with *minimal talent*.

Former NFL quarterback-turned-analyst Boomer Esiason is another national guy who can't get his Philly-facts straight. After the Eagles loss to New England in November of 2011 (the game in which the fans chanted *"Fire Andy"*), Esiason went on WEEI-radio in Boston and tried to absolve Reid of having any responsibility for the bad game and the bad season:

"Well, I know that he didn't put the team together. That's (former team president) Joe Banner. That's the guys in the front office. And I'm not ready to say that about Andy Reid, that he should be stepping down with dignity or any of that stuff. I think he's a terrific coach. He's just got a bunch of lunatics on his team right now … He's got an eclectic group of players there that don't seem to be playing for the team like they are in New England, so it's unfortunate for him, but I still think he's a great coach. I really do," [9] said Esiason.

Someone please tell Boomer that Reid's title was not merely head coach, but also executive vice-President of Football Operations! Ever since Tom Modrak was let go as the team's general manager in 2001, Reid had complete control of the front office. Reid acknowledged as much after a report surfaced in the L.A. Times that he was ready to leave the Eagles if he didn't have complete control.

"As far as the personnel control, I have had final say on personnel matters for quite some time here and that's never been an issue or a point of contention," [10] Reid said.

Yet the Esiasons of the world make him out to be the victim, refusing to recognize that Reid is the guy who had the primary say in bringing in the "lunatics" that Esiason talks about.

Then again, this is the same Boomer Esiason who said during the 2009 Pro Bowl that Philly fans wanted to see Donovan McNabb traded, and if it happened, those fans would rue the day because Donovan would show them how wrong they were. Then McNabb was, in fact, traded, and had a terrible year, throwing more interceptions than touchdowns for Washington before finally *getting benched after week 13.* He wasn't just benched, but demoted to third string.

Then McNabb landed with the Minnesota Vikings in 2011, and *was released after six games.* But I never heard Esiason admit that he was wrong (and that Philly fans were right). Instead, I heard him doing a radio interview on a Philly sports talk station the following year, in which he again questioned the knowledge of our fans because of our unhappiness with Andy Reid. He could've just queued up a tape with his comments about McNabb, and changed the name to Reid.

And isn't it interesting that Esiason criticized the fans for wanting to see McNabb traded, but had not a single critical word for the coach who actually engineered the trade. It shows just how gutless the national media can be in that they are afraid to criticize Reid, but find it easy to criticize the fans, so they wag their finger at *us* for things done by *him.*

Maybe the worst practitioner of this gutless approach is the guy who wrote an article on Bleacher Report titled "*14 Reasons Why Philadelphia Has The Worst Fans In Sports.*" [11] One of the "reasons" stated was "They Endorse Killing Dogs," which was accompanied by a picture of Michael Vick. Of course, it was *Reid* who brought in Vick, *not the fans.* At least in the case of Esiason, he could argue that fan criticism of McNabb might have influenced Reid, but there was virtually no senti-ment among fans urging the Eagles to sign Vick when he came out of prison. I don't recall any newspaper articles or talk show hosts say-ing, "Sign Vick." We were all surprised when it happened. Some fans accepted it, other people organized public protests, while others simply declared they could no longer root for the team. Yet the Bleacher Report writer makes the generalization that we all endorsed the move, while he bypassed any criticism of the coach who actually made the move. That writer only gives his name as "Neal" and I don't blame him for not wanting anyone to be able to identify him when he writes such utterly irresponsible nonsense.

During the time that Reid was the Eagles head coach, the team that plays across the street, the Philadelphia Flyers, made *six* coaching changes. Flyers owner Ed Snider, determined to get a Stanley Cup win-ner, fired and hired six coaches between 1998 and 2012. And he's done that despite the fact that the Flyers have made the playoffs 16 times in 17 years, because the only thing he really wants is a Stanley Cup. A drastically different approach from the Eagles, although the bottom line is that both teams, while occasionally coming close, have failed to win the big prize. But it certainly shows that Eagles fans were not unreasonable for thinking that after several seasons of "close but no cigar," a coaching change should've been made.

I understand why Lurie's friendship with Reid made him reluctant to make a change. He really is a good guy. I recall that, during my final days as a sports anchor, I did a one-on-one interview in which I told Andy that my frequent criticisms had nothing to do with any personal feelings, just a disagreement with his philosophy. And he said, *"Bill, you've done a great job for ten years here, and you'll do a great job (somewhere else) for ten more."* That was a classy thing to say to someone who has been a constant critic.

And it's true that Reid does have many good qualities as a coach. His players love him because he never publicly criticizes them. His rule of never re-signing players in their thirties, regardless of how well they played in the past, has proven to be the correct approach, as the players who signed with other teams experienced major declines in their performance time after time (with the possible exception of Brian Dawkins, who had a few decent seasons in Denver.) He has a reputation of being very good with quarterbacks (although Donovan McNabb's inability to ever adjust to throwing touch passes and Michael Vick's inconsistencies raise questions about the accuracy of that rep.) And he is a class act, unpretentious and even funny, if you meet him in person, away from his news conferences. But as we've seen, Reid also has his blind spots, and there's no reason to think he will suddenly see the light and make the adjustments needed to go from "near-winner" to champion.

Oh well. That's Kansas City's problem now. Reid is often accused of being a control freak, and he's managed to get complete power in KC, just as he had in Philly. Meanwhile, the Eagles new coach, Chip Kelly, came in the door talking about the importance of surrounding himself with people with a variety of experiences and viewpoints.

However, he also said something that was very disconcerting: Arriving in Philly after his hiring, Kelly hadn't even left the airport before he began joking with the media about Philly fans being the ones who threw snowballs at Santa. In reality, the fans are willing to give Kelly lots of latitude for a couple of years because we know it's going to take a while to remake Reid's roster of players who have little talent and even less heart, who flat-out quit during games late in the 2012 season.

But the national media will never give us the same latitude. Soon, they will break their silence and lift their heads up out of the mud, and without ever admitting that we knew what we were talking about with regard to Andy Reid, start shaping that mud into balls to throw at us. Or maybe they'll throw snowballs instead.

3

PHILLY FANS HATED
DONOVAN MCNABB FROM DAY ONE

He was called to the podium by then-commissioner Paul Tagliabue in 1999 as the second pick of the entire NFL Draft. A very proud moment for Donovan McNabb, who had just completed a stellar career at Syracuse University.

As his family and friends looked on, a huge crowd of Eagles fans welcomed Donovan to town in their typical way. BOOOOOOOOOOOOOOOOO!! The boos drowned out Tagliabue, or was it, Taglia-booooooooooooo.

This is a prime example of how Philly treated their best-ever quarterback who always produced for them, never complained, and was never embraced by his own hometown fans.

"The way they treated this man from day one, it's not justifiable. They will not treat any other quarterback in the NFL, like we said, Peyton Manning don't get treated like that."

- DEION SANDERS, ON EAGLES FANS FOLLOWING THE 2008 EAGLES-CARDINALS THANKSGIVING GAME.

RESPONSE: DENNIS BAKAY

Deion Sanders' opinion of Eagles fans as well as Philadelphia fans is that of an outside observer. This is a viewpoint shared by many in his position, as former athletes, so-called pundits, bloggers, and national reporters take any chance they can to malign and vilify the great fans of this town.

The debate over Donovan McNabb has been a very useful tool in the propaganda war against Philadelphia fans for over a decade. It's almost as if we needed to be reminded how great he was, including the multiple playoff wins and appearances in the NFC Championship Game and Super Bowl.

At the same time, we have been constantly reminded of just how little he was appreciated by the brutal Eagles fans.

When Donovan McNabb was booed at the 1999 NFL Draft, it became an instant national headline. The clip of him being serenaded by Eagles' boo-birds has become a go-to clip during many NFL broadcasts for over a decade. Throughout the past 13 years, it might have been played on TV more times than "The Catch."

At one time, I was one of McNabb's biggest supporters. However, when I look back on it, I couldn't see the forest through the trees. I blamed his choke job in the 2002 NFC Championship Game on his rust from a seven-week layoff following a broken ankle. I blamed his defeat in the 2003 NFC Championship Game on James Thrash and Todd Pinkston stinking up the joint. I even blamed his loss in Super Bowl XXXIX on the Eagles' defense failing to stop the Patriots' offensive machine in the second half as well as Coach Andy Reid's inability to think on his feet.

Despite the evidence against McNabb, I maintained that there was no way that he was the biggest reason for the Eagles' failure to win a Super Bowl. Unlike me, some people saw the forest— some more clearly than others.

"Some people are athletes, still good, but don't have that extra 'I'm willing to sacrifice my life. I'm willing to sacrifice what I have to sacrifice to win.' ... People never forgot when things happen, they see a guy crumble under pressure. Whether they throw up on the highway, whether they throw up on the court, whether they throw up on the football field, when people see that, that sticks in the back of their mind." [1]

-BERNARD HOPKINS ON DONOVAN MCNABB

I remember when Philly's own former Middleweight Boxing Champion Bernard Hopkins went on Howard Eskin's radio show on WIP to defend his remarks about McNabb. B Hop, as he is known to many, was fed up with McNabb's blunders in the playoffs.

At the time, I felt Hopkins (like a minority of vocal fans) was another "McNabb hater." What started out as just a few jabs turned into a full-blown bashing fest on Eskin's show. Hopkins ripped McNabb for producing hollow numbers, failing to be a leader, and coming up empty time after time.

Hopkins treated McNabb like one of his punching bags in the gym, and I was absolutely livid. How could he blame the Eagles' playoff blunders on McNabb? Didn't Andy Reid deserve some of the blame for abandoning the running game and failing to think on his feet? Didn't the defense need to be blamed for failing to come up in big spots? McNabb was the "leader" of this team, but many of the Birds' other leaders didn't step up with huge, game-winning plays when they needed them most. The quarterback takes much of the blame for losses, but this is a team game.

Like many of those national media types, I was towing the pro-McNabb line, defending him and dismissing his critics as mindless haters. I remember telling people that Hopkins took too many shots to his head, and how he had no clue about football. Upon closer examination though, Bernard Hopkins might have had a point—when you break down the Eagles' losses in huge games.

When analyzing the Eagles' losses in their biggest games with McNabb at quarterback, it's fair to place some of the blame on Andy Reid and the Birds' defense, but there is no doubt McNabb came up small along the way.

Take for instance, the 2002 NFC Championship Game when the Eagles laid an egg against the Tampa Bay Bucs in what proved to be their swan song at the Vet. The Birds dominated the Bucs during the Reid/McNabb era until that point, beating them four straight times, including two straight playoff victories. Temperatures were frigid that Sunday—with game time conditions in the 20's. Tampa had just one victory in their history when playing in conditions under 40 degrees and this victory came against the Bears during that regular season. There was no possible way that the Eagles wouldn't be on their way to the Super Bowl.

The team got off to a great start, with Brian Mitchell returning the opening kickoff 70 yards and Duce Staley running for a 20-yard touchdown just two plays later. This would turn out to be the Eagles' high point of the afternoon, as they would score just three points the rest of the day behind Donovan McNabb's endless string of three-and-outs. The Birds were down 20-10 and had a chance to make it 20-17 when McNabb threw the now-infamous pick-six to Ronde Barber, which cemented arguably the most devastating loss in Philadelphia sports history.

Number Five came up empty when the Eagles needed him most in the fourth quarter. The sight of McNabb watching Barber run up the sidelines for the touchdown leaves a lasting imprint in the minds of many Eagles fans. For Tampa, this was the moment when they finally got over the hump. For the Eagles, this would further cement their legacy as the "Poor Man's Buffalo Bills."

Fast forward one year later to the 2003 NFC Championship Game against Carolina, when McNabb eventually had to leave the game after Panthers defensive tackle Brenson Buckner delivered a nasty cheap shot to his ribs in the first quarter. McNabb fought through the injury and played for three quarters, before relinquishing the pigskin to Koy Detmer.

When McNabb was in the game, he was throwing passes that bounced off the receivers and into the hands of Ricky Manning, Jr. Furthermore, Duce Staley was the best player on the field that day, but was severely underutilized. The Eagles attempted 36 passes while managing only 26 rushing attempts, resulting in a 14-3 loss. With his three interceptions, Manning, Jr. went from a nobody to a playoff hero in just one evening. Let's be clear—this game was not just McNabb's fault. Andy Reid deserves some of blame for this one, but a great quarterback would have fought through the adversity and put the team on his shoulders.

Following the Eagles' third straight NFC Championship loss, Andy Reid went out and got Donovan McNabb the "Robin" to his "Batman" in All-Pro wide receiver Terrell Owens. The results were nothing short of spectacular. The Eagles' 2004 season was legendary – as they set a team record in points scored. They went 13-1 with T.O. in the starting lineup and were dominant on both sides of the ball. When they finally made it to the Super Bowl however, McNabb had one of the worst games of the year, throwing three interceptions—including one on the final play of the game. Not that there's any right time to throw an interception, but keep in mind McNabb only threw eight interceptions that entire regular season!

The result, of course, was the Patriots' third Super Bowl victory in four years, and the Eagles' second Super Bowl defeat in as many appearances. One of Philadelphia's all-time unresolved sports mysteries is whether or not McNabb vomited during the fourth quarter of this game. Former Eagles' center Hank Fraley claims he did, and so did some of his teammates. Others dispute the claim, saying he was gasping for air because he was winded from a punishing hit by Tedy Bruschi. Let's also bear in mind that there is no visual evidence of McNabb losing his lunch on the field, unlike the games in Jacksonville in 2002 and Tampa in 2006. To be fair, McNabb did throw a gorgeous touchdown to Greg Lewis during this frustrating drive, when it seemed like Reid was deliberately milking the clock despite this being a two possession game. Even though the Eagles scored on that drive and there was a lack of definitive proof, McNabb will be forever known for laboring during crunch time in the Super Bowl.

After the Super Bowl loss to the Patriots, things were never the same for McNabb and the Eagles, and in 2005 McNabb's leadership (or lack thereof) finally came to the forefront. The first sign of trouble came when a disgruntled Owens took his contract frustrations out on McNabb by calling him out on his lackluster Super Bowl performance. As the season went on, Owens single-handedly destroyed the team, as his antics and public tirades continued. Despite the team turmoil, McNabb allowed things to fester. There were many reports that McNabb didn't even communicate with Owens off the field or in the locker room. He just chose to avoid him. Could you imagine Joe Montana, Steve Young, Kurt Warner, or Drew Brees allowing a teammate to drag the entire team down without confronting a diva who was sabotaging his team?

McNabb seemed generally aloof and never really comfortable with the role of being the leader and face of a franchise, and this was a prime example. Sure, there was the whole *"I'm the captain of this ship"* speech after Owens went down with his ankle injury the previous December (which many believe was the time some tension actually started between the two), but there's the old adage that if you say you're a leader, you're not. It really speaks volumes that the locker room was divided between McNabb supporters and Owens backers during the 2005 season.

A sports hernia prematurely ended McNabb's season in 2005, and when he went down with a season-ending ACL injury in 2006, the Eagles appeared to be dead in the water. Backup QB Jeff Garcia took over the following week in a blowout loss to the Colts. However, something clicked the following Monday night against Carolina in a dramatic 27-24 victory. During the next several weeks, there was a special chemistry with this team which we hadn't seen since the 2004 season. They certainly weren't world beaters, but were playing as a team and getting the job done, the blue collar way.

Garcia helped lead the Birds to six straight wins (including one postseason win) and three straight road games against division foes. The Eagles 23-7 thumping of the Cowboys on Christmas will go down as one of the classic games in Eagles history. Many fans will never forget when Garcia said *"Hey Philadelphia: Merry Christmas"* in the postgame interview. This was a guy who really "got it." In just one season, Garcia understood what Philly fans were all about and he was able to connect with them on a personal level; something McNabb was never able to do. The Eagles wound up losing to the Saints in the second round of the playoffs, but the season will never be forgotten as they overcame a devastating injury to their franchise QB and went on an improbable postseason run.

During the offseason, Garcia signed with the Tampa Bay Bucs as a starter (which didn't sit very well with many Eagles fans) and Kevin Kolb was drafted in the 2nd round of the NFL Draft. After eight seasons in Philadelphia, it became clear that McNabb might not be spending his entire career here.

When McNabb returned in 2007, more controversy ensued when he allegedly told FOX reporter Pam Oliver that he didn't think he would return to Philadelphia for the 2008 season. McNabb later denied this, rattling off a series of he-said/she-saids between McNabb and Oliver.

McNabb's last legitimate shot at the Super Bowl came during the next season, when the Eagles flew out to the desert to take on the Arizona Cardinals in his fifth NFC Championship Game. Because of their 9-6-1 regular season record, this Eagles team snuck up on everyone, just like the Phillies did three months before when they won the World Series. The team reached the playoffs in miraculous fashion, winning four of their last five games as the Tampa Bay Bucs were upset by a putrid Raiders team, opening the door for the Birds.

In the game, the Eagles dug themselves into a 24-6 hole at halftime. But despite McNabb leading the team to three touchdowns in the second half, he failed to deliver yet again with the game on the line. For the fourth time out of five tries in NFC Championship Games during the Reid/McNabb regime, the Eagles went home empty-handed.

There is a common thread throughout the Eagles' losses in big games during the Reid/McNabb era: McNabb's inability to play a complete game and deliver in the clutch. He certainly wasn't horrible in the big games. Number Five had countless opportunities to get it done, but came up empty on many occasions. Yes, he hooked up with Freddie Mitchell on "4th and 26," but this amazing play has been overshadowed by far more failures. Could you imagine Eli Manning continuing to throw balls at receivers in coverage during that game against Carolina? No – he would adjust and find a way to lift the team. Could you imagine Tom Brady going three and out against the Tampa Bay Bucs on almost every drive? No – he would improvise and lead the team to victory. Could you picture Ben Roethlisberger laboring in the fourth quarter? No—he would do anything he could to pull off a touchdown drive in the clutch.

If the 2008 NFC Championship Game was McNabb's last chance to prove himself on the big stage, the Eagles' back-to-back losses against the Cowboys during the 2009 season proved to be the final nails in the coffin for his Eagles career. In the final week of the regular season, the Eagles were to square off against Dallas in a game with tremendous play-off implications. The Eagles were 11-4, while the Cowboys were 10-5. If the Eagles won this game, they would have ended the season with a 12-4 record and clinched the third seed in the NFC. The winner would win the NFC East and play at home in the Wild Card game six days later.

The Eagles never even showed up that day and were demolished 24-0, dropping them from a third seed to sixth seed. Worse yet, they had to play Dallas again for the second consecutive week on the road. McNabb's well-documented lack of accountability was fully evident in the post-game press conference, throwing his younger teammates under the bus and telling the media after the game they *"showed their youth today."* Typical McNabb: never putting the onus on himself and it was always clear that losses didn't tear him up as much as it did his teammates, let alone his diehard fans. Instead, he would constantly give the media the obligatory answers about how the Eagles were looking to win a championship.

The end of McNabb's reign in Philly seemed to be drawing closer. Either McNabb would step up and play lights out in their rematch against Dallas, or he would play his way out of Philly with a loss. Reid and McNabb began their ascension to the top of the NFC back in 2000 by blowing out the Cowboys in the season-opening "Pickle Juice" game.

Unfortunately, this is also where it would all end.

For the second week in a row, the Eagles were blown out by the Cowboys and sent packing following a 34-14 defeat. There probably wasn't a single fan in his or her right mind who believed that McNabb would return for the 2010 season. The back-to-back crushing losses to the Cowboys sealed his fate in Philadelphia.

Despite claims by Eagles' management that they were not parting with McNabb, on Easter Sunday, April 4th, 2010, he was traded to the Washington Redskins for a second round pick (used to select safety Nate Allen) along with an eventual fourth rounder in the 2011 draft that was traded to Tampa Bay.

In Philly, it's a pretty simple concept: If you win the big one, you're respected here forever. There are many choke artists in the history of Philly sports. There are also many teams, coaches, and players who are still held in high regard despite their inability to win a title: The 1993 Phillies, Allen Iverson, Ron Hextall, Reggie White, Buddy Ryan, Charles Barkley, and Dick Vermeil are still beloved in Philadelphia. Unlike McNabb however, they connected with the fans.

McNabb's lack of connection with the fans was evident in some ways, even early on in his career. In a 2002 game against Arizona, he broke his ankle on the third play of the game and still managed to throw four touchdown passes, which led the team to victory. Normally, this type of performance is the stuff legends are made of in a town like Philadelphia. Instead, McNabb was never seen as a hero for his gutsy performance. This may have been unfair to some extent, but proved to be a wiser judgment as the years wore on.

There was always a small group of fans who never really gave McNabb a chance. Maybe it was his aloof personality or his insistence on becoming a pocket passer, despite being blessed with an ability to make plays with his feet. Moreover, the national media seemed to run with this and assumed that Philly fans as a whole were rough on him. Hopkins became associated with the Philadelphia fans that were out to get McNabb and run him out of town.

Back in 2008 when the Eagles defeated the Arizona Cardinals on Thanksgiving night, Deion Sanders wanted to make it known just how poorly the Eagles fans treated McNabb. When he interviewed McNabb after the game, Sanders referred to Eagles fans as a bunch of phony idiots who were unsupportive of him:

"Can I tell them something for you? First of all, I would like to tell all these idiotic fans to shut-up. Don't get on his bandwagon now. You're the same guys who booed him on his first incompletion," [2] Sanders moaned.

As stated in the beginning of this chapter, Neon Deion wanted to remind us that McNabb was an elite QB who never got a chance with the fans and how this would never happen to Peyton Manning. Let's stop right there.

Sorry Deion, but Donovan McNabb was never in the class of Peyton Manning. Many analysts in the national media put McNabb in that class based upon his appearances in NFC Championship Games, but the bottom line is he never could get it done. The older Manning brother was a Hall of Famer before winning his first Super Bowl.

McNabb just sat there like a statue and didn't say anything in response to Deion's diatribe. The silence was deafening and spoke volumes about how Donovan McNabb really felt about the legion of Eagles fans that paid to see him play, cheered him on, and helped provide him with a luxurious lifestyle he enjoyed as a franchise player in Philadelphia.

Sanders is not the only one in the national media who subscribes to this viewpoint. ESPN's Tom Jackson said on countless occasions during *ESPN's Sunday NFL Countdown* how the Eagles fans had better appreciate McNabb. Co-host Chris Berman would constantly echo his sentiments. ESPN's resident Philly hater, Michael Wilbon, has openly stated how much he hates Philadelphia fans over the years. He also loves to remind everyone how those mean Philly fans never appreciated poor Donovan:

"We're talking about an 11-year veteran who was booed by Eagles fans from the moment he was selected," [3] said Wilbon in his column on April 5th, 2010.

ESPN columnist Jemele Hill reminded us how much Philly fans dumped on McNabb, and how he better be treated with cheers when he made his return to Philly as a member of the Redskins:

"In the 11 years McNabb was the franchise quarterback of the Philadelphia Eagles, many of the fans took every opportunity to dump on his accomplishments," [4] said Hill in her article on September 29th, 2010.

If we had a dime for how many times we were told we didn't appreciate McNabb by the national media pundits, we could all afford Eagles lifetime season tickets. Some of those playoff wins were all-time classics, but those disappointments in multiple playoff games were colossal to say the least. No fan in his or her right mind would enjoy coming so close, only to see their team come up empty time and time again.

If you want further proof that Philly fans as a whole were good to McNabb, all you have to do is watch his first game back at Lincoln Financial Field as a member of the Redskins. During the pre-game introductions, Eagles fans showed McNabb class and respect, giving Number Five a heartfelt ovation when he took the field.

Instead of showing class in return however, McNabb showed bitterness and a lack of appreciation for the opportunity he had as an Eagle, making it a point to rub it in after the Redskins' victory in the locker room, saying *"Everybody makes mistakes in their lifetime and they made one last year,"* [5] proclaiming that the Eagles made a blunder by trading him. Do you think Montana would have done that after he was traded to the Chiefs? He could have been bitter over how things went down with Steve Young, but he was a winner.

Despite this early season victory against his former team, controversy again followed McNabb in Washington. The Redskins struggled and he had a poor season, which culminated with Redskins' Coach Mike Shanahan benching him in the fourth quarter when they were trailing by six points with less than two minutes to go against the Lions in Week 8. For the first time in McNabb's career, the nation was able to see what we saw for eleven years; his inability to get it done in the final two minutes of a game. Shanahan also insinuated that McNabb did not know how to run his offense and acknowledged that McNabb's conditioning was the reason behind his benching.

"The cardiovascular endurance that it takes to run a two-minute, going all the way down with no timeouts, calling plays, it's just not easy. If I

thought it was the best situation to do, then Donovan would have run the two-minute offense," [6] said Shanahan.

The national media finally acknowledged this glaring weakness in McNabb's game following his benching, as this Associated Press article states:

"If McNabb hasn't grasped the offense enough to run a two-minute drill after seven months of study, there seemed to be only three possible conclusions: The offense is too complex, the coaches have done a poor job teaching it, or McNabb is a poor student…Or a combination of the three. One of the knocks on McNabb in his 11 years with the Philadelphia Eagles was his struggles in the two-minute offense – which came to light most embarrassingly when he took his time leading a drive late in the Super Bowl with his team trailing and the clock ticking away." [6]

When all was said and done, McNabb didn't assume any responsibility for the failed season, and was quite outspoken about his benching.

"I respect Mike's decision as a head coach, but I strongly disagree with it," [7] said McNabb in regards to his benching in Washington.

McNabb spent one season in Washington and headed up north to Minnesota in 2011, where he was benched in favor of rookie Christian Ponder following a dreadful 1-5 start. Naturally, he didn't assume any blame for the team's poor season either, and was released in December.

One of the saddest things about McNabb's career will be the grudges he holds, which in many ways overshadowed his play on the field. He's still upset with the Washington Redskins after playing there for just one season! During an interview in March 2012, McNabb ripped the Redskins when it was announced they would trade up for the No. 2 overall pick to presumably draft Heisman Trophy Winner Robert Griffin III. McNabb said Griffin will not succeed in Washington because of Mike Shanahan. When asked if Griffin will have a great career in Washington, McNabb stated, *"No…I say that because a lot of times ego gets too involved when it comes to being in Washington."* [8] It didn't take a genius to figure out McNabb was referring to Shanahan.

McNabb is very bitter about the downward spiral of his NFL career and claimed on Skip Bayless' show "First Take" that he's the most criticized player in NFL history. The back-and-forth began with McNabb discussing the severity of his criticisms when compared to Tim Tebow and Bayless stepping in to say Tebow receives more criticism than he deserves.

"Tim Tebow is the most unfairly, over-criticized quarterback in the history of this league," [9] Bayless said.

With that, McNabb interjected, *"Negative — I am."* [9]

"I am," McNabb continued. *"Nobody has been criticized as much as I have."* [9]

Ultimately, Donovan McNabb was the best quarterback in Eagles franchise history when you look at his body of work. He amassed 32,873 yards, 216 touchdowns, and just 100 interceptions in his 12 seasons with the Eagles. He led them to nine playoff victories, five NFC Championship Game appearances and one Super Bowl appearance. McNabb also made six Pro Bowls and was an MVP candidate several times.

You cannot take any of his accomplishments away from him. What eluded McNabb, however, was his ability to make the big play in those huge games. It says a lot when you look at his 1-4 record in NFC Championships and a Super Bowl where he turned the ball over three times. McNabb will go down as one of the most divisive figures in Philly sports history because the Eagles should have won multiple Super Bowls during his tenure here, but like so many teams have done in this town, they came up just short.

Bernard Hopkins was right all along about Donovan McNabb; he was incapable of bringing home the big one, and he will be forever associated with arguably the most disappointing era in Eagles history.

This is the cold, harsh reality of sports when you don't get it done. It doesn't matter what city you play in.

1st Intermission:

THE J.D. DREW INCIDENT

BY DAN BAKER

Dan Baker truly is a Philadelphia broadcasting legend. In addition to his public address announcing duties for the Phillies since 1972, he has also served as the Eagles PA announcer since 1985. In 2012, Dan was inducted to the Philadelphia Sports Hall of Fame. He is also a member of the BIG 5 Hall Of Fame and was the radio play-by-play announcer for the Drexel Dragons Men's basketball team before retiring in 2012. Baker has also worked behind the mic for all four major Philly sports teams, having filled in for legendary Sixers' voice Dave Zinkoff, as well as Flyers' PA announcer Lou Nolan. As of 2012, Dan is the longest tenured public address announcer in Major League Baseball. He has presided over two regular season no-hitters, one postseason no-hitter, two Major League Baseball All-Star Games, 12 Phillies postseasons, five World Series, and three Eagles NFC Championship Games.

Yes, Dan has pretty much seen it all in Philadelphia sports over the last four decades: the good, the bad, and the ugly—including the now infamous "J.D. Drew Battery Throwing Incident," which took place on August 10th, 1999.

One of the most respected men on the Philadelphia sports scene, Dan Baker sets the record straight in regards to the Drew controversy.

The J.D. Drew incident was something which I feel very badly about because I love Philadelphia deeply, as well as all of our teams and our fans. I've always felt that in the case of J.D. Drew, the Philadelphia fans, the Phillies organization, and myself as the PA announcer were portrayed unfairly, as if we orchestrated the fans against him. That was never the case.

I remember one of the announcers on ESPN was playing back my intro-duction of J.D. Drew and said *"Listen to how the PA announcer incites the Veterans Stadium crowd against J.D. Drew."* What I thought was really unfair about that was they just played my introduction. And it's true, I raised my voice level for this, so I could be heard above the cas-cade of boos throughout the crowd of 48,000 people. *"Now batting for the St. Louis Cardinals, number seven, J......D........Drew."* Any Phillies fan who has heard me announce knows that I pause for emphasis in between any player's name who uses initials. *"Now pitching for the Phillies, number 16, J.............C.........Romero,"* or *"Now batting for the Giants, F.......P.........Santangelo."*

Their booing of J.D. Drew for his perceived rejection of Philadelphia started when he came out to the on-deck circle without any kind of introduction. Philadelphia fans are very intelligent fans. They're very emotional and supportive of their teams. They know who they want to root for and who they don't. They were deeply hurt by J.D. turning down this city and maneuvering his way to St. Louis. That's what they were upset about, and when J.D. Drew went to the batters box, the boos increased dramatically.

Like the Philadelphia fans, I was disappointed that J.D. Drew and his agent Scott Boras acted like they never received the contract the Phillies sent them. To me, that wasn't right! I want every one of our sports teams in this city to win, but I want them to win fair and square. I do not approve of poor behavior, such as throwing things from the stands or cursing. If you want to boo somebody, you have a right to do that. You're a paying customer! In saying that, let your objection come in the form of vocalization, as opposed to intimidation or doing something inappropriate or illegal.

Some were critical of the way the battery throwing incident was handled, but I thought it was one of our best diplomatic moments in the sense that we helped diffuse the crowd's anger. As I recall, this was one of the largest crowds of the year. This wasn't one of the better years for the Phillies attendance wise, but they came out to let J.D. Drew know how they felt. I believe it was later in the game when the batteries were thrown close to J.D. Drew when he was in the outfield. Home plate umpire Ed Montague called me from the dugout and told me to make an announcement that if any more objects were thrown onto the field, the game would be forfeited.

As a fan, you didn't have to be a genius to figure out who was going to lose this game if that happened. I knew and respected Ed as I do all umpires and told him I'd make the announcement, but suggested that it needed to be said in a diplomatic way because we didn't want to incite the fans. He didn't care how I said it, he just wanted it done! However, I didn't want to say anything without checking with Dave Montgomery so he wasn't blindsided. I called Dave and told him about the announcement that Ed (Montague) wanted me to make. Dave told me to comply with what the umpire requested. I explained to him I didn't want to provoke the crowd into worse behavior with how the announcement was phrased. He agreed, and told me to do this as soon as possible. I finally remember saying something to the extent of *"Please don't throw any objects onto the field that could injure players from either team, the Phillies or Cardinals."* I made sure to mention the Phillies as well. I could have just mentioned the Cardinals, but that might have caused more negative reaction. During the time in which I talked with Ed and Dave, I was thinking what could be said that wouldn't be so volatile which would allow the fans to comply with this request and not over-react negatively.

I was in the press box as a statistician and later worked a post-game radio show at Franklin Field during the Eagles-Vikings game when Santa Claus was snowballed. Although there have been other fan-related incidents, that's always the one everybody goes back to. Growing up in Philadelphia, I felt badly that our sports fans were frequently maligned. This was not a proud moment for Philadelphia fans. Even though some felt Santa may have incited the fans with an inappropriate gesture, snowballing wasn't justified in any case.

Looking back, I always thought that the J.D. Drew incident was embellished. To the best of my knowledge, there were only two batteries thrown onto the field. In saying that, of course nothing should have been thrown. Because the Phillies always try to do the right thing, they hired additional Philadelphia police that night to ensure that fan behavior wouldn't go beyond acceptable limits.

Some Cardinals accused me of encouraging negative fan reaction towards J.D. Drew for several years after the incident. On one subsequent Cardinals' visit, Dave Montgomery called me about this. Apparently, there had been a complaint registered by someone from the Cardinals that I was continuing to incite the crowd. I can't remember when the next series against the Cardinals was, but Dave told me to please make sure my introduction of J.D. Drew was straightforward with no dramatics. What I did do because of Dave's concern was quicken my announcement of J.D. Drew by saying his name faster.

J.D. Drew certainly received enough negative reaction and didn't deserve any more. The Cardinals didn't deserve this, the Phillies didn't deserve this, and Major League Baseball didn't deserve this. In my opinion, the player and his agent's actions caused this negative chain of events.

J.D. Drew never deserved the overwhelming hostile reaction which he received; however, one can certainly understand what triggered the Philadelphia fans' emotions.

4

PHILLY FANS BOO ANYTHING AND EVERYTHING

Three things in life are assured: death, taxes and the boos of Philly sports fans. These miscreants constantly boo other teams and opposing players. When that doesn't satisfy their urges, they even boo their own players and fans. Parents in Philadelphia teach their babies how to boo before they are even capable of crawling. And yes, they learn to do it well, and quite often.

Philly fans boo throughout every season, and without rhyme or reason. They boo officials, referees, umpires and even go as far as booing the food, the beer and the vendors who serve them. So, what do they do after they come home? They boo their own kids, look at their calendars and count the days until they can boo Santa Claus again.

"You know what they do in Philadelphia when the game is rained out? They go to the airport and boo bad landings."

-BOB UECKER ON PHILLIES FANS

RESPONSE: JOE VALLEE
BREAKING DOWN THE 'BOO'

The art of booing is a very interesting concept. Perhaps more so in Philadelphia than any other place in the world. That's probably because people think the concept of the 'boo' was originated here. And while this might be disappointing to some of you, I'm here to break the news that it was not. Well, at least according to Wikipedia:

'The first written record comes from ancient Greece. At the annual Festival of Dionysia in Athens, playwrights competed to determine whose tragedy was the best. When the democratic reformer Cleisthenes came to power in the 6th century B.C., audience participation came to be regarded as a civic duty. The audience applauded to show its approval and shouted and whistled to show displeasure. In ancient Rome, jeering was common at the gladiatorial games, where audience participation often determined whether a competitor lived or died.' [1]

It also goes on to say that booing is quite common, no matter *where* it takes place. Hey look at it this way, at least we don't decide who lives or dies when we boo. That would really kill our reputation.

When you think about it, there's really a different kind of boo for almost every occasion at a sporting event. As a result, I decided to put together my own boo list. And while you might think I'm rationalizing things, at the end you'll get it, or at least I hope you do. Here they are, in no particular order of importance:

1. The Sarcastic Boo:

Now I fully admit, there are times when Philly fans play up their image of eternal boo birds- it's so obvious, but on those occasions it's all in good fun! Think of it as a rite of passage.

You sometimes hear these when a fan drops a foul ball, the t-shirt gun can't quite get that shirt over the glass at a hockey game, a ball girl botches a hot grounder, a fan gets a trivia question wrong when they're on the jumbotron, somebody can't sink a half court shot or kick a field goal in one of those half time contests, or if the person throwing out the game's ceremonial first ball doesn't quite make it to home plate.

Then there's arguably the most poignant example ever of a facetious boo in Philadelphia: **Billy Wagner** and the radar gun.

For those of you not familiar with the story, Billy Wagner was a flame-throwing left-handed closer who reached 100 miles per hour on the radar gun with regularity. When Wagner came to the Phillies for the 2004 season, fans would loudly cheer every time Wagner registered triple digits, which he did more often than not. However, there were some rare occasions when Wagner only hit 98 or 99 (MPH) on the JUGS gun. So naturally, the fans would boo (insert joke here).

However, in another case of a Philly athlete not "getting it," Wagner was under the impression that the fans were actually booing him, when in fact it was just meant to be in good fun.

"Those people, it doesn't matter how successful you are. I don't get it. They boo you. They scream at you. Anybody who's going to boo you when you don't hit 100 miles per hour, what does that tell you?" Wagner said in regards to Phillies fans. *"There are some fans who are fantastic, who were very supportive, and made you feel welcome there. But, for the most part, you had the guys who just came to the ballpark to yell at you. If you're having a bad season there, forget it. You can't get out of that funk. They won't allow you to. You have to go into Philadelphia and become so thick-skinned, somebody that you're not. It's hard."* [2]

What's even more bothersome was the fact that nobody took the time to tell Wagner the fans were joking, but I digress. There were lots of players on that 2004 Phillies team who didn't "get it."

The next year however, those boos became serious when Wagner couldn't come through when it counted most for the Phightins during the 2005 Wild Card race. Down the stretch, Wagner blew the two most important games of the Phillies' season to the Astros on consecutive nights. This included giving up a crushing three-run homer to Craig Biggio with two outs in the ninth inning of the second game. This was so heartbreaking that Harry Kalas, legendary voice of the Phillies, was practically reduced to tears. Furthermore, the fact that Wagner ditched the Phillies for the hated New York Mets the following offseason left the Philly faithful with a bad taste in their mouths as far as Wagner was concerned.

For Wagner to knock the Philadelphia fans about the radar gun is completely ludicrous, considering he might have been more popular with them than his own teammates (Wagner's highly publicized feud with Pat Burrell was well documented). However, there would be a happy ending for Phillies fans, as Wagner blew a crucial game against the Cardinals in the 2006 NLCS and several important games against his old team in 2007 and 2008. When Wagner retired in 2011, many of his former Phillies teammates had one more World Series ring than he did.

2. The Booing of a Certain Player or Team That You Absolutely Despise:

We could go all night with these. Maybe it's Joe Carter for killing the dream of the entire Delaware Valley in 1993, or Michael Strahan for giving Jon Runyan a hard time all those years with the New York Giants. One night it's Barry Bonds for simply being Barry Bonds, there's always Scott Rolen for obvious reasons, or maybe it was J.D. Drew for the biggest rejection in Philly sports history. You could be jeering Alex Rodriguez during World Series lineup introductions, Kobe Bryant for taking shots at Philly (more on that later). Don't even get me started on what a gnat Matthew Barnaby was. It might be Warren Sapp, who (when he wasn't spending time in Camden, NJ) was constantly reminding us why the Eagles should have picked him over Mike Mamula (remember when Sapp wore the Ron Jaworski throwback jersey as he got off the plane to San Diego for the Super Bowl?) or the New England Patriots, who basically beat our team in the Super Bowl by cheating. Maybe it's a team based out of New York, Boston, Washington, Dallas, or Pittsburgh.

Speaking of Pittsburgh, there should be a whole section here exclusively devoted to Sidney Crosby. Not only has Crosby kept the Flyers out of some potential Stanley Cups, but he blatantly took cheap shots at practically every Flyer (including hacking Claude Giroux's wrists- which required offseason surgery) that played on the ice during their first-round matchup against the Penguins in the 2012 playoffs. Crosby's performance combined with his postgame remarks throughout the series revealed how much of a baby he really is- to Flyers fans as well as the entire NHL! To the delight of the home crowd, Giroux famously got the last laugh in Game 6, propelling the Flyers to victory and sending "Sid the Kid" home.

If any sports fan reading this book can look us in the eye and say they don't have an issue with at least two of the athletes and/or teams mentioned above, you're either not from Philadelphia or you're not a sports fan. Unless it's some sacred figure who has absolutely nothing to hide whatsoever during their playing days (Bernie Parent, Dr. J, Jim Thome, Dale Murphy, Cal Ripken, Walter Payton, Hank Aaron) anybody or any team is fair game in regards to a boo. And yes, I did say *playing days*.

Keep in mind however, that if you come into our house and we don't know you, we won't make you feel at home, and that's exactly how it should be.

3.   The Booing of a Local Player You Absolutely Can't Stand:

Some local players just rub us the wrong way.

Take for example, **Shawn Bradley**, the former No. 2 pick of the Philadelphia 76ers in 1993. Bradley, who played only one year of college basketball at Brigham Young University before embarking on a Mormon mission, was picked directly behind future Sixer Chris Webber and before Anfernee (Penny) Hardaway (No. 3) and Jamal Mashburn (No. 4).

When looking back, you have to scratch your head and wonder what would compel the Sixers' brass to select a 7'6" inch wiry beanpole who hadn't played college ball in two years to compete with the likes of Shaquille O'Neal, David Robinson and Patrick Ewing on a nightly basis. The Sixers were clearly a glutton for punishment here. Sure they pulled out all the stops to try and bulk up/toughen up Bradley. Pat Croce, Moses Malone and Kareem Abdul-Jabbar were all part of the project at one point or another, but to no avail. Bradley was simply out of his league. Sure, he once put up 28 points against a hapless Clippers team, but then got schooled by the likes of Bill Wennington (who I randomly met one summer on the water slides at Dorney Park). By the time the Bullets matched up the lesser touted Gheorghe Muresan against Bradley in an early 1994 game, I had this sinking feeling that there was something seriously wrong here, that the Sixers had yet again made a terrible draft day mistake, and there was no going back.

When Bradley suffered a season-ending knee injury against Portland in his rookie year, it was almost a sigh of relief that we didn't have to watch him fall all over himself anymore. Although he was genuinely a nice guy, Bradley didn't even act like he wanted to improve his shoddy game. At least that's the impression I got from a guy the Sixers gave an eight-year $44 million dollar contract to. Nonetheless, the Sixers stuck with him until late 1995, when they finally realized Bradley would never be the player they envisioned him to be and traded him to the Nets for Derrick Coleman. Now I admired Coleman's talent (when he felt like playing), but man, did anybody win here?

In the end, Bradley had a respectable career as a defensive-oriented center with the Dallas Mavericks. It's safe to say however, that this was one experiment the Sixers and their fans wished they never took part in.

Then there's **Rod Barajas**, who absolutely stunk up the joint in his less-than-memorable season in Phillies pinstripes. As dreadful as Barajas was that year, however, it was more what he didn't do behind the plate as opposed to how he fared overall in 2007. Earlier that season (at whatever the Marlins' ballpark was named that particular month), Barajas, with ball in glove, sidestepped a sliding Hanley Ramirez at home plate with the game on the line, allowing him to score. What should have been the third and final out of a Phillies win turned into a nightmare, just because Barajas heard the footsteps.

Several pitches later, closer Brett Myers blew his arm out and the Marlins tied the game. Luckily, the Phillies won in extra innings, but all could have been avoided if Barajas simply sucked it up and took the hit that he's getting paid millions of dollars for. After the game (and I'm paraphrasing) Barajas said something to the effect that we'll all be able to look back at this and laugh about it. Rod, nobody was laughing that our closer had a strained right shoulder that further depleted an already horrendous bullpen, and part of it was YOUR fault. And we sure as hell weren't laughing when Phils GM Pat Gillick went and signed Jose Mesa a week later! Phillies fans never forgave Barajas for that incident. So naturally, he does what every lousy ex-Phillie does when they join another team: Torment us!

We obviously can't forget **Scott Rolen**, who we loved from 1997 until around mid-2001, when his prima donna attitude revealed how much of a miserable guy he really was. Much like another third baseman in this town (Mike Schmidt), the Philly fans appreciated his overall play, but we never really "knew" Rolen.

"If you want to get to know me, sorry about your luck," [3] was how Rolen once responded in regards to the fans in Philadelphia wanting to get to know more about him.

Kind of sums it up. Stay classy, Scotty.

Rolen's attitude was one of the main reasons why the 2002 Phillies squad floundered. One teammate even went as far as to call him a "cancer." Rolen didn't think the Phillies were committed to winning, but the team did finish 86-76 in 2001 and gave the Braves a legitimate scare in the race for the NL East crown that season, so it's not like they stunk anymore.

Rolen showed his true colors acting the way he did, and if you weren't in attendance at Veterans Stadium anytime in 2002 or 2003 when Rolen and J.D. Drew came to town as members of the Cardinals, you truly missed a boo bird's dream. When Rolen (now a Cardinal) asked to be part of a Phillies' Hall of Fame tribute to Harry Kalas before a Sunday afternoon game, he opened the car door for Kalas prior to his victory lap and the fans gave him the business. After the game, another target of the fans raised his ire at the Philly faithful.

"That was low class," said former Phillies first baseman Travis Lee in regards to the fans booing Rolen that afternoon. *"That was a day to honor Harry. I thought it took a lot of balls for Scottie to come out and hold the door. They can boo him all they want when he's on the field, but not when we're honoring Harry. That was ridiculous."* [4]

Travis, let me tell you something: we don't give a crap if Rolen was holding the door for the Pope. It took a lot of guts for him to pull what he did- before and after he left town. Everyone knows we weren't booing Harry, including Harry himself. And in a fit of irony, I recall that Lee's error helped cost the Phillies the game that day. And yet, he still felt like mouthing off about US.

Was Lee talented? Without question. You're not the #2 overall pick in the MLB Draft if you aren't. Lee did have some big home runs for those Phillies teams, like the Memorial Day weekend bomb against the Expos at The Vet and the ninth inning game-winner against the Orioles at Camden Yards right before the All-Star break in 2001. Defensively, Lee and Rico Brogna were the two best first baseman I've ever seen in a Phillies uniform.

In saying that, Travis Lee might have been one of the laziest (or indifferent) players to ever put on a major league uniform. No wonder Larry Bowa couldn't deal with some of these malcontents. The thing I couldn't stand about some of those players on those Phillies teams of the early 2000's is that they complained all the time, but never backed anything up. Lee never looked like he gave a crap, and that's probably another reason why we never liked him. As soon as Jim Thome was available, the Phillies rightfully waved goodbye to T Lee, who was out of baseball at 31 years of age.

Here are some others just for good measure:

Adam Eaton- The Phillies signed their former prospect to a three-year deal worth $24.5 dollars. During that time, Eaton promptly went 14-18, and decided to go home instead of pitching in the Florida Instructional League in October 2008. Eaton could have rejoined the team for the NL Championship Series and World Series if he swallowed his pride and went down with Kyle Kendrick and several other players on the roster who really had no business being with the team that October. As a result, the Phillies pretty much told him to stay home and not come back- not even for the parade. You might recall that Kendrick had a similar fall from grace that season, yet he was a team player, and was on the field at Citizens Bank Park after the Phillies won the World Series.

When Spring Training rolled around the next year, Eaton was promptly released after an interview with Todd Zolecki from MLB.com, where he stated that he frankly didn't care where he pitched in 2009.

"This isn't the only place I can pitch. There's a lot more teams out there that need pitching," [5] said Eaton during Zolecki's interview.

Several weeks after Eaton's release, he had the sheer audacity to show up to Citizens Bank Park to get his World Series ring in front of the 45,000 plus, who promptly showered him with boos. We're big on accountability with our athletes, and the fact that Eaton had basically nothing to do with that banner hanging in Ashburn Alley and was still present at the ceremony took a lot of nerve, and not in a way that Philly fans admire. So Taguchi practically had more to do with bringing home a championship to this town, and he hit .220 that season! The fact that Eaton made the hefty salary he did and then mailed it in at the end of 2008 did not sit well with the Phillies organization, or their fan base.

Say what you want about Philly sports fans, but we know a waste of roster space when we see one. Such as **Andy Ashby**, who once grabbed his crotch and cursed out some fans because he basically couldn't handle pitching in Philly.

4. Booing Because Your Team Really Does Stink, or a Player Does or Says Something Really Stupid:

We understand the fact that our teams are not going to win all the time.

Ok, I was being nice. Historically, everybody knows our teams rarely come out on the winning side of anything. If every Philly sports fan was paid a dollar for each time our teams have lost an important game, the city of Philadelphia alone could pay off the National Debt. With the exception of the 2008 Phillies, there have been 100-plus teams in this town since 1983 who have let us down when their seasons came to a close. Philly fans might be hardened, but a lot of times we have a right to be. Philly sports teams are almost like bad lovers you keep coming back to despite getting your heart ripped out over and over again. No sports city with four major sports teams has had as much heartache, and I'll debate anybody on the planet about this.

Despite decades of futility, however, what the national media doesn't get with our fans is so simple: If you play hard, give it all you've got, and act like you care, almost any athlete can be popular in this city. And despite our teams sometimes making us hang our heads in disappointment, shock, or overall disbelief (and not in a good way), we are always back next year cheering them on again! The Eagles have won nothing in over half a century, but there's still a waiting list for tickets at Lincoln Financial Field.

Then there are the times when athletes say and do things that are beyond the level of comprehension and give us no choice but to voice our displeasure. During the Phillies' championship season of 2008, Jimmy Rollins called Philly fans "front-runners." Now Rollins is a good guy, but he had to know he wouldn't exactly receive a standing ovation when the team came back from the West Coast. Even Harry Kalas gave him hell for that. Was anyone expecting us to cheer when Chris Webber and Allen Iverson ditched us on Fan Appreciation Night? You've gotta be kidding me. The fans cut Iverson a lot of slack over the years, but that was unacceptable!

As the years have passed, Philly fans have really warmed up to Phillies' starter Cole Hamels, the MVP of the 2008 NLCS and World Series, but it wasn't always that way, despite him helping Philadelphia win a championship. When Hamels got rocked in Game 3 of the 2009 World Series against the Yankees, he emphasized after the game how he couldn't *"wait for it to end"* [6] during postgame interviews. Philly fans or any fans really don't want to hear how you can't wait for your season to end when you're trying to repeat as World Series champions and you're trailing two games to one. In his first home start against the Mets in 2011, Hamels was practically booed off the mound after allowing six runs in less than three innings. During the Phillies' 2012 Home Opener, however, Hamels gave up four runs in a little more than five innings, but received a standing ovation from the crowd when Charlie Manuel took him out of the game.

Go figure!

Then there's former Sixer **Andre Iguodala**, whom Philly fans never really took to. Iguodala is a fantastic defensive player, but he was getting paid like a superstar by the Sixers, and his on-court results are similar to a player who is more of a number two or three option. Iguodala is also one of the worst fourth quarter free throw shooters in the NBA. That doesn't play well in Philadelphia when expectations are set high for someone with a lucrative, long-term deal who is supposed to come up big at crunch time. Moreover, the Sixers haven't exactly knocked on the door of the NBA Finals over the last decade or so.

It didn't help that in an interview with Sports Illustrated in 2012, Iguodala pretty much threw the Philly fans under the bus:

"In Philly, it's not about who you are, it's about what you do for us. You could be the worst person in the world, but if you score a lot of points or win a championship, you can murder somebody," [7] said Iguodala.

If there's anyone out there who knows what in the world Iguodala meant by that quote or who he was referring to, please let me know because I'm at a loss. First off, the only team to win a title in Philadelphia during his lifetime was the Phillies in 2008. The last time I checked, none of those guys have ever been on trial for murder one. The only person he could be remotely close to talking about is Michael Vick, who will never be completely embraced in Philadelphia because of his off the field actions. And by the way, the only team that ever used Lincoln Financial Field for a parade was the Phillies.

There have certainly been worse players (though not as highly paid) than Iguodala to wear a Sixers uniform, and just when he finally came through with a decent playoff showing in 2012, the Sixers shipped him out of town for Andrew Bynum. Iguodala, however, did make it a point to thank the Sixers fans after the trade. And as for Bynum, he received a thunderous ovation at the public media session that introduced him to the city. And in all likelihood, that will probably be the biggest ovation he ever gets from a Philadelphia crowd.

5. Booing a Bad Call:

We know people make mistakes. There are plenty of regular season contests in which seemingly easy calls go the wrong way and hurt your squad. However, if an official in any sport makes a call that is so atrocious and costs your team a game (or in some cases a championship) in the process, no fan in any city should be happy with this, and Philly has been the victim of some doozies.

There's **Black Friday 1977,** when the Phillies had a 5-4 lead against the Dodgers at Veterans Stadium and were one out away from taking a series lead in the NLCS. Dodgers' second baseman Davey Lopes hit a screamer that took a bad hop off Mike Schmidt. An ever-alert Larry Bowa picked up the ball and fired to first, apparently getting Lopes out to end the game. However, umpire Bruce Froemming called him safe, and the Dodgers tied and eventually won the game. The Phillies went berserk over the call and understandably so. Replays show Lopes was out, and to this day Bowa insists he got him. The next night, the Dodgers won the pennant at a soggy Veterans Stadium. At that time, the 1977 Phillies had won more games than any team in franchise history (101), and many believe that their entire season came down to that call. This call was so bad that the MLB Network ranked it as one of the worst blown calls of all-time on an episode of *Prime 9.*

In an interesting footnote to the story, Lopes became a popular coach when he joined the Phillies staff in 2007. During his time here, he helped establish the team's running game, which became one of the best in baseball history in regards to successful stolen base attempts. And in 2008, he became part of the second championship team in the history of the franchise. In what was considered a controversial move when his contract wasn't renewed in 2010, Lopes returned to the Dodgers, and received a warm ovation from the Phillies fans upon his return to Citizens Bank Park.

How's that for a happy ending?

How about the **1980 Stanley Cup Finals offsides no-call** in Game 6 against the Flyers. Leon Stickle's non-call (although he fully admitted after the game that he should have blown his whistle) resulted in a Brian Sutter goal, which many consider to be the turning point in the game. Even though the Flyers came back to tie the score, the Islanders eventually won the game and the Stanley Cup in overtime. It is known as one of hockey's all-time worst blown calls. In fact, 1980 Flyers coach Pat Quinn is reportedly still bitter over Stickle's faux pas.

Of course, Philadelphia isn't the only city that's been a victim of blown calls. Don Denkinger's blunder in Game 6 of the 1985 World Series between the Cardinals and Royals probably gave the Royals the championship. Imagine if Jim Joyce's blown call on what should have been Armando Galarraga's perfect game happened in Philadelphia instead of Detroit. That could have gotten real ugly. In an ironic twist of fate, Joyce found himself umpiring in Philadelphia two nights later!

6. Booing an Opposing Team for Beating Your Team in the Playoffs on Your Home Turf:

Philly has cornered the market on these moments the last few years. It could be the New Jersey Devils advancing to the Stanley Cup on your home ice because the Flyers blew a 3-1 series lead, the Lakers winning the NBA Finals the next year on the Sixers' home court, maybe it's Ronde Barber and the Tampa Bay Buccaneers, who shattered the Super Bowl aspirations of an entire generation. Let's not forget the Chicago Blackhawks, who just beat your team in overtime on a charity goal to win the Stanley Cup, or the Giants and Cardinals ending the Phillies' seasons at Citizens Bank Park two consecutive years.

Either way, do you really expect us to clap for these teams when they're prancing around on our turf as we sit there thinking about how our championship aspirations are crushed yet again? Get real. Call us sore losers, but we lost, we're mad, and now we're going to have to watch the enemy advance in the playoffs, or even worse, watch footage of their championship parade two days later on ESPN. If our teams had 11 championships like the St. Louis Cardinals have, then maybe we would be a little nicer. Unfortunately, our teams don't. In fact, Philadelphia doesn't have a total of 11 titles in any capacity!

7. Booing Because Your Team Didn't Execute When it Mattered Most:

I'm not going to sit here, be ignorant and say Philly fans never boo specific individuals. We have. Many, many times.

In saying that, just because we seem to boo a lot doesn't mean we're always booing an athlete. When the Eagles fail to score a touchdown in the red-zone (which has been a problem for decades), we might not have been directly booing Donovan McNabb. If a Phillies player grounds out with the bases loaded and the Phillies fail to score, we're not always booing Ryan Howard, we might be booing a wasted opportunity. If the Flyers fail to score on a power play, we're not necessarily booing Scotty Hartnell because his shot went wide. If the Sixers blow a ten-point lead, we might not have been specifically booing Andre Iguodala. We did that enough already.

"I just tried to let the players here know that if the fans boo when you're up with the bases loaded and you pop a ball up, they boo the fact that the Phillies didn't score any runs," says Larry Bowa, who has been exposed to the art of booing more than almost any other Philadelphia athlete or manager.

"If you wanna take it personally, that's fine," Bowa says. *"I really think the fans just want their teams to win. It doesn't matter how they win, if you don't do something in a crucial part of the game, they let their anxieties out and let you know that they're upset you didn't score any runs. Some guys can handle that, but some other guys can't mentally handle those situations."*

8. Booing a Player Who Intentionally Shows Up or Harms One of Your Teams' Players:

You don't steal second base when your team is up 9-2, as Barry Bonds once did against the Phillies at Veterans Stadium in a game during the summer of 1998. Whether Scott Stevens' legendary hit on Eric Lindros in the 2000 Conference Finals was dirty or not, it sure as hell looked that way. Though Stevens has long since retired, he will forever be despised by Flyers fans because of it. Now if the Flyers had won Game 7 and advanced to the Stanley Cup that night, would it still be held in the same regard? I guess we'll never know.

What about Cowboys' safety Roy Williams, who made a living out of horse-collar tackles? You know, like the one he pulled on Terrell Owens, which left him with a sprained ankle and fractured fibula just prior to the 2004 playoffs. Whether Williams meant to intentionally hurt Owens is debatable, but you all know how this story ended. Owens returned from his injury to perform valiantly in the Super Bowl against the Patriots. As strong as he was in that game, imagine how much better he would have been if he was playing with two healthy legs.

Remember Jose Reyes pointing that finger of his running around the bases after that Shea Stadium home run in 2008? How did you feel when Shane Victorino got plunked by the Giants' Ramon Ramirez in the summer of 2011? (As if we needed another reason to hate the Giants!). Even if these occurrences happen when our teams are on the road (like the Victorino or Reyes incidents), just wait until the opposition comes back into town. Philly fans have a long memory.

If Ryan Howard grounds out with the bases loaded and the Phillies fail to score, we're not always booing him, we might be booing a wasted opportunity.

9. **The Booing of a Popular Athlete Who Left Your Team Under Less Than Favorable Circumstances and Comes Back as an Opposing Player:**

When former Flyer **Eric Lindros** returned to the (whatever the arena was called at the time) Center after being traded by the Flyers to the New York Rangers in January 2002, he was literally booed right from pre-game warm-ups to every time his stick touched the puck come game time.

Why were the Flyers fans booing? Maybe it was because the Flyers had traded (what seemed like) half their team to the Quebec Nordiques, who went on to win two Stanley Cups as the Colorado Avalanche with those players they traded for Lindros. Maybe it was because the Flyers were supposed to win multiple Cups with Lindros and it never happened. Maybe the fans finally had it with Lindros, his parents and GM Bob Clarke for what seemed like a childish game that was unraveled for all of Philadelphia and the entire NHL to see.

Where do we begin with this one? Honestly, we could probably devote two full chapters to this. It was a shame that things ever got so bad between Lindros and the Flyers. After all, he's the guy who was pretty much responsible for getting that arena built! Much like Allen Iverson, Lindros rescued the Flyers from the doldrums of mediocrity (i.e. the worst stretch of Flyers hockey in their history) and gave the fans something to cheer about again. Sure, it took until his third year to lead the Flyers into the playoffs. But once he did, the Flyers became Stanley Cup favorites for the next half decade.

Sadly, a disappointing Stanley Cup loss to the Detroit Red Wings in 1997 was the farthest a Flyers team from the Lindros era would get to raising Lord Stanley. Shortly afterwards, things started going south with Lindros and the Flyers organization. A series of concussions had his meddling parents in a war of words with Clarke over how their son should have been treated. In the meantime, early playoff exits became the norm for these Flyers teams. And just when you thought it couldn't get any worse, one of the most tragic and understated sports stories in recent history unfolded in the 1999-2000 season.

The moment that perhaps foreshadowed the team's upcoming season took place in July, when young Flyers' defenseman Dmitri Tertyshny was killed in a freak boating accident. Then just a few months into the year, beloved head coach Roger Neilson, one of Lindros' biggest backers, was diagnosed with bone cancer. While Neilson underwent treatment for the disease, assistant coach Craig Ramsay took over. Neilson, while declaring himself fit to coach, never returned to the team and would watch the playoffs from the press box. Meanwhile, Lindros' subsequent criticism of the team's training staff for how they handled yet another concussion he suffered (by this time the count is believed to be four) saw Clarke strip him of the team's captaincy.

Despite the drama surrounding the orange and black, the Flyers came together (sans Lindros) and finished strong going into the playoffs. The Flyers won the first two rounds (which included a series win over the Penguins featuring the classic five overtime game) before squaring off against the hated New Jersey Devils (this is truly a team that will haunt Philly sports fans forever) in the Eastern Conference Finals. After dropping the first game, the Flyers reeled off three straight wins to take a commanding 3-1 series lead. After dropping Game 5, Lindros returned to the ice for Game 6 and his presence was instantly felt. Despite losing 2-1, Lindros scored the Flyers' only goal in the contest. He was the best player on the ice that night after not playing for two months. With Lindros back, it made the Flyers chances look pretty good for Game 7 at home, but this emotional rollercoaster of a season soon came to a crushing and bitter end.

Just minutes into the game, Devils' defenseman Scott Stevens delivered a hit on Lindros that is still talked about to this very day in Philadelphia. Lindros sprawled to the ice, suffered concussion number six (in what would be seven for his career) and was knocked out cold. The energy of the home crowd was reduced to being able to hear a pin drop in a matter of seconds. Lindros was eventually helped off the ice, and it was the last time he ever appeared in a game for the Flyers. You know the rest. Patrick Elias' goal late in the third period gave the Devils a 2-1 lead, and the rest is history.

Just like that, the season was over. While Lindros was eventually cleared to play in November 2000, he decided to sit out the entire season, which angered even the staunchest Lindros supporters. In the summer of 2001, Clarke finally traded Lindros to the Rangers, ending almost a decade of great moments, but ultimately expectations never fulfilled. Roger Neilson never returned to the Flyers, and eventually succumbed to his illness in 2003.

Although it seems Lindros has finally made peace with the Flyers, Philly sports fans will never forget that 1999-2000 Philadelphia Flyers season: arguably the saddest chapter of a franchise that has had its share of victory as well as tragedy. Nobody won here: not the Flyers, not Clarke, not Lindros, and certainly not the fans.

When I think of what transpired that season, I don't think as much about how the team came together through the adversity, or Keith Primeau's goal against the Penguins in the five-overtime game. Honestly, it's more a feeling of disappointment and sadness that everything turned out how it did. It's a cloud that quietly hung over the Flyers franchise for a long time.

As one superstars' era closed in this city, the Eagles, with second-year quarterback Donovan McNabb now at the helm, were making a meteoric rise to the top of the NFC East. However, after several consecutive championship game losses, Eagles fans began to long for the day McNabb would have a legitimate No. 1 wide receiver. This finally came in the form of **Terrell Owens** in 2004. As a result, McNabb had his best season statistically, the Eagles got off to a 13-1 start, and Owens finally gave the Eagles that long deep threat they so desperately needed. He also gave the team something they were sorely lacking—an edge. T.O. took this town by storm. If he would have run for mayor during the fall of 2004, he would have beaten Ben Franklin by a landslide. Owens was embraced immediately by Eagles fans and became a larger than life character in the city, instantly becoming more popular than McNabb ever was.

When T.O. overcame his gruesome injury that December, he rehabbed extensively to come back for the Super Bowl, in which he had nine receptions for 122 yards. It was practically a modern miracle that Owens was even able to step on the field considering the severity of his injury.

If the Eagles won the game, it would have been heralded as one of the greatest all-time performances in Super Bowl history. However, the Eagles lost to the Patriots 24-21, and this era of Eagles football would never be the same again.

Terrell Owens works his way through the crowd at Jacksonville during Super Bowl XXXIX Media Week in 2005.

Then came the 2005 offseason, where a bitter contract dispute eventually led to a war of words between T.O and McNabb (though most of the words came from Owens, with McNabb being his typical, passive aggressive self). Owens got kicked out of training camp and started doing a bunch of sit-ups outside his South Jersey mansion. T.O. was now wearing Michael Irvin throwback jerseys to press conferences and appeared on local talk shows saying he didn't care what the fans thought of him. Then came the alleged fight with Hugh Douglas in the Eagles' locker room, and finally more derogatory comments about McNabb and the Eagles' front office which turned out to be the final straw. The Eagles eventually deactivated him for the rest of the season and released him in the beginning of 2006. Owens had this town by the tail and he sabotaged it all within the span of a year. So who does he sign with shortly after he parts company with the Birds? Yep, the Dallas Cowboys. He even made a rap song about it (*"I'm a Cowboy now, no more black and green."*)

Anyway...

Whenever Owens returned to Philadelphia from this point, he was greeted with more boos than cheers, to which Owens replied *"There's a lot of love in those boos."* [8] And you know what? There might have been some truth to that. Part of Philadelphia still loved T.O. Many fans will never forget what he did during that memorable 2004 season. In the end however, the majority of Eagles fans were sick of his act. And truth be told, you can't blame any of them for feeling that way. When he got cut from the IFL at 38 years of age for refusing to play in several important games and being a no-show at a children's hospital, he officially burned every bridge you could possibly burn. T.O. had it all in Philly, as well as every place he ever played—and he blew it every time. Pretty sad.

Then there's **Jayson Werth**, the former Phillies right fielder who actually won a championship in this town. This was a strange case because originally, Werth didn't leave acrimoniously. Simply put, the Nationals offered him $126 million dollars, which was $48 million more than the Phillies offered him. As I previously mentioned, Werth already has a ring, now he has a lot of money to go with it. Lots of Philadelphia fans did not take kindly to this. On one hand, some were just upset that he left the team. Others however, were accusing Werth of "selling out" and "taking the money and running." Now I know Philadelphia is a blue collar town, but come on people! Each and every one of you would have done the same thing, and I personally never faulted Werth for this. Moreover, if Domonic Brown eventually gets his act together, we won't even have to talk about this, but I digress.

My beef and many other fans' beef with Werth started at his introductory press conference as a National, which was the beginning of several stories Werth couldn't seem to get straight. First, he said he signed the contract because of the on-field potential of the

Nationals, who were coming off a 69-93 record in 2010.

Meanwhile, the Phillies led the majors in victories with 97 that same season and would go on to win a franchise record 102 games in 2011. You would think the better chance to win would be in Philly. Little did Werth know that the Phillies were saving their money for a nice Christmas present, which turned out to be the re-signing of Cliff Lee. When Werth got wind of this, he texted Phillies GM Ruben Amaro showing his displeasure. At the press conference, he even made a note of it, mentioning how the Phillies *"got their boy back."* Werth came off as bitter, and still couldn't get the Phillies out of his mind.

Jayson Werth was a fan favorite, but now he's smoking victory cigars with the Washington Nationals.

Then came Spring Training 2011, where Werth then said he felt like he owed it to the Major League Baseball Players Union to take the best deal possible. He went on to say that if the Phillies had decided to extend Lee in 2009 prior to trading him to the Mariners, they could have kept him. This is the kind of rationale that has Phillies fans scratching their heads. Werth also made headlines when he was caught talking with Nationals GM Mike Rizzo near the batting cages about how he hated the Phillies. Although he may have been half-joking, Werth wasn't joking when he broke his wrist in Washington at the beginning of the 2012 season during a Sunday night game against the Phillies. After surgery the following day, Werth delivered perhaps the final knockout blow to a once strong relationship he had established with the Phillies fan base. In an email to Adam Kilgore of the Washington Post, Werth sent the following message.

"After walking off the field feeling nauseous knowing my wrist was broke and hearing Philly fans yelling 'You deserve it,' and, 'That's what you get,' I am motivated to get back quickly and see to it personally those people never walk down Broad Street in celebration again." [9]

Okay. There may have been a few idiots there who were cheering when Werth was walking off the field after his injury. I won't deny that. In saying that, do you really think those nimrods actually were sober enough to know he had a broken wrist? Have you ever been at a sporting event when a player is injured and you have to call or text your friends just to figure out exactly what happened on the field? It's a pretty damn tedious process.

Come on, Jayson. Instead of emailing Kilgore with a positive message for Nationals fans, it always comes back to us. For the record, there are lots of Phillies fans who will always be thankful for what you did for our team in 2008. You know, the ones who weren't booing when you hit the ground. Furthermore, chances are none of us will ever see $126 million dollars. Even though Werth somewhat softened his stance upon his return, he should just let it go.

And people wonder why we boo sometimes.

10. The Booing of a Player Because, to be Honest, They're Good, and *Not* Playing For Us:

Although the Sixers and Celtics squared off in the 1980 Eastern Conference Finals, Philly fans didn't get a real taste of **Larry Bird's** dominance until the next year's conference finals. In his second season in the NBA, Bird and the Celtics were down 3-1 to Dr. J and the gang when Boston took three straight, winning Game 7 at the Boston Garden on Bird's clutch jumper en route to his first,, and the Celtics 14th NBA title (as if the Celtics needed any more). Although the Sixers got revenge at the Garden in Game 7 the next year, many say that the '81 showdown against Philadelphia was when Larry "Legend" was born.

Over the course of four conference finals and a 1984 pummeling at the hands of Doc (with help from Moses Malone and a young Charles Barkley), Bird continued to torment the Sixers for the next decade. He was a sharp shooting trash talker, and arguably the best player in the

NBA- and we hated him for it because everybody knew it. Yes, he was introverted and aloof (just like a certain Phillies third baseman who played here for decades) but the thing is, there's not one person in the city of Philadelphia who wouldn't take Larry Bird on their team.

Bank on it.

One of the first commandments Philly sports fans are taught as a young child is to hate the Dallas Cowboys. And one of the players we hated the most on those Cowboys teams of the 1990's full of misfits and felons was **Troy Aikman.** Aikman's 10 concussions are a true testament to his toughness. He didn't even remember playing in Super Bowl XXVIII due to one of those concussions in the NFC Championship Game. Furthermore, he never got arrested for packing heat, was never busted for trafficking marijuana, and was never caught with any prostitutes.

After his retirement in 2000, Aikman went up into the FOX broadcast booth, and now talks as if he actually likes the Eagles. Yes, by all accounts, Aikman seems like a pretty decent guy.

So what was the problem? Do I even need to ask? Aikman was the quarterback on three Cowboys Super Bowl teams and an absolute Eagles killer. Two of those Dallas teams knocked out our Birds in the playoffs to raise the Lombardi Trophy.

The craziest epilogue to all of this is that Aikman was *thisclose* to coming out of retirement to play for the Eagles[10] after Donovan McNabb went down with his ankle injury in 2002. I wonder how that would have gone down in Philly.......

And of course, we can't forget the guy Aikman handed the ball off to all those years, running back **Emmitt Smith**. Like Aikman, Smith always stayed out of trouble, but he gave the Eagles nothing BUT trouble. In 26 regular-season games against the Eagles (remember the Halloween game in 1993?), his rushing yards were the best numbers against any opponent. The Eagles didn't have anybody close to Smith's talent at running back during that era, and fans couldn't help but wonder how much more effective Randall Cunningham could have been if he did.

If there's anything Eagles fans can take out of this, we'll always have 4th and 1 ("*They stop him again!*")

Speaking of Cowboys, how about **Deion Sanders** and his idiotic touchdown dances? And this was BEFORE he regularly egged on McNabb about how "awfully" we treated him. Much like Terrell Owens however, Eagles fans probably would have loved this guy if he ever suited up for the team. At the end of the day however, Sanders is an NFL Hall of Famer, so who am I to argue?

Maybe it's because he has the perfect life, a pretty boy smile and GQ outfits, his supermodel wife (Gisele Bundchen), and he beat the Eagles with the assistance of a video tape in Super Bowl XXXIX. But most of all, we hate **Tom Brady** because he wins all the time, and there's not a damn thing we can do about it, and we wish Donovan McNabb was the quarterback he was. As if it isn't bad enough for Eagles fans, we've had to watch the lesser of two evils play each other TWICE in the Super Bowl in the span of five years. I was hoping Brady and the Giants would lose (and that doesn't even really make sense). I dated a girl from New England once, and I made her take off her Brady jersey every time she came to my house- and we weren't even playing strip poker.

If it's any consolation, Brady is 0-2 in Super Bowls since the Patriots got caught watching other team's walkthroughs.

On second thought, it really isn't. We still despise him.

Then there's the guy who has beaten Brady in two Super Bowls and currently has one less ring than he does. Yes, the Giants' **Eli Manning** is an enigma to us all. Maddeningly inconsistent for the better part of his career, Manning and his *"aw shucks, I don't know where I am"* persona now has some experts discussing the possibility of a future enshrinement in Canton. In J.D. Drew-like fashion, Manning was drafted by the Chargers but demanded a trade to the Giants, where somehow, someway, he has managed to raise two Lombardi Trophies, winning both of them in miraculous fashion. If you're keeping score at home, that's one more than his older brother, Peyton.

As if we need another reason to hate New York.

A thorn in our side since Claude Lemieux broke our hearts in the 1995 Eastern Conference Finals, the Devils' **Martin Brodeur** has beaten the Flyers in three postseason series. Sure, Brodeur's off-the-ice escapades have gotten him into some hot water, but we hate him because he's won more games than any other goalie in NHL history, he just so happens to play in the Flyers' conference, and he has two of his three Stanley Cup rings at the Flyers' expense. Much similar to the Eli Manning/Tom Brady Super Bowl scenarios, who was the lesser of two evils in the 2012 Stanley Cup Finals? The Devils (who eliminated the Flyers in the second round of the playoffs) or the Los Angeles Kings (featuring exiled Flyers Mike Richards and Jeff Carter).

Can Philly fans ever truly win?!

When he first came up to the big leagues, I thought **Chipper Jones** was a cocky punk, and it didn't help matters that he played for the Atlanta Braves. Sure, they choked at the end of every year when it mattered most, but in the meantime they would put a beating on the Phillies en route to their hundreds of thousands of division titles. Jones had a lot to do with this. On second thought, Jones had almost everything to do with this from an offensive standpoint, flat-out dominating the Phillies more than almost any opposing player ever has. With his career winding down in recent years however, I fully realize and appreciate that Jones was indeed one heck of a player- one most certainly deserving of a first ballot Hall of Fame induction.

So how much did Philly fans despise Jones? Well, in the first game after the September 11th attacks, Jones was introduced by Phillies' PA Announcer Dan Baker and a cascade of boos erupted. To further complicate matters, Jones then launched a home run off Phillies' starter Robert Person. *"I knew then that the healing had begun."* [11] said Larry Bowa in regards to Jones' blast.

If there's one final indication that Philly fans respected Jones, it was evident the night the Phillies honored him during his last trip to Citizens Bank Park in September 2012, where he was given a standing ovation at a pregame ceremony by the Philly faithful. Sure, the next day the fans booed the heck out of him, but that's the beauty of it all.

Man, I'm really going to miss those *"Larrrrrrrrrrrryyyyyyyyy"* chants at the Bank.

Carlos "CHOOOOOCH" Ruiz

Yes, there are different reasons Philly fans can boo. But upon closer examination, I think you would agree that most of these are quite valid. Our reputation precedes us to the point that outsiders think we even boo our players when we're actually supporting them. So in a fitting conclusion to this chapter, I give you 10 past and present Philly athletes whose names have inspired cheers, not jeers:

1. Brian Boucher (BOOOOSH)

2. Duce Staley (DUUUUCE)

3. Lou Williams (LOOOOU)

4. Carlos Ruiz (CHOOOOOCH)

5. Raul Ibanez (RAUUUL)

6. Clarence Weatherspoon (SPOOOOOOOON)

7. Claude Giroux (GIROUUUUUX)

8. Bob Boone (BOOOOONE)

9. Hugh Douglas (HUUUUGH)

10. Jrue Holiday (JRUUUUUUUE)

5

PHILLY FANS EVEN BOO ANTI-CANCER ANNOUNCEMENTS

"Hi, I'm Sidney Crosby, leading the fight against cancer."

Perhaps, we should not even mention this one, as this seems even too low for Philly fans. Wink, wink. Of course, we'll mention it and please—milk it for all it's worth.

Yes, it's well established that Philly fans boo umpires, referees, opposing players, coaches and even their own athletes. But, a Public Service Announcement (PSA) against cancer is something that everyone can support, right? Think again: not in Philly.

Yes, it happened between periods of a Flyers game in 2011. As the NHL asked fans for support of their *Hockey Fights Cancer* initiative, the boos rained down, drowning out the life-affirming message. How outrageous...and it would have been even worse had Santa Claus made the announcement.

"So, yes, one could say that Philadelphia fans were booing a 'Hockey Fights Cancer' PSA."

- BAILEY JOHNSON, CBS NEWS SPORTS BLOGGER

RESPONSE: RYAN DOWNS

Oh brother, here we go again.

The Philadelphia sports fans have once again outdone themselves and unleashed their lack of class and overall disregard for humanity…by doing WHAT? Yes, ladies and gentlemen, Philadelphia Flyers fans booed a public service announcement promoting the fight against cancer.

Well, maybe not exactly.

On the surface, it seems ugly and unthinkable. Even more importantly, it really did occur.

Let's review the tape and take a good, hard look at the facts.

Fact: A *Hockey Fights Cancer* clip was shown at the Wells Fargo Center during the October 12, 2011 game against the Vancouver Canucks.

Fact: During the duration of said clip, the fans responded with a measurable amount of jeering.

Therefore, Bailey, yes I suppose you could say that the fans were booing the PSA. But what does this really mean?

Well, I'm glad you asked.

I think we need to break this down a little more to examine the true nature of the crime, before we dish out any punishment.

Essentially, to the naked eye (and ear), this is just another case of the ruthless, unforgiving fan base in Philadelphia embarrassing itself by spreading their standard, indiscriminant negativity. Incidents such as this would serve nicely to prove how spiteful and maliciously self-serving sports fans can be in a city not so loving of their brothers, it would seem. The thought of the same fans cheering wildly for Michael Vick and Brett Myers, then booing support toward cancer prevention is downright inexcusable and puzzling.

All of this seems undeniably true in this context, and it would be just as inexcusable and puzzling for me to argue against such a premise, unless the story here is that there should be no story at all.

Let's get one thing straight; regardless of interpretation, fans in Philadelphia need to be a little more careful before they cascade their vocal venom. If we didn't realize it before, we certainly know it now. There are eyes and ears focused on us at all times. The national media lurks when you least expect it, ready to pounce and make a story out of a virtual misdirection. Who even knew they played hockey games in October, right? I say this facetiously, of course. I certainly do– as do many of the legions of Flyers fans whose loyalty, enthusiasm, and support got them into this mess in the first place.

Herein lies the paradox.

This is just another example of pundits in the national media sticking their noses, mouths, and fingertips where they don't rightfully belong. Projecting the passion of hockey fans onto such a serious life and death issue is irresponsible, depressing, and entirely unfair.

The PSA itself began with quite a sight for sore eyes inside the (insert bank here) Center. As if in surround sound, the following words were blurted:

"Hi, I'm Sidney Crosby."

For those who don't follow hockey, this statement within the Flyers arena is akin to randomly rolling a clip of LeBron James at a Cleveland Cavaliers game. In fact, I would love to see footage of the same exact public service announcement, but instead it would be played loudly at Fenway Park and Bucky Dent would be the lead spokesperson.

How do you think *"Hi, I'm Bucky Dent"* would work in Boston? Perhaps we could team him up with Aaron Boone and Alex Rodriguez—what a trifecta that would be. I'm sure the out of context boo ratio would be skyrocketing.

Think it would even matter if Bucky was announcing that he discovered a CURE for cancer? I'm not so sure it would.

Not to poke fun at a very serious issue here, but it is clear that the fans preemptively booed the *Hockey Fights Cancer* portion of the promotion. Not only was it Crosby, but it was Ryan Miller and Jonathan Toews. All three have a healthy penchant for ending promising seasons for the Flyers, most notably Toews' Blackhawks, who skated around with Lord Stanley's Cup in this same building some sixteen months prior. Heck, it was Toews himself who first hoisted the Cup as captain. If that doesn't stick in a fan's craw, then they are either lifeless and impassionate, or simply not paying attention.

It is reasonable to conclude that the volume of the booing would have been decreased or nonexistent had the purpose of the PSA been evident before Crosby's mug was displayed for all to see, and subsequently jeer. Even more notably, it is certain that the crowd was jeering in the direction of Crosby and friends, and the timing was nothing more than pure coincidence. Heck, it could have very easily been *"Hi, I'm Sidney Crosby, and I drink Gatorade."* Would the arena then be filled with Gatorade haters? I think not.

At its core, the incident proved nothing more than the healthy rivalry between cross-state foes. The brewing hatred and competitiveness between the Flyers and Penguins in recent years is exciting for fans all over the Keystone state.

The individual fans that chose to channel that disdain were merely victims of circumstance. They were in a building filled with meddling pen pushers and internet gossipers, clamoring to create a story to fit the narrative. After all, this is where they booed Santa Claus and threw batteries.

The natural reaction became an unfair and absurd accusation, and the only good reason was because people needed to create an easy story. Well, sometimes, stories can cause damage. No individual person was a victim of libel in this case. Rather, this was mass libel.

Interestingly enough, many of the published articles argued against themselves. For instance, an article entitled *"Flyers Fans Boo 'Hockey Fights Cancer' PSA"* featuring rival players gives this little nugget of wisdom:

"So Flyers fans did what came naturally when they saw those players: they booed them, despite the fact they were representing and speaking to a worthwhile cause which I am confident most Flyers fans wouldn't boo had it not been for those players' appearances in the spot." [1]

Or try this one on for size:

"It's easy to take potshots at Philly fans for their, shall we say, spirited reaction. No one is suggesting Philadelphia hockey fans are pro-cancer. But, guys, come on. Maybe tone it down a little and it wouldn't be so easy." [2]

Tone it down a little? Quite frankly, I find it maddening to read about an "incident" in which the prosecution goes on the defense. If the intent was not to portray Philadelphia sports fans in a negative light, the article would either be titled differently, or not written at all.

Simple as that.

These fans were not guilty of any sort of disdain or lack of humanity. Instead, there was passion and excitement, surely a thing of beauty to suits in the NHL league office. Sadly, today's blogosphere and overall media circus have created an atmosphere where the lazy and uncreative prevail. If anything that can be portrayed as negative happens in Philly, it will be reported, no matter the context.

No matter the severity. No matter the harsh sensitivity.

Some people, like Yahoo! Sports' Puck Daddy Greg Wyshynski steadfastly defended the Flyers fans.

Wyshynski exclaimed, *"We're as guilty as anyone for taking whacks at the Flyers fan piñata. But please tell us Flyers fans aren't now going to be labeled pro-cancer? Please?"* [3]

However, that being said, why did this incident even warrant reporting or defending of any kind? Puck Daddy wrote an article essentially begging his peers to stop the rapid fire labeling and irresponsible accusations. The irony here is that his article was a response and was only borne of the fact such knee-jerk nonsense already existed, filling up internet homepages everywhere. Yes, the mere fact that he had a story to defend was ludicrous in its own right.

Tweets everywhere were calling for this to be the "new Santa" in Philadelphia. Now, that is actually amusing.

Was it mildly insensitive for fans to boo? Not really, given the chronology and all the facts. Should Philly fans be a little more "careful" before they boo? Possibly. Uh, wait, check that.

Definitely.

But is this incident really front page news? Not even close.

The situation has now become crystal clear. The Flyers fans on this particular night were guilty of one thing only. They were in Philadelphia.

Maybe the NHL should recruit Santa Claus to do the next announcement.

WE'LL GIVE YOU THAT/ YOU GOTTA GIVE US THESE!

WE'LL GIVE YOU THAT:

SEVEN PHILLY FAN INCIDENTS THAT NOT EVEN WE CAN DEFEND

Now granted, this book was written to defend ourselves and poke fun at the national media who always give us Philly fans a hard time. In saying that, the following incidents don't exactly do much to dispel the notion of unruly fan behavior in the City of Brotherly Love. We'll concede defeat on these.

1. Beating Of Rangers Fans At Geno's Steaks Following Winter Classic- January 2nd, 2012.

The Philadelphia Flyers had just lost to the New York Rangers in the 2012 NHL Winter Classic. It's always difficult to lose to an archrival, but up until the infamous Geno's Steaks incident, the Flyers and their fans had received well-deserved kudos for staging a terrific two-day event.

A short time later outside Geno's Steaks—one of South Philly's iconic outdoor cheesesteak establishments—an orange-clad (alleged) Flyers fan and his dim-witted buddies thought it would be a wonderful idea to pay a homeless, "squeegee" guy to spray at least one of those two Rangers fans he spotted with his bottle.

What happened next was not so much an altercation, but a full-out criminal assault in the street as one of a gang of three (and possibly four) morons came from behind to cold-cock a man wearing a Rangers' No. 24 jersey. From there, (as captured, and spread virally on youtube. com) we all cringed watching the video of these idiots landing numerous shots to the man when he was already down on the street, while also getting in their shots against his friend. The one man suffered serious injuries and could have been left for dead on the street.

This horrific incident was somehow even worse when one considers that the Rangers fan wearing No. 24—who in no way precipitated this assault—was identified as Neal Auricchio Jr., a police officer from Woodbridge, New Jersey. Officer Auricchio, 30, fought two tours of duty in Iraq, returning to war even after a sniper in Fallujah blew apart one of his calf muscles. His second tour of duty started the day after he graduated from the Woodbridge Police Academy. Among other things, he won the Purple Heart for his heroism, served his community honorably as a police officer and even served as a volunteer fireman. Oh yeah, he was also a new dad just trying to enjoy a game and a cheesesteak with his buddy.

This may have been the most embarrassing and despicable example of fan behavior ever displayed by Philadelphia fans. Turns out this nimrod had a prior criminal record. Lock this guy up and throw away the key, please.

2. Barfman (aka Matthew Clemmens)- April 14th, 2010

The Chicago Cubs have Bartman; we Phillies fans have Barfman. Yuck!

Steve Bartman's cluelessness and overzealousness may have cost the Cubbies a trip to the 2003 World Series. Barfman stained Philllies fans with a gruesome black eye, not to mention that he intentionally showered a poor 11-year-old girl with his vomit at an April, 2010 game at Citizens Bank Park. If you are disgusted reading this, so are we in recounting this atrocity.

The girl was the daughter of Easton, PA police Captain Michael Vangelo, who had asked ballpark security to remove Clemmens from his seat because he was spitting and cursing. After being ejected, Clemmens intentionally shoved his fingers down his throat and in Vangelo's words, committed the *"the most vile, disgusting thing I've ever seen, and I've been a cop for 20 years."* [1] Meanwhile, Vangelo suffered a bruised ear from Clemmens while attempting to force him away from his daughter, so kudos to the Philly fans for getting some shots in on Clemmens prior to the police arresting him.

Barfman was sentenced to three months in jail, and we would have applauded if Vangelo flattened this 21-year-old loser. That may be a slight exaggeration, but Clemmens is not only a disgrace to the Philadelphia fan, he might be a disgrace to anyone who has ever paid admittance to any sporting event. Clemmens' acts were so disgusting that he should be banned from all sporting events. Not only in Philadelphia, but everywhere else.

3. Bottle Rocket Man - November 10th, 1997

This was the scene. Veterans Stadium, November 10th, 1997: The Eagles hosting the San Francisco 49ers. Now, one might reasonably expect many home fans at a Monday Night Football game to be inebriated.. A few, admittedly, might even be high as a kite. But, nobody expected any fan—yes, even an Eagles fan—to try to turn The Vet into Cape Canaveral.

Well, let it be recorded that a fan simply to be known as Bottle Rocket Man decided to launch a bottle rocket from his seats and that this act of monumental stupidity (and aeronautic mediocrity) in turn launched the infamous…

4. Judge Seamus McCaffery's Veterans Stadium Courtroom: 1997-2003

Seamus McCaffery was your typical municipal court judge in Philadelphia with an atypical venue—the lower level of Veterans Stadium at Eagles home games. Due to the antics of Bottle Rocket Man and other more traditional rowdies, it was decreed that a courtroom be established at Eagles home games, with the honorable McCaffrey presiding. He held court for the remainder of the 1997 season and five more years until the Eagles moved into Lincoln Financial Field to start their 2003 campaign.

An offender would typically sit in the stadium jail for the duration of the game, forfeit his season tickets and be fined up to $400. McCaffrey, who was born in Belfast, Northern Ireland and served as both a Marine and a Philly cop, now sits on the Supreme Court of Pennsylvania. We are incredibly impressed with his credentials, but somewhat ashamed that his services were ever needed in one of our stadiums.

5. Flyers Fan Vs. Tie Domi - March 29th, 2001

Tie Domi was a tough-as-nails right wing for the Toronto Maple Leafs known much more for his big fists and strong chin than for his deft scoring touch. In his storied career, he scored 104 goals and logged over 3,500 penalty minutes. Domi literally made his living with his fists. For God's sake, he used to drop the gloves like we put our socks on! Domi's career was highlighted by his fierce heavyweight battles with the late Bob Probert, as well as a penalty box scuffle with Chris Falcone, a concrete worker from Havertown, Pennsylvania.

Really.

Perhaps, Falcone was trying to determine if Domi's dome was made out of concrete during the third period of a March 29th, 2001 Flyers-Leafs game. Responding to some heckling, Domi squirted his water bottle at fans sitting behind the visiting team's penalty box. The rather absurd scene played out with Falcone leaping in from the second row to try to scale the glass between the glass and the sin bin.

Well as luck (or no luck) would have it, Falcone managed to break the glass, leaving him and Domi by themselves in the penalty box. Domi got some shots in before being restrained by the referees.

We have no idea on earth what Falcone was thinking, but nonetheless, he was escorted from the arena with two black eyes: one for him and another for Philly fans.

Unfortunately, Judge Seamus was not there to dish out more justice to this clown.

6. Bounty Bowl II: Eagles Fans Pelt Jimmy Johnson And Other Dallas Cowboys With Snowballs - December 10th, 1989

As you may have heard, Philly fans and snowballs have a long history. Unlike the Santa Claus incident however, there was plenty that was captured on tape in the "Bounty Bowl" sequel. Just weeks after the original "Bounty Bowl" (a Birds 27-0 thrashing of the Cowboys on Thanksgiving), where Birds coach Buddy Ryan reportedly placed a bounty on former Eagles kicker Luis Zendejas, Buddy's boys and "America's Team" were at it again.

Although this game was a lot closer than its predecessor, the Eagles swept the season series with a 20-10 win. But let's get to the point: the only image many remember from "Bounty Bowl II" is that of Cowboys first-year coach Jimmy Johnson being escorted from the field by Philadelphia police as he was being pelted by a barrage of snowballs and beer following the Eagles victory. One can only imagine what first-year NFL commissioner Paul Tagliabue was thinking as he watched this unfold in front of his very eyes. However, when you combine the Veterans Stadium crew failure to remove snow off most of the 65,000 seats of a stadium along with some drunken fans, it was a recipe for disaster. And oh yeah, it probably didn't help that CBS' pregame show featured various members of the Eagles and Cowboys featured on make believe wanted posters. Truth be told, this makes the "Santa Claus" incident look like an episode of Romper Room. Even future Governor of Pennsylvania Ed Rendell got in on the action, which might be a reason why it's not talked about so much anymore (Sorry, Gov). Yeah, not one of our better moments.

As savage an incident that "Bounty Bowl II" was made out to be, it was kids stuff compared to the snowball incident at Giants Stadium in 1995, where people were seriously injured. But then again, that was New York, so they get a pass, of course...

7. The 700 Level

We simply don't have enough time for this one.

YOU GOTTA GIVE US THESE!

SEVEN INCIDENTS THAT
EVEN OUR CRITICS APPLAUDED

Let's face it: Most of the time Philadelphia fans are mentioned, it's usually for incidents that don't portray us too favorably.

And while we're never one to refrain from a well-deserved boo, fact of the matter is there isn't a greater fan base on the planet than Philly fans when the stakes are high or when an opponent is on the ropes. We have also stood up quite tall and proud for our country, and even for a rival superstar who courageously stood up to a dreaded disease to return to the ice.

Here are seven of the greatest displays of Philadelphia fandom that come to mind. And I must say, going over these has further reinforced the fact that despite often coming home empty-handed, we're still proud as hell to be Philly sports fans. We wouldn't have it any other way.

1. Phillies Fans Singlehandedly Boo Burt Hooten Out Of Game 3 Of 1977 NLCS Against The Dodgers - October 7th, 1977

Philly fans always smell blood, as they did when Dodgers' starter Burt Hooten ran into some trouble with his location during the second inning of this Friday afternoon playoff game at The Vet. When Hooten, who once no-hit the Phillies in just his fourth big league start in 1972, snapped at home plate umpire Bob Engel for supposedly pinching him in regards to balls and strikes, Phillies fans smelled that blood, and it was on like Donkey Kong.

A cascade of boos permeated The Vet, and Hooten proceeded to issue four consecutive walks to Phillies hitters, resulting in three runs without the ball ever leaving the infield and the Phillies taking a 3-2 lead. Dodgers rookie manager Tommy Lasorda, who had given Burt the nickname "Happy Hooten" because of his supposedly dour demeanor, removed him from the game and replaced him with Rich Rhoden. After he walked off the mound in utter humiliation, Hooten could be seen firing his glove in the dugout afterwards in sheer anger. Arguably, Phillies fans had more to do with the team scoring those runs than the actual team. And to this day, it might be the best example of the overall power and influence of the Philly sports fan when it matters most.

We'd like to tell you the Phillies went on to win the game and the pennant the next night, but you know we'd be lying, because happy endings don't often happen in Philly and they don't call this game Black Friday for nothing (See Chapter 4).

2. Burt Hooten 2.0: Phillies Fans Get To C.C. Sabathia In Game 2 Of The 2008 NLDS- October 2nd, 2008

After a 3-1 win against the Brewers to kick off the 2008 MLB playoffs, it was assumed by many that the Phillies would head to Game 3 in Milwaukee having split the first two games of the series. This was due in large part to C.C. Sabathia, whom the Brewers acquired in the middle of the summer to boost their then-sagging playoff chances. Sabathia was an absolute beast for the Brew Crew, going 11-2 with a 1.65 ERA. He was even more impressive down the stretch, going 2-1 with an 0.83 ERA as the Brewers clinched a playoff spot on the season's last day.

As effective as he was however, you had to wonder if Sabathia's yeoman-like effort during the month of September would result in him running out of gas.

It didn't help matters that Phillies starter Brett Myers had a shaky first inning. Myers walked in a run before getting Brewers right fielder Corey Hart to hit into a rare inning-ending 1-2-3 double play on the first pitch with the bases loaded.

Phillies third baseman Pedro Feliz had tied the game 1-1 in the bottom of the second before Myers, a career .116 hitter (and .069 hitter during the regular 2008 season), stepped to the plate. What followed was the most improbable and possibly the most pivotal at-bat of the entire 2008 postseason.

Phillies fans knew of Myers' batting history (or lack thereof), so when he was constantly fouling off pitches after getting buried 0-2 in the count, we were more than appreciative of Myers' "battle" with Sabathia and started cheering him loudly. Where this was going, we had no idea, but we knew Myers was putting up a fight and Sabathia was wasting pitches. When Myers someway, somehow drew a walk, the fans at Citizens Bank Park were waving their rally towels in an absolute frenzy.

The walk to Myers messed up Sabathia's concentration something fierce. With every pitch, the fans cheered even louder. Much like Burt Hooten in 1977, Sabathia wasn't getting borderline pitches. He walked Jimmy Rollins on four pitches, setting the stage for Shane Victorino. And with the count 1-2, Victorino sat on Sabathia's next pitch and launched the first grand slam in Phillies postseason history over Ryan Braun's head in left field. 5-1 Phillies. They had effectively slayed the beast. Myers coasted the rest of the way and the Phillies flew to Milwaukee with a commanding 2-0 series lead. With Victorino's four-bagger, they had made a statement not only to the Brewers, but to all of Major League Baseball. And Phillies fans were starting to feel that maybe, just maybe, things could be different this time.

And the great part about this was, they had a lot to do with it.

Unfortunately, almost every happy story in Philly has an epilogue, and Sabathia got his revenge on the Phillies the next year as a member of the Yankees, who took the Phillies in six games to deny them of a second consecutive World Series title.

3. USA! USA! USA! Osama Bin Laden Is Killed, And Phillies Fans Show Their Pride On Espn Sunday Night Baseball – May 2nd, 2011

It was late in what would be an extra-inning game between the Phillies and the Mets when people started receiving news updates and text messages that 9/11 mastermind and international terrorist Osama Bin Laden had been killed. As the news spread like wildfire, fans started with loud chants of *"USA! USA!"* throughout the stadium.

For once, Phillies fans were displaying the raw emotion that the entire country was feeling, and it was on live display at Citizens Bank Park. It's safe to say that night made everyone in attendance extremely proud to be a Philadelphia Phillies fan, and even prouder to be an American.

4. Flyers Fans Cheer President Bush During A Preseason Game – September 20th, 2001

It was a little more than a week after 9/11, and the United States was still reeling in the wake of the terrorist attacks. President Bush was set to address the nation during the second intermission of the Flyers' preseason game against the Rangers. During this time, Flyers' PA Announcer Lou Nolan told the audience that the President's speech could be seen in the concourse.

However, that wasn't good enough for Flyers fans, who booed and chanted *"leave it on!"* as they lobbied to keep the speech on for its duration. And that's exactly what happened. Instead of playing the third period, the Flyers and Rangers watched President Bush address the nation from the ArenaVision jumbotron. The arena fell silent, with the exception of occasional chants of *"USA! USA!"* It wasn't about hockey that night; it was about the return of the USA to prominence. The fans gave the President a standing ovation, the two teams shook hands and agreed to end their contest in a tie, and in what was perhaps the most unlikely scenario of the entire evening, Philadelphia saluted New York.

5. Phillies Fans Show Their Best In First Post-9/11 Game Against Braves – September 17th, 2001

Braves starter Greg Maddux said he never saw Philly fans as polite as he did in the game that followed the 9/11 attacks. And he was right.

For all in attendance, it was truly an experience we will never forget. There was a feeling of unity between the fans, players, opposing players—just about everyone. Phils' skipper Larry Bowa even managed to bond with Scott Rolen, who (reluctantly, and absurdly so) agreed to a rare curtain call after his second home run of the night off Maddux. The image of the hard-nosed Bowa wiping tears from his eyes was one symbolic of the entire country as well as the Philly fans. The Phillies won the game 3-2, moved another game closer to the first place Braves, and we all forgot about the troubles the United States faced— at least for a little while.

6. Flyers Fans Stand Up And Cheer The Return Of Mario Lemieux – March 2nd, 1993

We may not have a *"BEAT LA"* moment to rival the Boston Celtics fans' unexpected show of magnanimity—perhaps, for the only time in their history, way back in 1982—but Flyers' fans really showed their class and appreciation for a courageous superstar during a regular season home tilt against the rival Pittsburgh Penguins on this date.

You must understand that the Penguins had been a bitter, cross-state rival for many years preceding this late-season clash. They were also the two-time defending Stanley Cup Champions, and while their great captain, Super Mario, had never received the type of treatment that a current captain with a pencil-thin mustache and whiny ways (named Sydney) has inspired, he was not exactly exempt from boos during his nine years of appearances at the Spectrum.

This night was different, as Lemieux returned to the ice after undergoing 22 radiation treatments for Hodgkin's Disease, including a five-minute session that very morning. In all, he had been out of the lineup for two months from what started as *just* a back injury. So, when he came out of the tunnel behind his teammates to warm up for his first game action since January 5th, Flyers fans really let Number 66 have it. He was serenaded with a stirring, 90-second standing ovation that caused the stoic megastar to look up at the stands and raise his stick in a show of mutual appreciation.

For the record, Mario would miraculously—if seemingly effortlessly for a player of his singular gifts—tally a goal (which produced more thunderous roars from the fans) and an assist, but the Flyers' fanatics would also be able to cheer a 5-4 win by the orange and black, helped in part by a late, third-period save of a Lemieux shot by Tommy Soderstrom. It was the Flyers' first head-to-victory over the Pens in 15 tries.

All in all, just a wonderful night in South Philly.

7. Eagles Fans Show Andy Reid Support In Wake Of Son's Passing – August 9th, 2012

Despite the well-documented troubles of Eagles coach Andy Reid's oldest son Garrett, his sudden death sent shock waves throughout Eagles training camp and the entire Delaware Valley. Just two days after burying his son, Reid returned to work the following Thursday for an Eagles preseason game against the Pittsburgh Steelers. The Eagles paid a tribute to Reid's fallen son prior to kickoff. Then during a timeout in the first quarter, Reid and his wife Tammy appeared on video screens thanking everybody for their support with their tragic ordeal. Reid received a long, loud standing ovation, with the fans chanting *"Andy! Andy! Andy!"* In a rare public display of outward humility, Reid was clearly touched by the crowd's sentiment and support.

Despite an often rocky relationship with the fans, Andy Reid wasn't the Eagles football coach on that night, he was Andy Reid the grieving father. And for one brief moment, the entire community had Big Red's back and the two came together—perhaps more so than ever before. Whoever says we don't have a heart can go pound some serious sand.

6

PHILLY FANS HAVE NO CLASS

When it comes to sports fans, there is the high class, the middle class, the working class and then...you guessed it...Philly fans.

Class means conducting yourself with a sense of decorum—if even just a little bit. Philly fans are usually too drunk and obnoxious to bother with such minimal standards.

In other cities, fans of opposing teams are given good-natured ribbing; in Philly, they suffer broken ribs.

You get the point, media members. Philly is not the king of the hill and the top of the heap like New York, or my kind of town like Chicago. It's just a city and a fan base devoid of class.

"Just mustard packs? That's better than AA batteries."

TONY DEMARCO- MLB EXAMINER

RESPONSE: MATT GOLDBERG AND JOE VALLEE

MATT:

The national narrative has been used recklessly to define us as a fan base with no class, and my first move in response is to ask this question:

How do you define class?

If your definition of class is *informal excellence or elegance, esp in dress, design, or behaviour*—as defined by thefreedictionary.com—then perhaps, Philly's not your kind of town. And while we're at it, we don't spell the ending of our words with that British *our*. So clearly, that definition does not do us any favors, or favours.

Now if your definition of class is in keeping with dictionary.reference.com's informal one—*of high quality and integrity*—I would tell you that Philly fans embody it. In great numbers.

Let me explain. Philly fans are not about elegant behavior. As a rule, we do not go to the ballpark to impress people with our elegant fashion sense, unless that fashion sense makes room for a vintage Reggie White, Dutch Daulton (not so sure about Lenny Dykstra anymore), Allen Iverson or Rod Brind'Amour jersey. And yes, even our men wear them as well.

When it comes to food and drink, we don't come to the ballpark to show off our use of a salad fork or to tuck a napkin under our chin. We eat our cheesesteaks and Schmitters with gusto—calories and LDL counts be damned— and if we drip some glop on our Reggie White jerseys, well, the more the better.

We come to the ballpark on a mission to support our teams. I'll ask you this: What other fan base supports all four of its pro teams with such fervor and passion? To me, that is the hallmark of high quality and integrity. Integrity is showing up at the ballpark in any kind of weather to root for players and teams—even when they are overmatched on paper. Philly fans should take pride in the fact that we turned out to support our teams in great numbers despite their not earning us a single victory parade between 1983 and 2008. If you're counting, that was 25 years and close to 100 combined seasons of futility.

Technically, there were only 98 champions crowned during those would-be 100 combined seasons. But consider this:

* In 2004, the Flyers were just one game away from ousting the Tampa Bay Lightning to advance to the Stanley Cup Finals against a very beatable Calgary Flames team. Due to a lockout, there was no NHL season in 2004-05. Agonizing!

* Major League Baseball had no World Series in 1994. So yes, Phillies fans had 365 extra days to *savor* Joe Carter's World Series walk-off homer versus Mitch Williams in Game 6. Excruciating!

In fact, you could forgive us fans for thinking that it was *more* than 100 years between sips of champagne. During those 100 combined seasons of futility, the fans kept flocking to the parks, buying jerseys and putting our own civic pride on the line with our teams—game after game, season after doomed season. How is that for integrity, loyalty—and yes, class?

JOE:

Matt, I think it really speaks volumes for the passionate Philadelphia fan. Year after year, heartache after heartache, Philly fans still come back with the hopes that maybe, just maybe, this will be their year. In fact, the product that ownership puts out on the field has to be pretty damn dreadful for fans to stay away in droves (ie: Phillies: 1988-1992, 1994-2000, Sixers: 1992-1997). The Flyers' 2006-2007 season was the worst in the history of the franchise, yet the team still finished seventh in the NHL in attendance that year. The Eagles haven't been a major contender for really anything since their Super Bowl season of 2004 (and no, I'm not forgetting about the 2008 NFC Championship Game, but that was lightning in a bottle more than anything), but the waiting list for season tickets is still just that—a waiting list. And last but certainly not least is the Phillies. Build a World Series champion however, and they will come. All I have to say is this: 257 straight sellouts- the longest streak ever in National League history and the third-longest in Major League Baseball history!

The Phillies' sellout streak of 257 consecutive home games currently stands as the longest in National League history!

In fact, Sports Index ranked Phillies fans as the most loyal in baseball, according to Brand Keys President Robert Passikoff in an interview with Bloomberg.

"With the Phillies, every game seems to count to the whole team. They seem to take it more personally," [1] says Passikoff. And yes, the Flyers were ranked second in the NHL behind the Red Wings, who win Stanley Cups like we drink water (see 1997 Stanley Cup Finals).

As far as elegance is concerned, you're 100% right, Matt. If you're looking for the prim and proper, chances are you will not find it at a Philadelphia sporting event. Personally, I think it's way cooler if my girlfriend wears a Phillies jersey to a game as opposed to taking three hours to get ready for a Business Persons Special. Whether it's good or bad, we definitely don't try to be somebody we're not in this town, whereas that is not the case in some of those other cities. It doesn't mean we don't have class; there's just a time and a place for everything. I'd rather sit with a bleacher bum at Wrigley Field any day than some uppity CEO in a Yankee Stadium suite. Unless of course, he wants to throw some money my way.

Now in saying that, it doesn't mean we are slobs and have no class. We just don't have the stuffiness of New York (I'm looking at you, Mr. Yankees fan) or even Washington, and they don't count because they're mostly all transplants down in the nation's capital, anyway. New York is a big money city; Philly is a blue collar city. That will never change and neither will the perception. It's the haves versus the have-nots.

And speaking of Yankee Stadium, two good friends of mine basically had their lives threatened as they were leaving Game 6 of the 2009 World Series. The team that those fans were rooting for just won the World Series, and they still had to get off by trying to intimidate the fans of a team they just beat? At least we never spit on player's wives like somebody reportedly did to Kristen Lee (wife of Phillies pitcher Cliff Lee) at Yankee Stadium.

I remember reading that Phillies fans threw mustard packets (Do they even have mustard packets at Citizens Bank Park?) at Rays' Manager Joe Maddon's granddaughter during the 2008 World Series, a beer was poured on a nine-year old and family members were harassed. Like I said, if that's true, there's one in every bunch, and it's certainly not justi-fied. If that were my daughter, the gloves would be off. In saying that, if they were all animals at The Bank, Maddon surely wouldn't have been joking around with some fans in the stands asking them why they were drinking Coors Light in Philadelphia.

I was at every game of that World Series that was played in Philadelphia. And with the exception of Game 4 and Game 5: Part Deux, there was a LOT of rain, which gave fans plenty of time to lubricate their throats.

Seriously, I don't care whether you're in New York, Seattle, Cleveland, or at a Wilmington Blue Rocks game: anybody can drink too much and do stupid things when that much booze is available at your disposal and you have that much free time on your hands. I have several friends in the Phillies organization, and despite reports to the contrary, not once did I hear of any major issues of fan misconduct.

When you think about it, how many other rain delays can you think of in recent memory that occurred during a World Series game with fans in attendance? Game 4 of the 2006 World Series, but that was in St. Louis, where no fan in the history of the world has misbehaved. Game 6 of the 2011 World Series was postponed, but that announcement was made in the afternoon. Other than that, I can't think of anywhere else. It had to happen in Philly. Come to think of it, actually **EVERY** World Series in Philadelphia since 1983 has been hampered by rain!

One thing we *did* do, however, was intimidate the ever-loving hell out of the Rays. Those *"Eva"* chants directed at Evan Longoria were absolutely classic. Personally, I would have rather had Eva playing third base, but mostly for visual reasons. Fact of the matter is, whether it was Eva or Evan at the hot corner, someone with the last name of Longoria went 1 for 20 during that series (identical to some third baseman named Schmidt in the '83 Fall Classic), and a lot of that had to do with the Philly fans getting into Evan's head, Carlos Pena's head (2 for 20) and most of the rest of the Rays. Just look at the differences in the dugouts when you watch the 2008 World Series highlight film. The Phillies are laughing and joking and so are the Rays—prior to going into Citizens Bank Park, where they suddenly turned stiffer than Andy Reid at a press conference. After the World Series, Longoria and Pena were really classy guys, and never once pointed their fingers at the fans of Philadelphia as a possible reason for their lackluster performances.

Truth be told, I think there was a small time frame when the Philly fan base softened a bit. Finally winning a championship after that long drought will do that to you. And even though the Phils lost the World Series to the Yankees in 2009 and several months later the Flyers lost the Stanley Cup to the Blackhawks, fans didn't spew venom the way they did prior to 2008. However, the way the Phillies' 2010 and 2011 seasons ended followed by the debacle of the Eagles' 2011 "Dream Team" seems to have given the fans their edge back.

MATT:

Well said Joe, and with the type of high quality and integrity (our definition of class) that defines Philly. And one more thing: If that *were* Eva Longoria at third base, that would truly be the *hot* corner. Hey, with the Phillies' lack of offense the last few years, I'll take either Evan or Eva over there.

7

PHILLY IS A TOUGH PLACE TO PLAY

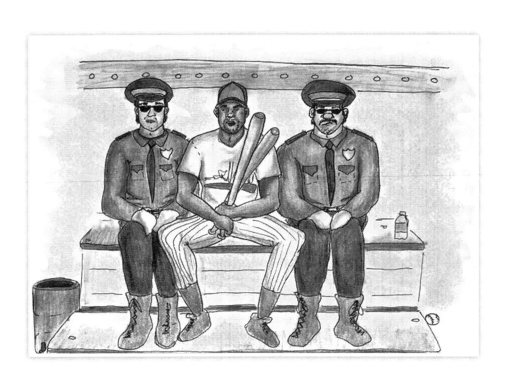

Who would ever want to play in front of the Philly fan base? They have overly high expectations for all their players and teams, yet no standards for their own behavior.

There is a reason why free agents in all sports have turned down bigger money to play elsewhere. Not only are they tough on opposing players, but they never even give many of their own athletes a chance to shine in this town.

Sports is filled with pressure already. How would you like to play in Philly, where every strikeout, missed free throw, incomplete pass or goal through the five-hole will be lustily booed. You may even have to dodge snowballs while you're at it.

"The problem with Philadelphia fans is that they want you to play every game like it's your last one."

-Shawn Bradley, former 76ers center

RESPONSE: JOE VALLEE AND MATT GOLDBERG

JOE:

Philadelphians live and die by their sports teams. You can tell just by speaking to somebody on the street whether the Eagles won the previous Sunday, or whether Roy Halladay threw a three-hitter or gave up a three-bagger the night before. When our teams lose, it's like all of us just lost. You hear it all the time, just in our daily interactions:

"I can't believe we blew that game!"

"We let up that easy goal."

"We really need to play better in close games."

As previously mentioned, Philadelphia is a blue collar town and there's no getting around this. A silver platter doesn't exist in our vocabulary. If something comes too easy, we wonder when the bottom is going to drop out. Where else does the final game of a World Series take three days to win? Exactly. We had to earn that, too!

Back in 2005, Eagles fans took second mortgages out on their homes just to buy tickets to the Super Bowl in Jacksonville. I was there, and I can't begin to tell you how many establishments I frequented where hundreds of fans would randomly break into E-A-G-L-E-S, EAGLES! chants at the drop of a hat. I've never seen anything like that.

Eagles fans invade Jacksonville for the Super Bowl.

To the national guys, outsiders or even transplants, if you aren't from here, you won't completely 'get it' and you never will. It's difficult to explain, really. It's not an act of snobbery; it's just the way it is. We work hard here for everything, and we expect the same from our athletes. And when they don't, we let them know it. And personally, I don't think there's anything wrong with that. To know us is to love us, and we're tough because we care. And nobody, I mean NOBODY, cares as much as the Philadelphia sports fan.

Think about it. Philly sports fans relate more to somebody like Brian Dawkins or Larry Bowa, who scratched and clawed for everything he ever achieved in a major league uniform as opposed to somebody like Mike Schmidt, the 6'2" natural athlete who looked like everything came easy for him. The same goes for Bobby Clarke, whom scouts didn't think would ever play in the NHL because of his diabetes. Clarkie, however, outworked everybody on the ice when he stepped on it, and along with Bernie Parent, became arguably the most beloved Flyer of all-time.

Bobby Clarke

Is it unrealistic to simply ask a player to go all out all the time? Yes and no. It's unrealistic because there are simply some who don't have it in them because they're lazy, simply don't feel like it, or don't want to get injured with that potential new contract on the horizon. That's just the type of player they are, and they usually don't last very long in Philly. Aaron Rowand left part of his nose on the Citizens Bank Park outfield wall for his team, and he'll be forever loved in Philly because of it. Not every athlete has done that, but we remember the ones who give just a little more. When players start dogging it and play with their head up their *"you know what,"* Philly fans (as do any other group of fans in the country) have every right to give them some serious business.

On the other hand, it's realistic because this is what they do for a living, and one would think that athletes might take some pride in doing their jobs well. At the end of the day, we're ultimately rooting for our guys to win, and with the ever increasing salaries to play a kid's game, the expectations to perform to their best capabilities are set higher than ever, as it should be. You're getting paid the big bucks by ownership for a reason.

Don't believe me? Ryan Howard makes more money per at-bat than most people make in a year. When you break it down in those terms, it can be tough for somebody living in Sioux City, Iowa—let alone an opinionated city like Philadelphia, to digest. And don't get me wrong, I'm not going to sit there and say I never blamed him for his shortcomings when it mattered most. I have, but overall, I am a Ryan Howard backer. I admire Jimmy Rollins' swagger (most of the time), I love the way Chase Utley plays the game, but I stop whatever I'm doing to watch Howard hit.

I think the issue Phillies fans have with Howard is that his greatest asset is also his greatest liability. He's a slugger, and unless you're Albert Pujols, chances are you're going to strike out a lot. While Howard can carry a team for weeks, he's also capable of going cold—sometimes at the worst possible moments (including the 2009 World Series and his lack of offensive production in the 2010-2011 postseason). Unfortunately, this can make a lot of good he's done seem less important—and Howard has done a lot of good for the Philadelphia Phillies.

How many times have you heard people say at the bar, water cooler, or even in your own home *"The money he gets paid, he should hit that ball out of there with his eyes closed."* Philly fans can be tough, but we want the best from our players. If you think we're too hard at times on somebody like Howard, let me introduce you to the likes of Chris Gratton, Lance Parrish, Gregg Jefferies, Andy Ashby, Steve Everitt, and Adam Eaton. These players didn't have half of Howard's talent, but they are on the long list of many who didn't live up to expectations after signing very nice, lucrative deals.

While there have been plenty of athletes who couldn't cut it here, there are also some who became legends in this town and will be forever loved by the Philly fans.

One of those players is Bowa, a former Phillie who was not immune to hearing boos at times despite his legendary status he established for himself on those great Phillies teams of the late 1970's and early 1980's. The fans gave Bowa the business when he and the Phillies struggled in the early part of 1980, before he finally turned things around that summer. Those boos however, quickly turned to cheers that October, as

Bowa's .375 average and record-setting seven double plays in the 1980 World Series was a major factor in the Phillies raising the trophy for the first time in their long-suffering history.

After finishing his career with the Mets in 1985, Bowa became a long-time Phillies coach and manager. His hard-nosed style of play combined with his fiery temperament almost make it seem like he was destined to play here. Bowa never took a play off, and gave it everything he had on the field in every capacity he served as a Phillie. I can still hear the chants of *"Larry, Larry"* whenever he came on the field to show his displeasure at an umpire's bad call during his managerial tenure. Yep, it's safe to say Phillies fans "got" Bowa, and Bowa "got" the fans right back.

"My relationship with the fans (in Philly) is really good. You play hard, give it everything you have, and let them (the fans) know you're passionate about the game and you'll do nice there," says Bowa, now an analyst for MLB Network. *"You have to be mentally tough to play on the east coast. When things go bad, that's part of the game. If you get booed, that's the way it goes. But when you do well, it also goes to the other end of the spectrum—the fans (in Philadelphia), they're unbelievable. You like coming to the park every day when there's enthusiasm and energy in the stands. That's the way Philadelphia was when I played and managed there."*

Now contrary to what the general population thinks, Philadelphia doesn't boo everyone.

Just ask Pat Burrell,[1] who the fans (for the most part) gave a free pass to for the majority of his nine years as a Phillie. After having a breakout season in 2002 when he hit 37 home runs and drove in 116, the Phillies opened their checkbook and signed Burrell to a six-year, $50 million dollar contract. With the addition of Jim Thome to the Phillies lineup, many expected Burrell to better his power numbers in 2003.

Unfortunately, the exact opposite happened. Burrell slumped to 21 home runs and 64 RBIs (a little more than half his 2002 total) and his average dropped from .282 in 2002 to .209. If Burrell hit even .235 in 2003, the Phillies make the playoffs. Instead of being one of the players to lead the Phils to the postseason however, Burrell was targeted as being one of the main reasons (if not THE main reason) the Phillies lost the Wild Card to the eventual World Series Champion Florida Marlins. Despite his rough year, Phillies fans treated Burrell pretty well throughout his ordeals. The following season, Burrell regained some admirers when he played through a serious wrist injury that should have ended his season. The Phillies however, once again missed out on the playoffs, costing Larry Bowa his job.

After having solid seasons with the Phillies in 2005 (in which he finished second in the league in RBIs and seventh in the MVP voting) and 2006, the boo birds finally caught up with Burrell (don't get me wrong, it's not like the fans never booed Burrell prior to this, but now it was consistently). After a decent April, he struggled mightily through the first half of the 2007 season, hitting just .157 after April. He lost his starting job, and became the subject of several trade rumors.

Then, something clicked, and Burrell went on an absolute tear, finishing the season hitting .257 (100 points higher than his May and June average!) as the Phillies finally ended their postseason drought and staged one of the greatest September comebacks in the history of the game by overtaking the Mets for their first NL East crown in 14 years. While this was a complete team effort, I believe to this day that Burrell led the way by driving in 65 runs in the Phillies' last 75 games. And although Burrell had just two hits as the Phillies were swept in the NLDS by the buzzsaw known as the Colorado Rockies, the groundwork would be set for some of the best baseball this town would ever see from the Phightins.

In 2008, the Phillies won the NL East again. Burrell's playoff showing wasn't all that great, but his two home runs in Game 4 of the NLDS against the Brewers help send the Phillies to the NLCS against the Dodgers, where his Game 1 home run broke a 2-2 tie and proved to be the game-winner as the Phillies won, 3-2.

Perhaps Burrell's final hit in a Phillies uniform was the most telling. After going hitless in 14 at-bats in the World Series against the Rays, Burrell ripped a long fly ball to the deepest part of Citizens Bank Park in the seventh inning of Game 5: Part Deux for a LONG double. To this day, I still don't know how that ball didn't leave the yard because it came up inches short. Burrell was replaced by pinch runner Eric Bruntlett, who eventually scored the World Series-winning run.

When Burrell was drafted out of Miami, people had him pegged as the next Mike Schmidt. Much like that ball he hit in Game 5 however, Burrell's career didn't quite reach the level many thought it would. But nonetheless, Phillies management chose him to lead the World Series parade two days later. The majority of athletes who come through Philadelphia never get to even experience victory, let alone leave town a winner. Pat Burrell managed to do both. If you would have told me after the 2003 season that his Phillies career would have ended with him riding down Broad Street on a World Series float with his bulldog Elvis and some Clydesdales, I would have looked at you like you had five heads. Only in Philadelphia.

During Burrell's years in Philly, I often wondered from time to time why Phillies fans were rather easy on him compared to other athletes that have played here. When it comes down to it, I think a lot of it has to do with effort. As many times as we saw the "Burrell shuffle" as he looked at a called third strike or tiptoed his way around the base paths with his ailing knees, everybody in the stands knew he was trying hard. Despite his often surly demeanor with the media and sometimes the fans, Burrell was known as having one of the best work ethics on the Phillies. Sure, his career wasn't what many thought it would be, but there's only three other players in the history of the Phillies franchise that have hit more home runs than Pat Burrell (Mike Schmidt, Ryan Howard, and Del Ennis). Not too shabby.

Philadelphia has always taken to hard-working players. While winning is the cure for everything, it's always been effort over result here. When you've lost as much we have over the years, it kind of has to be. Maybe I'm biased, but shouldn't it be like that everywhere? I don't think it's too novel of a concept, really: Play hard, play smart, make a great impression, and give it your all. It's what you're paid to do!

When the Eagles won their last championship in 1960, players started working their offseason jobs the next day. These were blue collar guys who identified with this city. And it's not like the Flyers were making a king's ransom when they were winning Stanley Cups back in the 1970's, either. It's safe to say it was more of a pride factor than anything, and that's one of several reasons Philadelphians were so in love with that team. And while we're on the Eagles, do you think it's a coincidence that after 25 years, fans still favor the days of Buddy Ryan and arguably one of the greatest defensive units in the history of the NFL over the Reid/McNabb-led Eagles teams of recent years? The latter was the greatest stretch of Eagles football in their history. Meanwhile, those Eagles teams under Ryan never even won a playoff game!

Then there's the 1993 Phillies, the greatest Philadelphia team who never won it all. In saying that, they're still my favorite sports team of all-time. They adopted the attitude of this city, made no apologies for how they played the game, and most importantly, they 'got' the three million plus who came to Veterans Stadium that year.

"It was a party every day, and 50,000 people joined us every night. It was unbelievable," [2] said Phillies Wall of Famer John Kruk at his induction ceremony speech when speaking of that magical year.

Kruk's final words that night in August, 2011 were arguably the greatest tribute ever from a Philadelphia athlete to his fans.

"The luckiest people here are these 25 guys right here (as Kruk pointed to the 2011 Phillies in the dugout). *They get to play in front of the greatest fans in all of sports every damn night. You hear players, media people say it's tough to play in Philly in front of these fans. To those people, I say, you didn't have the guts to succeed here."* [2]

Right on, Krukker. Right on.

MATT:

Joe, I should give you and the Krukker the last word, but I am one of those loud, opinionated guys—I'm not from Sioux City, Iowa —who wants to get a word in edgewise. And, I'm doing so in full agreement with what you and Krukker said.

I have often, at least internally, debated as to whether it takes a certain breed to make it, let alone thrive, in Philadelphia. My debate is ongoing, but here is where it now rests.

If you are either an underachiever or perceived as just coasting, Philadelphia is probably the last place you want to play as a professional athlete. If you spill your guts and *leave nothing in the locker room*, then Philadelphia is definitely the town where you want to earn your paycheck.

Let me offer this apology to Philly fans. A certain Philadelphia Eagles coach named Rich Kotite talked about his team *leaving nothing in the locker room* and he was hardly beloved here, despite a winning record (36-28). Of course, there were many reasons for our antipathy toward *Richie the K* including his thick New York accent, his unbridled arrogance and his idiotic, mind-numbing excuses—the *best* one being the time where he did not know whether to kick an extra point or go for two because his cheat sheet for such situations wasn't laminated, and it was raining. Strange but true, and still maddening.

Now, Eagles fans did revere players who put everything on the line for their team and their rabid fans. One of our favorite players of the Kotite Era was a former Heisman Trophy winner and future Olympics bobsledder named Herschel Walker. By the time he played his home games in Philly, Herschel was no longer the megastar who once churned for 1,500 yards for the hated Dallas Cowboys. He *was* a reliable, hard-running back who also played his heart out on special teams.

Philly has taken so many of its teams and players to heart over the years, not only because they won (and, of course, we have had precious few parades outside of the Mummers here) but because, to adapt our famous advertising slogan, they loved us back. If these athletes did not say so with their words, they communicated it with their actions on our fields, courts and rinks.

The way I see it, there are several paths to winning the hearts of Philly fans, and these pathways should not be all that hard to navigate.

Here are four of them:

1. Play all-out with most, if not all, of the same passion and fire that we bring to the stadium as fans. We admire superstar effort just as much as superstar performance—maybe even more.

2. Be a part of a terrific, winning team

3. Have a strong presence in our communities

4. Throw a bouquet to the fans every now and then. As tough as we are, we are not unforgiving or hard-hearted. We just need to be respected and loved once in a while.

A great current example of the above is Phillies' lefty co-ace Cole Hamels, who became a hero in this town in 2008 when he captured the NLCS and World Series MVP Awards while leading his team, and city, to its first major pro championship in 25 years. This was followed by a puzzling 2009 season in which Hamels struggled—somewhat in the regular season and mightily in the postseason. If Hamels even partially resembled the brilliant pitcher of the year before, odds are that the Phillies—bolstered by midseason acquisition Cliff Lee —would have repeated as World Series champions.

Hamels compounded this apparent felony by making statements that were interpreted as him not being exactly amped up to pitch in that postseason when things weren't breaking his way. To many fans (and a local reporter or two) Hamels was seen as being *soft*—which can be the kiss of death, here or elsewhere. In retrospect, the label may have been unfair, as Cole was just being brutally honest, as he often is. At the same time, negative labels can be very hard to shake, and it seemed to take all of 2010 (including a five-hit shutout in Cincinnati to clinch the NLDS) for him to regain the good graces of Philly fans and put the *soft* label to rest.

Fast forward to 2012, and a frustrating season in which Hamels was the only pitcher out of the Halladay/Lee/Hamels trifecta of aces to resemble one. This also coincided with two other factors that made the homegrown talent a greatly valued commodity among Major League Baseball teams as the July 31st trade deadline approached. For one, the Phillies—after five straight seasons atop the National League East—were floundering, with even a wild card spot relegated to the status of a remote possibility. For another, the Phillies and their de facto ace had not come together on a contract, leaving the likelihood that Hamels might be pitching in another uniform come July 30th or so.

All of this served as the backdrop for a July 21st matchup at Citizens Bank Park with the San Francisco Giants and their own ace, right-hander Matt Cain. In a strange game in which Cain and Hamels homered off one another but also gave up three bombs and five earned runs apiece, Cole was removed from the game with two outs in the bottom of the eighth inning, having surrendered a run in the frame that knotted the game.

So, how did the fans respond to the man who was rumored to be enjoying testing the waters of free agency? Fearing that this would be his last appearance in red pinstripes, the Phillies faithful showered him with a long, loud ovation as he headed to the dugout.

Four days later, the Phillies announced that they inked Hamels to a six-year, $144 million contract extension. The pitcher, who has also spearheaded many local charitable efforts via his Hamels Foundation, remembered the fans and threw them a nice bouquet at the press conference:

"Words can't really describe the emotions that you get, and the way the fans were standing and cheering, that was ultimately the deciding point to be here." [3]

If you're still thinking that Philly is a tough place to play, you may also want to consider the following three teams—in three different sports—who got us close to a victory parade, but came up short on the biggest stages.

Despite some rough patches, Phillies fans' didn't want to see Cole Hamels leave the team via free agency. And it turns out Hamels didn't want to leave, either.

The 2000-2001 Philadelphia 76ers electrified this town during a playoff run that ultimately ended in an NBA Finals loss to the heavily favored Los Angeles Lakers. To say that this squad made a lot of new fans and believers along the way would be an understatement. In many respects, the team was embodied by three men, only one of whom suited up to play. Allen Iverson, despite whatever his flaws were on and of the court, was absolutely magical that season, capturing another scoring title and winning the regular season MVP Award. Coach Larry Brown, almost as quirky as his superstar guard, constantly preached to anybody who would listen about the virtues of *playing the right way*, while charismatic owner Pat Croce would do anything and everything to both promote his team and give the fans an entertaining, winning product.

Beyond those three stars, Iverson's supporting cast endeared itself to this town by, indeed, playing the right way while displaying the type of suffocating defense (led by the likes of Dikembe Mutombo, Eric Snow, George Lynch and local favorite, Aaron McKie) that even an Eagles fan would be proud of.

Phillies fans still love Macho Row and those scraggly 1993 Phillies of Dutch Daulton, John Kruk, Lenny Dykstra (well, we didn't know he was *that* crazy back then), Mariano Duncan, Curt Schilling and Mitch Williams. Yes, the same Mitch Williams who served up that soul-crushing Joe Carter dinger. He was also a standup, no-excuses guy who seemed to put full effort into every single pitch, ill-fated or not. Plus, *Mitchy Poo* and that wild bunch also happened to knock off those big, bad Braves of Atlanta in the NLCS.

Philly has always revered the 1980 NFC Champion Philadelphia Eagles who got blown out by the Oakland Raiders, 27-10, in Super Bowl XV. Head coach Dick Vermeil is still worshipped in this town, as are players ranging from the great (linebacker Bill Bergey and running back Wilbert Montgomery) to the good (tight end John Spagnola) to the overachieving role player (undersized back Louie Giammona.) And it didn't hurt any that they walloped the Dallas Cowboys in the NFC Championship Game.

But as much as Vermeil is now revered in Philadelphia, Eagles fans were quite skeptical of the rookie coach during the summer of the Bicentennial.

"There was a lot of trepidation about him from the fan base," former Eagles linebacker Frank LeMaster says in regards to Vermeil's arrival in the City of Brotherly Love.

"First of all, he was coming from the West Coast (having coached at UCLA) to the East Coast, and back then the papers and the news they played it up as this golden California boy coming into the pit of blue collar America. Now, Dick looks like a young guy even today, but I was 24 at the time, and he looked like he was 24, too, although he was in his late thirties. I think once we got into training camp and the fans saw his organizational skills, how hard he worked, and how strict he was when compared to other teams of the past, it really started to grab the fans' attention, and they're still packing the stadium."

Why was that Vermeil-led Eagles team so highly regarded, even though they lost the Super Bowl by a much wider margin than the 2004-05 Andy Reid edition? Some of it may be explained by the different eras in which they played, but I also think that the Vermeil team hit upon all four of the pathways to the fans' devotion. They played with passion and fire; they were a terrific winner (and also an underdog, as were the 2000-01 Sixers and the 1993 Phillies); they were visible in the community and they showed their appreciation for the fans.

When it comes to Philly fans, you don't have to win it all, make multiple All-Star teams or even donate millions of dollars. Just respect and somewhat duplicate our passion, and chances are you won't be crying that *Philly is a tough place to play.*

Indeed, you will be supported more than you would in any other town, and you may very well even love us back.

7TH INNING STRETCH:

IF PHILLY IS SO BAD, WHY DO SO MANY ATHLETES STAY HERE?

Unfortunately, it's not too often that Philly brings home a winner. In saying that, chances are you'll never have to buy a beer or dinner here for the rest of your natural born lives if you perform well in this town.

One way or another, these guys have made their mark on Philadelphia sports lore. Some of them have been here most of their lives, some made the Tri-State area their home since their playing days have ended, and some have even had movies made about them!

Let's hear it from the men who felt the love from the Philly fans, and loved us right back.

EAGLES

Vince Papale

Eagles Wide Receiver/Special Teams: 1976-79

Inspiration for the movie *Invincible*

Lifelong Tri-State area resident

Father, motivational speaker, author and fundraiser

On staying in the Philadelphia area:

A lot of people don't know this, but I had an opportunity when I was done playing to do some television in Chicago. This is my hometown, though. I knew people and felt more comfortable here being a big fish in a small pond, so I chose to stay. I wasn't all that confident that the little homegrown Philly kid would have made it under the glare of being out there in the Windy City.

On how the national media seems to not always take too kindly to Philadelphia:

I don't get it, you know? I guess you could say it's like when I'm talking to my kids and someone comes up and tells me that somebody said something nasty about you that isn't true, and you wonder *'Well where did they hear that?'*

Maybe they're jealous or envious of you, so they said something about you that's not true. Who knows? It could be just the fact that some really dumb, stupid fans have done things that, for whatever reason, have gotten the attention of the national press and it has been blown way out of proportion. They're less than one percenters, but the squeaky wheel gets the grease, and apparently that's what it is.

The Philly fans are tough fans. They're so passionate, they're so involved, and they've really invested a lot in their teams. It's more than just money. They've invested their families, their soul, their heart, all of their passion. And it seems like each year regardless of whether it's the Phillies, Flyers, Sixers, or Eagles, there's been a few exceptions, but mostly disappointments. And yet, the promises that have been made by their organizations that say *'Hey, this is gonna be our year. This is when we take it to the next level.'* And we as sheep have a tendency to think *'Ok, we're gonna follow this and believe in it,'* and then it doesn't happen. And once it doesn't happen, they start getting cynical and negative, and then the fans get labeled and ridiculed. *'Look at those fans. They're nothing but a bunch of jackasses. They don't get it.'*

But the thing is, if you're from outside of Philadelphia, you don't get it. You really don't get it, unless you've been here and been part of the disappointment and frustration and culture. For me personally, I'm excited all the time for the sports, games, and wins that we get here and have been given. And I'm not so frustrated that we haven't won the Super Bowl, Stanley Cup, World Series, or NBA Championship. To me, it's fun being competitive, being at the games, and getting excited that way.

On his Eagles season tickets:

My season tickets go back to Franklin Field in 1966, when I was a sophomore at St. Joe's and season tickets were 60 bucks. My friends and I were like those guys in the movie *"Fever Pitch"* when those guys got their Red Sox tickets and they were all excited about it. We were the same way. Four of us would sit together, just look at our tickets and go *'Wow!'* We'd plan our whole fall based upon what the schedule was. Everything came in the mail and what you read, you read in The Bulletin. They didn't have morning newspapers. All you had was Channel 6, Channel 10 and Channel 3. Everything was so pure and basic. I go way back.

146

Frank LeMaster

Eagles Linebacker: 1974-82

Local Delaware Valley Resident: 36 years

Current Occupation: Regional Sales Manager at FieldTurf, Birchrunville, PA

Thoughts on Philly:

I came up here to stay after Coach Vermeil arrived in 1976. Growing up on a horse farm in Kentucky, I migrated towards Chester County, which reminds me of where I grew up. It's got roving hills, trees, fields, horses. I just fell in love with Philadelphia. First, it was the fans, the people, and then the area. When I got here, there was some culture shock.

Coming from Kentucky, I still have a southern twang. One of the things I loved was the diversity in the ethnic groups and the ethnic foods. Kentucky is more Middle America and there wasn't a lot of that out there. My mom was the best southern cook you'd ever meet. However, you can't eat that every day. All the food here was just unbelievable. The first time I went to this nice Italian restaurant, the waiter gives me my pasta, and asks me if I want some gravy. I

said *'Gravy? I don't see any gravy around here.'* I'm used to sausage gravy. My mom's idea of spaghetti sauce was buying Ragu, and back then that was watery tomato sauce. Of course, now I know they call sauce gravy around here, so there were little funny things like that.

On the Philly Fans:

Much like Pittsburgh, Philadelphia has always been known as a blue collar town. The media has to write about something. And when you're winning, and you're a reporter or sportscaster in the media, there's lots of positive things to talk about. But when you're losing, the only thing anybody does is draw on the negatives. So over the years, from the 60s until the Eagles started winning in the late 70s, all they had to talk about were the Eagles fans and how they're really tough, and not to wear your colors when you go there because you're going to get beat up.

I think after all the national talk, the fans eventually started to carry that as a badge of honor. They became proud feeling that they were very astute when it came to the game of football, and they were going to let you know about it. If you're playing well, they're going to cheer for you. If you're not playing well, they're going to boo. So I think it perpetuated itself. Every city in the country gets slapped with a certain type of title if you would, but I think the fans are very proud of the heritage here, and we consider ourselves very tough nosed.

Favorite fan moment:

The best time ever for both the players and the fans was in the 1980 NFC Championship Game against the Cowboys. The electricity in the air was just unbelievable. I knew walking down the tunnel, I could feel the chemistry in our team, I could feel the energy, my adrenaline was pumping so hard that I could not feel my legs. I couldn't wait for the first play. That was caused by the fans and the chemistry Dick Vermeil built.

Mike Quick

Eagles Wide Receiver: 1982-1990

Philadelphia Eagles Color Commentator: 1998-present

Between the time that you retired as the Eagles star wide receiver and the time that you were hired as their color analyst on the radio, you remained in the Philadelphia area, rather than return to your native North Carolina or somewhere else. Why?

I never left. I played my entire pro career here. That's nine years. And there was really no real reason to go anywhere else. I think we all like to go where we're loved and I knew that I was loved here.

How did the fans show you that love?

Just in my everyday life, the way I was treated by people that were rabid fans. That's what we have in this area. We have people that, once you're a professional athlete in this area, you're a Philadelphian. I was born and raised in North Carolina, but I really grew up in Philadelphia. This is where I became a man.

But you must have had some bad experiences with fans during your years as a player or as a broadcaster?

Yeah, but it hasn't been so bad that things really stick out for me. The good always outweighed the bad.

How well do Philly fans know their sports history? Do those who were too young to see you play have a clue who you are?

It's been 21 years since I played. Fans that didn't get a chance to see me play may have heard of my name. They know their father saw me play or their father said I was a good player.

After playing, moving into the broadcast booth really just gives you a second life with the fans. People who don't know me from my playing days will say *'That's the guy on the radio with Merrill!'*

Ken Dunek

Eagles Tight End: 1980-81

Philadelphia Stars: 1983-85

Mt. Laurel, New Jersey resident: 30 years

Current Occupation: Publisher of JerseyMan Magazine

On the Philadelphia area:

I met my wife Terri while visiting Merrill Reese at his radio show in Deptford, NJ in 1982 (she was the restaurant manager). We got married in March of 1983. I love the area for its history, culture, restaurants, and proximity to the shore, mountains, and other major cities.

On the passion of the Philadelphia fans:

The national media has picked up on the Santa Claus snowball incident and blown it way out of proportion. Philly fans care deeply, and at times the frustration boils over. I can relate, I've been a Chicago Cubs fan my entire life!

FLYERS

Bill Barber

Flyers Left Winger: 1972-1984; Assistant Coach: 1985-1988; Head Coach: 2000-2002

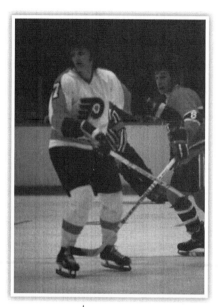

Resident of the Tri-State area for the better part of 40 years

Current Occupation: Flyers scouting consultant

You played your last game in 1984 after undergoing knee surgery. You could have punched your ticket anywhere in the NHL. What made you want to stay in the Philly area?

You end up falling in love with this area. I think the two Stanley Cup teams combined with the warmth and appreciation given by our fans, friends you meet outside of hockey as well as raising my son and daughter here all factored into staying here in this area and not go elsewhere. I was very fortunate that the Flyers gave me the opportunity to stay on board and keep me active here in different capacities, thanks to Bob Clarke. For 12 years I never played anywhere else as a player. The Flyers are a great family and I can't thank Mr. Snider enough. My heart goes to Keith Allen (former Flyers coach and general manager) and Fred Shero (former Flyers coach), who are special, special people in my life. I'm a lucky guy to have the opportunity to stay in the area.

Describe your relationship with the Philly fans, and why do you think their image is portrayed the way it is by the national media?

I think the Philly fans are great, great fans. They're very supportive and passionate for the sport that they cheer for. Whether it's hockey or football or baseball, when they come into one of our sports arenas, they bleed orange and black just like the players did. I think sometimes it gets tossed into an area where they seem harsh, but they're really not, they're just passionate. That's the one word I keep thinking of. They want to see the city or the team win, and you can't be critical of that. If you really love the sport you're involved with, and for me it was hockey, I lived and died for it.

When I came into the Spectrum and stepped on the ice, I knew I had to go out there and give it the best that I could do. You're not always going to be on top of your game, but if you do that, the fans will love you forever, and I love them. When I first came here, we had a large contingent of hard working people who took the time to support us, we went on to win championships, and I think the love affair still holds up today.

Bob "The Hound" Kelly
Flyers Left Winger: 1970-1980
Current Occupation: Flyers' Ambassador of Hockey

Came here as a 19-year old and 40 years later, he never went home.

The Broad Street Bullies are probably the most beloved Philadelphia sports team of all time. There was the HBO documentary made about the team as well as a major motion picture. Why do you think people in Philadelphia related to you guys so well and still do to this day?

I think because Philly was known as a city of losers and we were able to take a new franchise that was seven years old and win the Stanley Cup. People jumped onto our blue collar approach to the game and what we gave back to the community through local softball games, golf outings and various other charity events. Winning the championship here raised the bar for the rest of the pro teams, and they also got better and had a great following restored. People felt good about the city again.

You witnessed the pure passion of Flyers fans during the Broad Street Bullies era of the 1970s. Given the consistent increase in player salaries combined with the corporate takeover in professional sports, do you feel it is possible for Flyers fans of this era to have a similar feeling about their team?

Each team has their own following and I would say the Flyers fans are the best fans in any sport in any city. Mr Snider (Flyers owner Ed Snider) is still the team's first owner and for years has laid down a role model of hard work, passion, commitment to a team concept, loyalty, respect, and to be the best you can on and off the ice. Sometimes you don't know what you have here till you go to another team!

Many of the Flyers you played with ended up making their homes in the Tri-State area after they finished playing hockey. Even though you ended your career with the Capitals in the early 1980's, you settled here after you retired as a player. What was it about Philadelphia and the surrounding area that made you want to stay here?

The fact that most of our players in that era played six or eight or ten years together, got traded away, then came back was because our kids were in school and we didn't want to uproot, we got embedded in the community and if there was a chance for employment, why not here where people knew us? It was a win-win situation staying here. You live in a great city close to the shore, the Poconos, New York City. We have great restaurants and tremendous history here. No wild fires, no real earthquakes, no mudslides, hurricanes or tornados of great danger.

Bernie Parent

Flyers Goalie: 1967-71; 1973-79

Local resident: 40 years

Current Occupation: Available for motivational and inspirational speaking engagements. More info can be found at www.bernieparent.net Follow Bernie on twitter @Bernieparent

Why is the Philadelphia area special to you?

The love of ocean and boating. The fact that I had roots in the Philadelphia area raising my children.

Is the national media wrong in regards to Philadelphia fans?

The Philadelphia fans are intelligent, passionate fans. In my opinion, the best fans in all of sports.

Brian Propp

Flyers Left Winger: 1979-1990

South Jersey resident since 1979, when drafted by the Flyers.

Current Occupation: VP of Strategic Account Management for The Judge Group, which provides Technology Consulting (SAP & Microsoft) Staffing (IT, Engineers, Finance, Accounting, Medical and Food Industry) Corporate Training and Unified Communications/AV.

Why did you decide to stay in the Philadelphia area after your playing days ended?

I decided to live and work in Philadelphia after my playing career because I loved the area and had a number of career choices here. My wife is also from the area and I enjoy bringing up my children in this area. The Philadelphia area has a lot to offer as far as cultural history and summer relaxation with the Jersey Shore.

Why do you think the national media has such a negative perception of Philadelphia fans?

The national media has a negative perception towards Philadelphia fans because their sports teams are always good and competitive. Philadelphia has awesome fans and they stand behind their teams. They don't like rival fans because they love their own teams so much. The Philadelphia teams all play with an edge and everyone hates them, but in other cities the sports arenas are sold out when Philadelphia comes to visit. A lot of places wish their fans were as passionate as the Philadelphia fans.

PHILLIES

Larry Bowa
Phillies Shortstop: 1970-1981; Third-Base
Coach: 1988-1996; Manager: 2001-2004

MLB Network Studio Analyst

On being a Delaware Valley resident for 40 plus years:

This area is something I really adapted to when I first came up in 1970. I like the change of seasons. I get back to California to visit relatives, but this has been where I reside.

On why the national media is hard on Philly fans:

I have no idea because I've seen just as much stuff go on in Boston, New York, and Chicago. There's a lot of ballparks you go to where the mannerisms of the fans are the same. I guess ever since the so-called booing and throwing snowballs at Santa Claus incident, it sort of expanded from there. What happened to the San Francisco Giants fan particularly sticks out in my mind. You've got a guy that's still in the hospital where he got jumped in Los Angeles on Opening Day. It's written about, but if it happened in Philadelphia, it would be front page news every day for the next five years.

On the 1980 World Series Parade:

It was unbelievable. Just to see all those people whose smiles you put on their faces, the people crying as you're riding on those floats saying *'I wish my mom and dad or grandmother and grandfather could be here right now.'* If someone would have told me that before it happened, I would have said *'Yeah, right.'* And then you go into JFK Stadium after the parade route, and there were 100,000 there. It was completely jammed. It was something that you take to your grave with you. It was overwhelming for me. It's something that you can't bring back and you can't describe the emotions.

Marty Bystrom

Phillies Pitcher: 1980-1984

Local resident: 32 years

Current Occupation: Phillies Post-Game Television Analyst; Broker Development Coordinator - Aflac Pennsylvania

You last pitched in the majors with the Yankees. Why did you decide to stay in the Philadelphia area after you retired?

I love the city, the people, the restaurants, and it's a great sports town. There are also many options within a two-hour drive.

Why do you think Philadelphia fans are given such a hard time by so much of the media not living in the Tri-State area?

Because they are not here to experience the passion the Philly fans have for their teams on a consistent basis. They tend to focus on a couple of negative moments that happened here.

What stands out in your mind as the most (good or bad) in regards to Philly sports fans from your playing days?

They never forget a winner! I still get people who come up to me to this day and thank me for the 1980 World Championship. That makes you feel appreciated.

Where is it tougher to play; Philly or New York?

I can't say one over the other. They are only tough to play in if you are not performing up to their expectations.

Larry Christenson

Phillies Pitcher: 1973-1983

Local Delaware Valley Resident: 26 years

Current Occupation: President at Christenson Investment Partners, Conshohocken, PA

On the end of his playing days:

It was in Spring Training 1983 in Clearwater, Florida, that I started to notice my elbow literally coming apart. There was a gap between my radial head and humerus bones. I had already had three elbow operations and over 20 bone spurs and chips removed from my right elbow. The regular season was starting.

After warming up in the bullpen in San Francisco, I took the mound for my start against the Giants. It was the same night as the opening of Club Enchante in Cherry Hill, New Jersey, which I was a 25% owner. The first pitch of the bottom of the first inning, I felt my arm tear apart. The pain was intense and my mind was whirling. I had signed a three-year free agent contract and I was not about to walk off the mound. The tendons had torn off of my radial head and the tendons like spaghetti in my outer forearm under the skin. For the next six starts, I had to lift my arm with my glove hand to throw a pitch and the real pain was after every pitch. It would take about 20 seconds or more before I could throw the next pitch. My last start was in San Diego and my arm was in spasms between innings, and the trainer, Jeff Cooper, was very concerned. He was going to put a stop on me pitching anymore.

In about the fifth inning, Pete Rose came to the mound because he knew I was in pain and he said to me *'if it throws, don't hurt.'* Tony Gwynn got the last hit off of me and I could not throw anymore. I started a process of getting several second opinions about fixing my arm. Dr. Marone in Philadelphia had done the first three operations and I always came back strong. I visited Dr. Parks in New York and Dr. Papas in Boston. They sent me on my way because they could not fix my elbow.

Dr. Frank Jobe in Los Angeles said he could fix my elbow with an outside Tommy John operation. He transplanted a tendon from my left wrist, wrapped it around the radial head, and drilled a hole through the humerus bone to connect the two. He removed about seven to 10 chips and spurs and cut a piece of bone out of the back of my elbow so I could straighten it. He also moved the ulna nerve. I woke up with both arms hanging up on hooks. My recovery took months and I did not heal well. He went in again to try to move some tendons around, which was my fifth and final surgery.

Meanwhile, Bill Giles called me on my birthday, November 10th, 1983, and released me. My arm was in a cast, a steel brace, and then a sling until early 1984. I went to Clearwater the spring of 1984 because I had a condominium on the beach and to 'be around for Spring Training.' The Phillies invited me but my arm was not healing well. I exercised, but there was no pitching or hitting. I had a long way to go.

That spring before camp broke, my teammates and friends held a kind of going away party for me at my condo on Indian Rocks beach. I packed up the condo and headed to Ardmore, Pennsylvania, where I also packed up my belongings. I sold my Ardmore condo to Richie Ashburn, a friend I will never forget, and moved to Washington State where I originally came from. I moved into the house I invested with my 1972 bonus, which was a real good investment. I kept working out to attempt to try and make another comeback.

Fast forward to pre-spring training of 1985. I'm still in Washington State, I come back to Philadelphia to work out at Veterans Stadium and I'm throwing really well. However, my arm was still loose, it's falling apart, and then it got to be where I was upping my pitches, but the recovery took longer and longer each time, it wasn't right anymore and it was just a mess. Technically, I knew I wasn't going to pitch again and proved to myself I could no longer pitch professionally. I missed Philadelphia. Things had changed and it wasn't the same in Washington State anymore. So I turned around from Washington State and came back to Philadelphia and started in the investment business. I have been doing so for 26 years and started my own company in 2004.

On the Phillies organization:

From the Bob and Ruly Carpenter era to the Bill Giles era, to the Dave Montgomery era, the Phillies are a great, first class organization full of first class people. Paul Owens was my guy. Then there was Danny Ozark, who was the manager for most of my career, then there was Dallas Green and Pat Corrales. To this day, I'm a season ticket holder and have all the respect in the world for this organization. I was fortunate that I was with one great organization my entire career. I'm second in line with Mike Schmidt, he having 16 years with the Phillies and only the Phillies, and me having 11 years. Now, Jimmy Rollins has even more time than that under his belt. I told him *'You don't want to be anywhere else. You want to finish your career in Philadelphia,'* and he agrees. Guys like Ryan Howard, Roy Halladay, Cliff Lee, and Cole Hamels all are saying the right things. These guys do not want to play anywhere but in Philadelphia. They have a fan base like no other.

On the Philly fans:

Fans in Philly don't give you a long time, they give you whatever time they give you, but once you win them, you've got them. Just look at Charlie Manuel. Just look at how was he originally received and how things are now. They love him. Philadelphia fans are the most knowledgeable fans. They even recognize people out of uniform. They know everybody. It's absolutely amazing.

To see all those fans in JFK Stadium during the 1980 World Series parade was just awesome. We pulled around in there and saw all these fans standing up just roaring in that giant stadium. From all the way down Broad Street, there was just a sea of people. It was a bright, sunny day and just a really awesome time to see the fans react. They needed it, and they got it.

As far as today goes, the atmosphere at Citizens Bank Park is unbelievable. I brought Pete Rose to some of the games, and to this day, he is mesmerized at the electricity in Philadelphia with the fans. He said he's never seen anything like it, and that's a testament to the Phillies fans.

On the perception of Philly fans:

Just like there's good guys and bad guys, there's good fans and bad fans. The bad can come out in anybody and those fans can take it way too far. In Philadelphia, they want to continue carrying on this reputation of being tough, but they're very sophisticated fans. They know what the games are about, they know what sports are about. It's an integral part of their life and I commend them for their loyalty to their teams. It's time consuming, but I love to go to the games and watch them become electric. Fans become quiet when things aren't going well. You can feel them worry, you can feel them exuberate, you can feel them growing with excitement, you can feel it build. They know what to do to spark the team, they know what to do to tell them they're not happy. Phillies fans know how to show their appreciation and boy, can they ever show their appreciation!

SIXERS

World B. Free

Sixers Guard: 1975-1978; 1987-1988

Current Occupation- 76ers Director of Player Development/Ambassador

As part of your job description, meeting fans is a part of your job requirement. From your experiences with Philly fans, what do you think is the biggest misconception about them?

They say that Philadelphia fans are not passionate or that they are stone cold mean. All of that is just like any other fans in any major market. You know, I feel like the Philadelphia fans are some of the greatest fans in America. Just like the players need to come to work on the court, the fans come to work when they come in to this building. I think they get a bum rap... Philadelphia fans are great.

Back during your playing days, did you really pay much attention to the passion and support of the Philly fans? Or is this more something you've taken notice of after you retired?

Yes I did. Sometimes I would come to the games and I'm not feeling

right, but when you walked into the Spectrum the people would go crazy because they wanted our layup line. We had THE best layup line in the history of basketball with our slam dunks and everything and the fans got into that and they got us going. They were truly that sixth man.

Allen Iverson has made a lot of questionable decisions off the court that other players in this town would not have gotten away with. In saying that, Philly fans seemed to be forgiving in regards to his behavior. Besides the fact that he was such a talented player, what do you think it was about him that most Philly fans have always given him a pass?

A guy like Allen Iverson was a guy like myself back in the day. He was from the inner city, never really left the inner city; his body might have but his mind was always there. He went out and played his butt off every night on the basketball court. People in Philadelphia, as long as you don't kill anybody [laughs] or go really, really crazy... they could accept it because of his work ethic on the basketball court. That's where you separate Allen Iverson the human being from Allen Iverson the basketball guy.

Assist: Earl Myers

Aaron McKie

Sixers Guard/Forward: 1997-2005;

Sixers Assistant Coach; 2008-present

2001 NBA Sixth Man of the Year

Temple University: 1991-1994

Lifelong Delaware Valley resident

Having grown up in Philly, what were your thoughts when you were traded to the Sixers in December '97?

I was just like *'I'm going back to Philly, one of the worst teams in the league, and they got Allen Iverson and Derrick Coleman,'* and I thought that was the worst thing in the world that could happen. In hindsight, it was the best. Those guys were great.

And what about the fans? What were you expecting as far as how Philly fans would be?

I think my college coach didn't like the idea of me playing back here. He always had his thing with Philadelphia fans, but I was just a basketball player. I (played in) Portland and the fans were great, then went to Detroit and the fans were great, so I'd never been on a team that was below .500. The 76ers team that I came

to under Coach (Larry) Brown, we scratched and clawed each night, and I think we won the hearts of our fans. Other than Allen Iverson, we didn't have an abundance of talent, and I think that's how we won the respect of our fans.

The college coach you're referring to is John Chaney, who coached you at Temple. Why was he concerned about you playing pro ball here?

John Chaney is like a father figure. He didn't want me to come back here and be in a situation when things don't go right. He was just protecting me.

But the reputation of Philly fans is that if you give them a great effort, they'll appreciate it, even if you don't always win.

But at the end of the day, they want to win. They're very knowledgeable. Some of these other places you go to, they're not knowledgeable. They only understand wins and losses. They don't understand the building process. But Philadelphia fans...this is a blue collar city. They aren't accepting anything less than guys giving it everything they have.

During that memorable journey to the 2001 NBA Finals, what did their outpouring of support mean to you as a key player on that team?

It was great. I got the opportunity to see both sides of Philly fans. Growing up here, I never got that opportunity to go to games and be in that atmosphere. But growing up in the neighborhood, you always talk sports. You didn't have NBA TV back then. Now you have fans living in Philly that are Orlando Magic fans. But when I was coming up, you only saw Sixers games. We always had our favorites and we went out and tried to emulate those guys, whether they were doing good or bad, in baseball, basketball and football. So the dynamics of sports has changed tremendously from the time I came out in '94 to now.

With Philly's reputation for being a difficult place to play, what would you tell an NBA free agent about the experience of being a Sixer?

It's a great atmosphere to play in. You gotta play your ass off every night. Period. But you should want to do that anyway. It's a tough town. Players talk across the league, but I'll tell you this: If our team continues to move in the direction that we're moving in, there are guys that...would love to be in a Sixers uniform.

As a native Philadelphian, what do you think another NBA championship would mean to basketball fans of this city?

I think the fans would be super supportive. They showed that in 2012 with how supportive they were with our team. We're still missing some pieces, but they enjoy watching our team.

8

PHILLY FANS MISTREAT THEIR OWN SUPERSTARS

It is important to relate the story of the greatest everyday player in Philadelphia Phillies history and the man often proclaimed as the greatest third baseman in Major League Baseball history. His name: Mike Schmidt.

Schmidt played his whole career in Philadelphia, was often booed and never felt the warmth of the fans. All he contributed was three league MVPS, 12 All-Star selections, 10 Gold Gloves, 548 home runs and a world championship. He even won the World Series MVP Award, yet all the fans could do was call him a *choker*. Or, they said that he coasted and was too cool.

In any other town, he'd have been lionized; in Philly, they almost booed him out of town. The same could be said for a bunch of other great players: Charles Barkley, Allen Iverson, Eric Lindros, Donovan McNabb...Kris Kringle.

"Philadelphia is the only city where you can experience the thrill of victory and the agony of reading about it the next day."

-MIKE SCHMIDT, 1974

RESPONSE: MATT GOLDBERG

Mike Schmidt, almost inarguably the greatest Philadelphia Phillies player of all-time, famously uttered the above words over 30 years ago. While the target of his ironic words was the perceived-to-be overly aggressive Philadelphia sports media, many fans also felt their sting. And if that shot was more subtle in nature, there were other occasions in which Schmitty really let us have it.

There was this gem from 1989—just a couple months before he abruptly, and tearfully, announced his retirement from the game.

"If you're associated with the Philadelphia media or town, you look for negatives. I don't know if there's something about their upbringing or they have too many hoagies, or too much cream cheese." [1]

Ouch! So was Michael Jack Schmidt's diatribe justified? And what about the other superstars, or would-be franchise players, that have played for the Philly faithful over the years? Would they have been justified in leveling their own attacks? Well, yes and no—and mostly no.

The national narrative is that Philly fans will boo anything and everybody and still have enough oxygen in their leather lungs to vent on other unworthy targets of their collective wrath. The story is told that we are also incredibly demanding of our own superstars and want to heckle them out of town. An examination of the last 40 or so years would indicate that this is not the case, even if we felt disconnected from a couple of our greatest performers over that span. In fact, we've been very appreciative and supportive of the great majority of our superstars.

In presenting a list of the greatest Philadelphia athletes of the past 40 years, I've included a few from each of the four major teams. Together, they encompass a few different eras. Some of you may argue that others could be added, but there's only so much space and this is a very representative list. Others may even argue that some of these players were not superstars, per se; I would counter that they were, or are, all franchise players or at least carried that burden, solely or jointly, during their tenure here.

And no, if you're looking for Shawn Bradley, who was drafted No. 2 overall in 1993 to be the Philadelphia 76ers' centerpiece, you won't find him here. Nice guy or not, Sixers fans may have justifiably greeted him with the occasional catcall. 7'6" guys who play like 6'3" guys aren't exactly Philly favorites.

So, what of Mike Schmidt?

There used to be an urban legend of sorts that Mike Schmidt hit so many homers…fill in a number between 300 and 548…and none of them was ever hit in the clutch. It was silly and obviously untrue, but it did speak to the lack of appreciation that many Phillies fans had for the greatest all-around third baseman to ever play the game…for any team.

Of course, to even suggest that all Phillies fans felt that way would be just as silly as the urban legend itself. Still, I believe it to be almost a point of fact that the once-skinny kid from Dayton, Ohio who played so brilliantly here for 17-plus seasons was both underappreciated and overly criticized during the great majority of his playing days. We Philly fans share in some of that guilt.

Undoubtedly, there were some reasons, or at least good excuses, for this lack of affection. Some of it may be traced to the way that Schmidt carried himself on the field. His persona was that of *Mr. Cool*. To the fan, the game seemed to come almost too easily for him—whether it was making that marvelous barehanded throw to first on a swinging bunt or catapulting a ball over the wall of the Vet with a flick of his mighty wrists. At the same time, he seemed to saunter on and off the field with a nonchalance mixed with arrogance that we just could not relate to. Schmitty did not usually let us in on his emotions, and…wouldn't you know it.....the ultimate, demonstrative overachiever—peppery shortstop Larry Bowa—lined up just forty feet to his left.

It always seemed as if the fans took to other players more than they did Schmidt, despite the incredible achievements and accolades that he amassed. While No. 20 was cementing his legacy as arguably the greatest Phillies player of all-time, it seemed that our collective hearts were won by a great collection of players, including Bowa, Greg Luzinski, Steve Carlton, Manny Trillo, Bake McBride and Garry Maddox. Even the once-despised Pete Rose endeared himself to us quickly with his hell-bent-for-leather, bowl-over-the-catcher hustle.

And, I did not even mention the electric, buoyant Tug McGraw, who wore his heart and humor on his sleeve and struck out the Royals' Willie Wilson to win us the 1980 World Series for the first time in our mostly futile 98-year history. The Tugger was already a truly beloved figure—and that was even before he told the New York fans to *stick it* at our championship parade.

But Schmitty? Well, it appears that the prevailing view was that he was supposed to produce like a superstar, and these lofty expectations served to highlight all those late-inning strikeouts and failures in the playoffs. Of course, this was a very harsh view, even if Michael Jack did not exactly tear the cover off the ball in his first four NLCS appearances (1976-1978, 1980). Fans seemed to zero in on the fact that Schmidt did not hit a single homer, and only drove in five total runs in those 16 games. It didn't seem to matter that the perennial All-Star and Gold Glover did more than anybody else to lead us to the postseason. And yes, this was the first postseason action Phillies fans had seen since the 1950 Whiz Kids were swept by those damn Yankees.

After years of playoff frustrations and heartache, the Phillies finally climbed to the top of the baseball mountain in 1980 and Schmidt, who won his first regular season MVP, found some postseason magic in the World Series, hitting .381 with two homers and seven RBI to help defeat the Royals. Schmidt was awarded the World Series MVP for his heroics, and it appeared that the proverbial gorilla had been lifted off his back. In retrospect, the gorilla may have been lifted, but his relationship with Philly fans never was all that harmonious.

Certainly, there were some great moments to come after 1980, as Schmidt would collect two more regular season MVP Awards and lead us to two more postseasons, including a World Series appearance in 1983. On the downside, the Phillies (featuring the *Wheeze Kids* of Pete Rose, Joe Morgan and Tony Perez) went down in five games to the Baltimore Orioles. The 1983 Fall Classic was a reminder that the legendary third baseman's postseasons didn't always match his regular season dominance. Schmidt contributed an anemic one single in 20 at-bats. I guess you can't have it all.

What about our personal connection to the guy? It seemed that there were only a few moments over the years where Schmidt revealed his true emotions. One played out on April 18th, 1987 at old Three Rivers Stadium in Pittsburgh, when he buried an offering by Don Robinson into the left-field seats for the 500th homer of his illustrious career. Schmidt allowed himself, and us, a little joyful bicycle kick down the first base line before going into a respectful trot which culminated in emphatic high-fives to his teammates.

The irony of this moment was that many remember Phillies broadcasting legend Harry Kalas' great call as much as they do Schmidt's milestone home run. While Kalas was simply nailing the call (as he always did), our affection seemed greater for the broadcaster than for No. 20. While the fans certainly admired Schmidt's impressive feat, they loved Harry's call.

Through it all, and for whatever criticism Schmidt endured here, it never got to the point where Phillies fans wanted him out of town. Yes, some wanted to boo him and still others never gave him enough credit, but the great majority of fans knew they had the privilege of seeing the full career of a surefire first-ballot Hall of Famer.

Philly fans in particular and baseball fans in general were almost blindsided by Schmidt's sudden retirement announcement, made from a clubhouse in San Diego on May 29th, 1989. Not only was it a shock that the greatest Phillie was retiring one-third of the way into his 18th season, but his short announcement was equally remarkable for one thing: the sheer emotion that he displayed. The man who had played with very little outward feeling for almost the entirety of his big league career dissolved into tears less than 20 seconds into his address. The man who kept our passionate fan base at arm's length with his sometimes prickly personality showed, quite viscerally, how much he cared about his profession and the game that he loved.

In retrospect, perhaps Phillies fans would have been more appreciative of the greatest player to ever wear red pinstripes if he had shown more of his passion and emotion along the way. Another telling quote of Schmidt's revealed how his apparent indifference and graceful, clean-uniform style of play belied how hard he worked at his craft.

"If you could equate the amount of time and effort put in mentally and physically into succeeding on the baseball field and measured it by the dirt on your uniform, mine would have been black." [2]

This was a great quote from a legendary player who never quite clicked with this town. Did Phillies fans miss the boat a little bit on the "skinny kid from Dayton, Ohio with two bad knees?" Yes, although it would be an exaggeration to say that we wanted to run No. 20 out of town.

The arc of Schmidt's career makes for an interesting contrast with that of the franchise's current slugger, first baseman **Ryan Howard**. While Schmidt started slowly (batting just .196 with 18 homers and 136 strikeouts in 1973), Howard exploded on the scene, winning the National Rookie of the Year Award in 2005, after compiling dynamic stats—a .288 batting average with 22 homers and 63 ribbies—in just 88 games. That was just a prelude to the damage that the man known as *The Big Piece* would do the very next year: a monumental line of .313/58/149 that would earn him the NL MVP. In doing so, he became the first Phillie to garner this piece of hardware since Schmidt won his third award in 1986.

It would be an oversimplification to say that Howard has never matched the monstrous numbers that he put up in his first full season. In truth, he hasn't, although what exactly does one do for an encore after shattering the team record for homers, and almost eclipsing the hallowed territory of Babe Ruth and Roger Maris in the process? The big man also knocked in the most runs in franchise history since a Hall of Famer named Chuck Klein drove in 170 in 1930. What Howard did was plenty, becoming arguably the top power hitter in baseball from 2006-2009, posting the following homer/RBI totals in successive years: 58/149, 47/136, 48/146 and 45/141. Even with drop-offs the next two years, he didn't exactly fall off the map while exceeding the still relevant 30/100 benchmarks to put up 31/108 in 2010 and 33/116 in 2011. The Baseball Writers Association of America seemed to always hold Ryan in high regard when it came to MVP voting; after winning the award in 2006, he finished in the top ten in each of the next five seasons.

A case can be made that Phillies fans have also been a little unappreciative of Howard's contributions over the years. A lot of effort has been spent among some insatiable fans in focusing on all the things that he doesn't do particularly well. He'll never be a Gold Glove first baseman, and one still cringes whenever he needs to throw the ball to second or third. He has only topped the .300 mark in that ridiculous 2006 campaign, and yes, he does strike out too much. These criticisms have some validity; although, when you wield one of the three most potent bats in the sport, should you be expected to excel at all of these other phases of the game? Unless your name is Albert Pujols—who ironically held down first base in Howard's hometown of St. Louis from 2001-2011—you probably won't meet all of (or even most of) these categories. Driving in the most runs, and being the most irreplaceable Phillie in a lineup that usually boasted another All-Star or two should have been enough for even his harshest critics.

Most Phillies fans, it appears, do seem to *get it* with Howard, and to his own credit, nobody could ever fault the Big Piece's work ethic or attitude. In addition to that, he truly seems to be the proverbial gentle giant, and he can easily be described as affable and genial. And yes, unlike Schmidt, his next controversial statement will be his very first.

One similarity with Schmidt is that Howard makes it look so easy to hit home runs off major league pitchers. When he connects and propels the ball into orbit, it just doesn't look like any park, including Fairmount, can hold it. So, there are some fans who focus on the strikeouts—and the fact that he will be paid $25 million per season through the 2016 season—and wonder why he doesn't do it more often. Like, perhaps, *just* 58 times every year.

Howard's postseason record is sometimes viewed a little harshly, and it has been his cruel fate to make the very last out of the 2010 and 2011 postseasons—both times in quite inglorious fashion—with both games played in Philly against teams the Fightins were expected to dismiss. Yet this is part of his record, every bit as much as the five straight division titles and two World Series appearances (and one parade) that he helped to bring to Philly in his first six full seasons.

It should also be remembered that Howard was responsible for one of the more dramatic moments in Phillies postseason history. The visiting Phillies had just surrendered three runs in the bottom of the eighth to fall behind the Colorado Rockies 4-2 in Game Four of the 2009 NLDS. If the Phils lost, they would have to return home for a deciding Game Five. It was at this point that Howard exhorted his teammates to *"just get me to the plate, boys."* His boys did, although they were still trailing 4-2, with men on first and second and two outs. The Big Piece laced a two-strike double to tie the game and would come around to score the game-winner on Jayson Werth's follow-up hit. All that was left for the team to advance to the NLCS was for closer Brad "Lights-Out" Lidge to shut the door, which he did. Howard would be one of the stars of the ensuing NLCS against the Dodgers, hitting .333 with two homers and eight RBI to capture the NLCS MVP and lead them to a second consecutive Fall Classic.

In contrast, through 2011, Howard has only slugged two more homers in his last 20 postseason games, and some fans exhibited short memories, seeming to forget about his earlier heroics. To categorize the feeling of Philly fans towards the run-producing first baseman, it would be *slightly unappreciative*, but not nearly to the extent to which many approached the great majority of Mike Schmidt's career.

If Howard hasn't always been appreciated as much as he should be, his longtime teammate, **Chase Utley**, has had no problems whatsoever in clicking with Phillies Nation. Together, they have manned the best right side of the infield in the game for most of their tenure, and the majority of Phillies historians would place both of them in their all-time Phillies lineup. Of the two, Utley seems to have soaked up his share of the adulation.

Chase "The Man" Utley

One of the mysteries of sports is why fans sometimes pit star players against one another, as if there is only enough love for one or the other. It seems silly, especially when there is no conflict between the two, as is the case with Howard and Utley. In 1961, fans of the New York Yankees apparently *had* to choose between Mickey Mantle and Roger Maris as they were both vying to break Babe Ruth's legendary mark of 60 homers. But even with no records on the line, we still often pick our favorites, as if we can't quite (to return to former hometown dilemmas) adopt both Schmidt and Luzinski or Eric Lindros and John LeClair. In any such tandem, it would be hard to find a superstar more tailor-made for Philly than Chase Utley.

While Howard has been the top dog when it has come to driving in runs, Utley has been a superior all-around player, and also something that Howard can't be due to his massive size—scrappy. Utley defines "scrappiness"; at his best, he combines the hustle of Larry Bowa with a Schmitty-like penchant for launching baseballs with his compact swing. He contributes all of that, and better-than-average defense, while playing with an almost perpetual sneer and a command of all the little things that define a winner on the diamond.

Utley's statistics, let alone his intangibles, made him the top second baseman in the game from 2005-2010, as evidenced by his five All-Star game appearances and four Silver Slugger Awards, given to the league's top hitters at their positions. Injuries and wear-and-tear have depleted some of Chase's production in the last few years, but his approach to the game (as well as his Hall of Fame-like play in his prime) will always be celebrated in this city.

Chase's double play partner, **Jimmy Rollins**, is a little harder to sum up. It is fair to come to the conclusion that J-Roll, like Howard and Utley, is the best to ever play his position here. For a franchise that once featured his former manager and mentor Larry Bowa, that is not an easy distinction to hold.

Philly's longest-tenured current athlete flirts with controversy much more than his fellow All-Star infield mates. As mentioned, Howard is quiet but always pleasant and never one to boast, while Utley, essentially, doesn't say much of anything. Rollins? Well, he doesn't mind stirring the pot. It should be noted that none of them, unlike a few Philly superstars yet to be discussed, have had any major off-the-field indiscretions.

Rollins is a bit of an anomaly. He is the little big man who somehow gets the team going from the leadoff spot, despite a career on-base percentage that is well under a respectable .350 mark. He also plays with maximum effort the great majority of the time except for...well...when he doesn't. There have been at least three or four instances over the years when Rollins has appeared to "dog it" on the bases—situations when manager Charlie Manuel has had to either bench him, give him a private talk or even yank him from a game. The funny thing about these incidents is that they appear to be totally inexplicable, as Rollins usually busts it, both offensively and defensively—where he has always excelled.

By the time he retires, Rollins may very well be the team's all-time leader in hits (he's already amassed over 2,000) and he will challenge for franchise supremacy in runs and stolen bases. As a shortstop, he has had few peers (four Gold Gloves) and his three All-Star appearances and 2007 MVP Award will get him some votes, if not a plaque, in Cooperstown.

As for the fans, it appears that Philly has gotten it right when it comes to the little shortstop. We loved him when he tweaked Mets fans (and players) prior to the 2007 season, saying we were "the team to beat" and well, he backed it up with his best season as our rivals from New York collapsed down the stretch. We have also expressed our hurt and anger when he referred to us as "frontrunners," and even let him have it a little after those few occasions when he didn't leg out those ground balls. Mostly a hero, with a bit of renegade and anti-hero in his DNA, Rollins and Philly have been a good match.

Of the list of superstars that Philly treated unfairly, Mike Schmidt represented the biggest disconnect, followed closely by a more recent player in another sport—the Eagles franchise quarterback, **Donovan McNabb**.

With full disclosure, I will offer that I am probably the biggest McNabb fan among the co-authors of this book. In general, I support the premise of Chapter 3 because I don't believe that the national media has delved too deeply into all of the reasons why there was lots of tension between the franchise quarterback and Eagles fans.

Jimmy Rollins is slowly but surely becoming one of the all-time great Philadelphia Phillies.

While I would not put McNabb's career in the same stratosphere as Schmidt's, there is a case to be made that he played at a borderline Hall of Fame level during his time in Philly. While many would dispute this point, others would see his overall success (his high winning percentage, how he often carried the offense and even his relative playoff success, if one can ignore the lack of a Lombardi Trophy) and compare it favorably with other signal callers—Jim Kelly, Dan Fouts and Warren Moon come to mind—who made it to Canton without a championship.

More relevant to this discussion is that all but a few of McNabb's most ferocious detractors would concede that he had, at minimum, a very good career in Philly. Given the relative success of his tenure here and his spotless conduct off-the-field, I would be hard-pressed to find another Philly athlete in the last 40 years who has been so similarly scrutinized and assailed from all possible angles.

Similar to Schmidt, McNabb made it hard for a lot of fans to warm up to him. While he always was civil during media sessions, he came off as either insincere (taking pains to inject humor, often belying his true feelings) or displaying the chip that often lodged on his shoulder. On the field, his manner sometimes came off as nonchalant, although I often felt that it masked the fire and resilience he truly had. How else could he successfully rebound from all the injuries and all the criticism?

Whatever the reasons for our collective lack of regard for McNabb—and even 50 pages may not be enough to do justice to this chapter subplot—I do think that Philly fans overly criticized him, and also underestimated just how terrific a player he was. But, did we run him out of town with a steady stream of boos? Not at all. By every indication, McNabb—who was coming off a terrific 2009 regular season, if one that ended with a deflating playoff loss—wanted to come back to Philadelphia for a 12th season in 2010. The fans did not toss him out by any stretch; Eagles management felt that it was time to turn over the keys to Michael Vick...or was it Kevin Kolb at the time?

The downward spiral of McNabb's career since he left Philly (to say nothing of the downward spiral of many of his underthrown passes), should not negate what he accomplished as an Eagle. His lack of success in Washington and Minnesota seems to have warmed the hearts of many somewhat vindictive Eagles fans. In my mind, Eagles fans came up a little small when it came to Number Five, and it will be fascinating to see how he is regarded five or 10 years down the road. It will be equally intriguing to see how he feels about Philly fans by then.

So, perhaps Philly fans treated Mike Schmidt and Donovan McNabb somewhat unfairly, but over the last 40 years, these two players have been the outliers. Contrary to popular belief and the overall national narrative, it is hard to find other great players who weren't adored by the majority of local fans. And yes, this even extends to our most controversial athletes.

Charles Barkley and **Allen Iverson** were two of the most colorful franchise players to ever suit up in South Philly. Both of them came into town with great fanfare, gave us between eight to ten seasons of stellar play and ended up being traded to other cities without carrying their respective teams to a championship. Both players—and one might even add mercurial Eagles' quarterback **Randall Cunningham** to this list—had ever-so-slightly disappointing careers here (mostly because of that one glaring hole in their resumes where a championship would be listed) yet both were, on the whole, recipients of great adulation.

When examining reaction to these players, it is wise to consider the great majority of the fans. There are a certain percentage of fans—and this is not unique to Philly—who will look to bury franchise players for any misstep they make on and off the *field.* There is another group of fans on the other end of the spectrum who would be capable of defending their favorite player even if he were convicted of murder. While this is not a scientific

Sir Charles Barkley

185

survey, I am mostly considering the other, more pliable, middle tier of fans—that other 10%. Just kidding. Call it 80-85% of the fan base, even among Philadelphia sports fans.

For all of his controversial comments and doings, Sir Charles lit up the arena like very few before or since. His career overlapped with the amazing **Julius Erving**, and he represented a much different kind of central figure. Barkley was as raw as Doc was polished, as bombastic as Doc was majestic, and as irrepressible as Doc was conciliatory. And in large part, we loved Barkley for the way he spilled his guts on the court and how he entertained us off of it. He sometimes made us cringe, but he also delighted and disarmed us with an almost boyish, cheeky sense of humor.

Fans in the know lay blame for the Sixers' decline at the feet of their (mis-) management, and understood why Charles had enough, and essentially talked his way out of town. Such was our respect and adoration for Barkley that we serenaded him with "M-V-P" chants when he returned to the Spectrum for the first time in 1993 as a member of the first-place Phoenix Suns. The fans had it right; Barkley won his only league MVP Award that year, leading his team to the NBA Finals.

When it came to sheer excitement, it is hard to imagine that any player could pack as much pure energy and pizzazz in such a small package as the electrifying **Allen Iverson**. Iverson, even before his collegiate days at Georgetown, was always a controversy waiting to happen. But man, could he leave it all out there on the court and whoop the crowd into a frenzy.

In considering Iverson, it is important to remember that 85% of fans who could overlook the superficial—his mode of dress, his entourage and his disdain for even *talking 'bout practice*—and just marvel at the magic he performed on the hardwoods. Iverson and the Philly faithful forged a sometimes unreal love affair. Despite his misdeeds, when the lights came on, we just clicked.

To root for Iverson, one had to ignore his many off-court flaws and incidents, or at least put them into some kind of perspective. As often as the diminutive guard earned free throws due to his fearless play on the court, it seemed as if the great majority of Philly fans gave him even more *free passes* from his various controversies. Where exactly do we begin and end with AI's indiscretions, which ranged from parking in handicapped spots to problems experienced by his outsized entourage to explosive, homophobic rap lyrics? There was also a marital dispute that made front page news, including helicopter coverage of events surrounding his palatial home. And if all that weren't enough, in 2002, there was the surreal *"we talking 'bout practice, man"* (not a game… not a game…not a game…) press conference which seemed to show just how far apart he and his old school head coach, Larry Brown, were. And, I didn't even mention the April 18, 2006 Fan Appreciation Night that AI and Chris Webber (never a superstar in *this town)* arrived late for. In retrospect, the last indiscretion may have been a bit of a final straw for the Sixers organization; Iverson was traded to Denver in the early stages of the 2006-2007 season.

One of the many fascinating aspects of Iverson's career was that he never seemed to *get* some of the professionalism that went along with being a superstar in the NBA. His legendary disdain for practice was such that he appeared to not understand that building such chemistry may have helped him blend his incredible talents with those of his supporting cast when it really mattered. That complaint aside—and overlooking that Fan Appreciation Night blow-off—he did seem to get Philly and the type of on-court effort and love we savor in our superstars.

As infuriating as each and every one of his flaws could be—from his late night escapades to his hatred of practice—he was a galvanizing force whenever he took the court. Philly admired and loved that the smallest man on the court (generously listed at six-foot tall and 165 pounds) could repeatedly lead the league in scoring and even minutes played. So what if he begged off practice, man. And the little guy, who seemed to represent us in the starting lineup of the All-Star Game each year, even took his scoring up an extra notch in the playoffs.

Iverson's game brought the city sheer joy, along with one surprising appearance in the 2001 NBA Finals. That postseason run, featuring an unlikely trio of owner Pat Croce, coach Larry Brown and Iverson was one of the most thrilling rides in recent Philly sports history. AI seemed to enjoy every minute of it, while letting us in on all of his emotions;

indeed, who can forget the way he cupped his ear to the fans, encouraging us to unleash our celebrated passion.

A case can be made that Philly fans took Iverson—despite his various indiscretions—to their hearts as much they have any player in the last 25 years. It would be a gross misstatement to assert that our often maligned fans did anything to run AI, or Sir Charles, out of this town.

Unlike Iverson, **Eric Lindros** had a quiet, even dull, personality, but his career was bathed in controversy and expectations before he even arrived in Philly. Refusing to play for the team that drafted him (the Quebec Nordiques...remember them?), an arbitrator awarded his services to the Flyers over the challenge of the hated New York Rangers. Lindros was advertised as the next great player and, when healthy, he performed like it for his eight-year tenure with the orange-and-black.

On the ice, when firing on all cylinders, Lindros could be a one-man wrecking crew, whether scoring, assisting, burying opponents with board-rattling checks or dropping his gloves—usually inflicting some damage with some punishing rights. His game was designed for Philly fans. For all his amazing gifts and great play (he won the league MVP in his third year, at age 22), Lindros led the Flyers to only one Stanley Cup Finals appearance, where they were promptly swept by the Detroit Red Wings.

Lindros could be a lightning rod for criticism, although most of the controversies were behind the scenes, and waged between No. 88's overbearing parents and the team's iconic general manager, Bob Clarke. Somewhat tragically, his Flyers career, which started with almost impossibly high hopes, ended on a down note off the ice, including all kinds of grievances aired by Clarke in the local press. If that wasn't enough, his last shift on the ice ended on a borderline dirty hit by New Jersey Devils defenseman Scott Stevens.

When we next saw Lindros in town, it was a year-and-a-half later as a member of the...oh, cruel irony...New York Rangers. And no, the arena that Eric helped build did not erupt in cheers (as it did for Barkley, who had the advantage of playing for a team out west, in a year that the Sixers stunk), although he did receive at least a smattering of applause. During the years that Eric suited up for the Flyers, he was held in great esteem by the great majority of fans. His controversies were between him (or his parents, Bonnie and Carl) and management, and most fans continued to support him, even throughout that messy divorce-in-the-making. Lindros did not carry us to a Cup, but did make the Flyers one of the most exciting and compelling teams during his never-dull eight years here. He still has earned our appreciation for that.

There is another large group of superstars in the last 30-plus years that enjoyed great support here and were positively adored by Philly fans. By sheer numbers, this group would suggest that Philly fans treat their superstars with great appreciation—in pointed contrast to the way the national media depicts us.

During the same era that Mike Schmidt was earning his membership in the 500-homer club and leading the Phillies to contention and beyond, there was a bit of a golden era for all Philadelphia teams. Yes, Schmitty sometimes had a rough go of it with the fans, but when he looked into his own dugout, he would see the almost larger-than-life presence of **Steve '*Lefty*' Carlton**—a pitcher who the fans practically worshipped. The Hall of Famer, who won four Cy Young Awards here, was bathed in mystery—which may have worked to his advantage. An iconoclast who refused to talk to the media and embraced his own Eastern training techniques, we only asked for Lefty to excel every fourth day, and he did. In retrospect, it might be a good thing that some of his bizarre philosophies were not publicized back then. He showed up on the hill, had the most devastating slider in the game, and got results. Period. And we loved him for it.

The Flyers led the sports renaissance during the early 1970s winning back-to-back Stanley Cups in 1974 and 1975. While Schmitty was sometimes vilified for his lack of clutch play and nonchalance at the Vet, in the Spectrum, we idolized the Flyers' gap-toothed captain, **Bobby Clarke.** Clarkie was everything we love in an athlete: a smallish, overachiever who even overcame diabetes, a bona fide superstar who won three NHL MVP Awards, and a gamer who would seemingly do anything to earn a victory for his team. Clarkie, the player, is still a god-like figure, even if Clarkie 2.0, the GM (now known as Bob Clarke) who never could earn us another parade, was treated like a fallible being.

The Broad Street Bullies: arguably Philadelphia's most beloved alltime team!

Bernie Parent between the pipes

Between the pipes, there was a superstar goalie named **Bernard Marcel Parent**, smaller than most, but blessed with a preternatural quickness and guts in the crease. It did not hurt that Bernie absolutely peaked in our Stanley Cup years, winning both the Vezina Trophy (for best regular season goaltender) and the Conn Smythe Award (MVP of the playoffs) both years. With an endearing personality and a self-effacing sense of humor, a bad word has never been hurled Bernie's way. The man is forever a Philly hero.

Julius Erving flew above mere mortals on and off the court during his 11 years in the Sixers' red-white-and-blue. Although we did not expect to wait seven years after his arrival to win a championship, Dr. J—who could have easily won a mayoral election here—was never blamed for those shortcomings. Doc was held in great esteem around the league, and fans felt privileged that he made most of his house calls in South Philly. When the Sixers swept the Lakers to capture the 1983 title, they reserved their loudest cheers and happy tears for the high-flying, regal Erving.

With apologies to Bill Bergey, Wilbert Montgomery, Harold Carmichael and Ron Jaworski, the Eagles of that Golden Era—a unit coached by Dick Vermeil who improbably made it to Super Bowl XV—did not have a player of the singular stature of Schmidt, Clarke, Parent or Erving. Montgomery may have been the team's best all-around player; for those who missed this era, think of Brian Westbrook with a little more durability as a runner. The quiet Montgomery was loved by fans. "Jaws," a Hall of Fame competitor and Philly citizen who has become one of the best analysts of the game, did endure his share of boos at home games. To some degree, it goes with the position, and with the territory of playing for a passionate east coast fan base. Those catcalls aside, he never, in my estimation, was attacked on all possible angles as McNabb was.

Even before the legendary Chuck Bednarik patrolled the middle of the field, Eagles fans have always loved hard-hitting defensive players, and the two greatest defenders of the last 20 years have been the team's most popular players during that time. Both **Reggie White** and **Brian Dawkins** left town without leading us to a parade, although fans would blame at least 100 other factors before thinking about criticizing these two icons.

Julius "The Doctor" Ervinggggg"

On the right day, one can still hear diehard Eagles fans grumbling about how hated owner Norman Braman let Reggie sign with Green Bay and how Andy Reid and Joe Banner cut B-Dawk loose to ink a deal with Denver.

The late, great White was almost a force of nature at defensive end, the likes of which this town had never seen. Indeed, an easy case can be made that no player in NFL history has ever played that position so well. A gentle giant with a childlike sense of humor off the field, the Minister of Defense was revered in this town.

How much, you ask?

One indication of the reverence was the March 3, 1993 rally that was held for Reggie, as fans feared that he would soon be leaving owner Norman Braman's tight-fisted clutches and moving on to another team. Staged by radio station WIP, the "Rally for Reggie" featured thousands of fans screaming *"Reggie, Reggie"* in appreciation for his superlative play and selfless, charitable service in the community. If the fans had their way, Reggie would have completed his Hall of Fame career in Philadelphia; as fate and money (and possibly God?) would have it, he signed a lucrative deal one month later with the Green Bay Packers.

Dawkins, the heart and soul of a very strong defense, appealed to fans as much as any Eagles player over the last 40 years. Fearless, ferocious and demonstrative, Dawk launched his body into players with the kind of reckless abandon that Philly loves. It did not hurt any that he wore his heart on his jersey, from his animated, Weapon-X/Wolverine player introduction all the way through his candid post-game media

sessions. Dawkins never left any doubt about his love of the game and his appreciation for the Philly fans.

B-Dawk, listed at a relatively small 6-foot-even and 210 pounds, was one of the most punishing hitters of his era in the NFL. His all-out playing style was a perfect match for Philly, and he was, in turn, very appreciative of his fans. Brian did at least three things—in addition to being a phenomenal, eight-time Pro Bowl free safety—that made him so popular in this town:

1. He was the ultimate team player that regularly sacrificed his own body to make play after play for the good of the team and the delight of the fans.

2. He sincerely saluted and honored the fans, on the field and off.

3. He was honest and secure enough to take blame for his own play and that of his own defensive unit. He looked every bit as pained by Eagles' losses as the fans that cheered him.

And so it was that Philly sports fans collectively mourned when Dawkins (going on 36 at the time, but still capable of good play) accepted an offer to play for the Denver Broncos. To this day, it never felt right to see Dawk suiting up in anything other than midnight green, and while the safety gave it his all for his new team, his heart always seemed to be with the Birds and their fans. Those three seasons outside of Philly will always be on his resume, but both parties did the right thing, enabling him to sign a one-day contract in April, 2012 to retire as an Eagle. Of course, Dawkins displayed his trademark appreciation, toughness and raw emotion at that ceremonial press conference.

Ironically, Dawkins wore No. 20, as did the man who started this discussion—the great (and underappreciated) Mike Schmidt. Schmidt, in my analysis, is—along with Donovan McNabb—one of only two superstars who Philly fans seemed to have missed the boat on over the last 30-40 years. But as illustrated above, the fans were highly supportive of so many other franchise players.

In retrospect, one wonders how Phillies fans would have embraced Schmitty if he would have, like Dawkins, shown his love for the game more often. Admittedly, it's probably easier to do this as a 16-game-a-year safety than as a 162-games-a-season third baseman. But, the point remains. Philly may, indeed, be the *town that loves you back*, but we are a little sensitive and like to feel that love in return from our greatest sports heroes.

Since he retired, Michael Jack Schmidt has spent time in Philly at some of our most important celebrations as well as our times of sorrow (including the memorial service for Harry Kalas at Citizens Bank Park), and the mutual admiration between player and fan has been great to see. It would be nice to say that this was the prevalent

Mike Schmidt's statue outside Citizens Bank Park is a true testament to his legacy.

feeling during his playing days, but the clock cannot be turned back to the 1970s. The greatest third baseman of all time expressed it best when he addressed the fans on the night of his number retirement ceremony.

"I want to tell you straight from the heart, how I feel about you and your influence on this game. As athletes, we're disciplined, we're focused, we're even tough. But I know of no athlete who is immune to fan reaction, positive or negative. Yes, you fans affect the game in a 'big' way. Calling Philadelphia fans spectators hardly describes your impact. You help mold the spirit of a team. Your positive feedback is crucial in the Phillies' quest to stay on top. You know, I'm often asked what I miss most about the game. It's tough to sort out all the wonderful memories and come up with a definite answer. But I can tell you this; I'll always miss the goose bumps I got when you cheered me. I've collected eighteen years of those goose bumps, from my first hit back in 1972 to the welcome you gave me tonight. To right now. That feeling can never be recreated, but that feeling will always be remembered." [3]

So, say what you want about Philly fans, but we don't run our superstars out of town with boos. And to those who care to notice, we inspire some serious goosebumps.

9

PHILLY FANS CHEER INJURED OPPONENTS (THE MICHAEL IRVIN INCIDENT)

It is important for you as members of the media to point out that Philadelphia fans are savage enough to even boo injured players from opposing teams. These fans once booed Michael Irvin when he was dying on the field one year. Such atrocious behavior has happened countless times in Philadelphia, not that you have to go into great detail or any kind of reasonable perspective here.

Please Always Remember: Too much detail and any kind of balanced perspective may not only dilute the clarity of your narrative, but it may hinder your ability to retain your own coveted, prestigious position.

It is an accepted common courtesy that an opposing player—no matter the intensity of the rivalry—is a human being with a life and a family. A hush should come over the crowd when he goes down and fans should rise to their feet in applause and gratitude when he recovers. This is true in every city across the nation, but not in Philly. This is also important to point out whenever you see a seriously injured player, whether the game is being played in Philly or elsewhere.

Please use this incident as a reminder of the classlessness of Philly sports fans, and point out that this happens *all the time* in the City of Brotherly Love, and nowhere else. There is no need to research further. And this happened to Michael Irvin, one of the most self-effacing, classy, clean-living gentlemen in the history of the sport—and a future Hall of Famer.

To be *fair* to Philly fans, you may want to balance this by saying that Philly fans have never booed their own injured players. Now, **here** is an area that you may wish to research. You know: these are the same people that kept pelting Santa Claus with snowballs.

"By cheering Dallas Cowboys receiver Michael Irvin as he lay motionless on the turf Sunday with a neck injury, the fans brought the city's reputation for boorishness to new lows."

-ASSOCIATED PRESS, OCTOBER 1999

RESPONSE: RYAN DOWNS

I was nothing more than a lanky college senior in a yellow jacket. The jacket said "STAFF" on the back, but it would have more accurately read "FAN." Beneath this faux authority was a kid gladly and dutifully serving his fraternity's philanthropy by appearing as a security guard at Veterans Stadium, a concrete-filled sea of beer and testosterone. I waltzed in on that October day hoping to fulfill my role. And in doing so, see a free Eagles game.

It didn't work out exactly according to plan, but it did leave me with this story to tell.

The 1999 Eagles were less than spectacular, but any matchup against the rival and perennial powerhouse Dallas Cowboys was intense. The Birds were a pitiful bunch led by journeyman Doug Pederson, and the season appeared to be lost before it started. Yet, I was still a big Eagles fan and I very much valued the experience simply as a Sunday at "The Vet."

My assignment was simple and exciting, with an ironic twist. I was to stand on the sidelines and monitor fan activity. It was my first—and only opportunity to stand on an NFL field during actual game play.

Best gig ever, right? Well, sort of. The remainder of my assignment involved facing the fans in the stands with my back to the field AT ALL TIMES. For a person in my position at the time, it was simultaneously exhilarating, frustrating, and tempting. Most of all though, it gave me an incredibly unique perspective to one of the most memorable moments of the last few decades of Philadelphia Eagles history: *"The Michael Irvin Incident."*

Michael Irvin was a lightning rod of a man who played wide receiver for the hated Cowboys. If you worshiped the 'Star,' you loved the man. Irvin was talented, charismatic, and produced Hall-of-Fame results for the entire decade of the 1990's. If you were not a fan of America's Team however, you focused in on his incessant hot dog routine, his taunting and whining, as well as off the field endeavors involving drugs and an alleged sexual assault.

By October, the Eagles were futile and hopeless, steadfastly awaiting the on-field emergence of first round pick Donovan McNabb to take Pederson's place. The Cowboys were on the downside of their run of brilliance that began in the early 90's following the drafting of Troy Aikman, Emmitt Smith, and Irvin, as well as the trade of Herschel Walker that eventually bolstered the roster with many more young, talented players. Still, they were the Cowboys, and the sight of them in the old Vet was nauseating to an Eagles fan. Hating that star was a religious experience of sorts.

When Irvin was crushed on a solid hit by safety Tim Hauck in the first quarter, the collision was naturally appreciated by fans. Irvin was our nemesis, and had been torturing Eagles fans for over a decade with his on-field brilliance. Quite simply, Michael Irvin was hated in Philadelphia for what he did on the field, and far from liked for what he did off it. The people of Philadelphia wanted to see Irvin get smashed hard enough that he wouldn't get up.

They got their wish on this day.

The fans cheered mightily. I saw it with my own eyes—they cheered and cheered. I couldn't turn around, nor did I actually see the play unfold. All I could do was listen, feel, and watch the fans. After minutes of Irvin lying motionless, people began to slowly focus their thoughts toward its true ramifications. Football emotion evolved into human emotion, and most fans started to become concerned. They slowly sat down, some with hands to their chins, feeling somewhat remorseful for their previous wishes. In some small circles, as widely reported, fans continued to cheer until the stretcher carried Irvin off the field.

However, in the section I looked toward, I saw passion turn into compassion and sports-related hatred turn into humanity. It was actually alarming to watch, considering the fact that I could essentially not see behind me. It was the sports equivalent of going to see your favorite artist in concert, and spending the entire duration waiting in line for the bathroom on the concourse. All I could do was hear and feel, and I remember feeling proud of the way people behaved because I knew how easy it would have been to cheer for this particular man's demise. I was, needless to say, astonished by what I would hear and read the next morning.

Naturally, following in-stride with true Philadelphia form and lore, the reports following the game documented our fans as vile and insanely evil, with all signs pointing toward the cheering of Irvin being lifted onto a stretcher.

Hello? News flash! The truth is, in large part, that the cheering was a sportsmanlike display. Let's face it, if you put 65,000 people from any city into any building, you are going to have a few thousand jerks. That's just the way it is. Law of averages.

But on this day in mid-October 1999, the jerks won out. And so the beat went on, cementing the reputation of Eagles fans as violent, abrasive detriments to society. Is this true of some people in that stadium that day? Sure. The circumstances dictated it to be an almost absolute truth to some degree.

But was it true of the fans I saw with my own eager, impressionable eyes? No, not at all. That one's for the birds.

Although I think I did see someone chuck a snowball at Santa Claus. With my back to the field however, I sadly may never know if he or she hit the intended target.

BOTTOM OF THE 9TH

BEHIND THE MIC:

THE THOUGHTS OF PHILADELPHIA'S MOST WELL-ESTABLISHED AND LEGENDARY SPORTSCASTERS

From Wilt Chamberlain's 100-point game to Brad Lidge striking out Eric Hinske, to Rick MacLeish's game-winning Stanley Cup goal, to the Miracles at the Meadowlands and almost every play Allen Iverson ever made as a Sixer, they are the voices that bring you the great (and not so great) moments in Philly sports from behind the microphone—and we have them!

Even though they brought the calls to you, what were they really thinking? While some voice their opinions for all to hear on the radio or TV, some are heard only seasonally. Ever wonder what they really think about some of Philly's most notorious and memorable incidents? Let's not forget, while they are professionals in their field, they most likely got into this business because they were fans!

Dan Baker

Phillies/Eagles PA Announcer; Big Five Hall of Famer

On the Michael Irvin incident:

When Michael Irvin went down and didn't get back up, my recollection was there were many people who cheered, but it wasn't the whole stadium. As far as percentages go, I couldn't tell you the amount. I would say it was pretty high! But I also didn't think they were cheering because he suffered a career-ending injury. The basis of their reaction was that, without Michael Irvin, it would be harder for the Cowboys to win. Could there have some people in that 65,000 sellout crowd that were happy about the injury? Yes, there could have been a few, but I think that was a minority.

My feelings are tempered with hope and desire that Philadelphia sports fans can be thought well of. I don't want them to be thought of as the boorish individuals that some may portray them to be. Something which upsets me is that incidents like this in other cities take place, and they don't receive anywhere near the bad press that Philadelphia gets. I don't think there's a place for bad behavior in Philadelphia or any other city. These kinds of incidents happen everywhere. It's not unique to Philadelphia, but I prefer it didn't happen anywhere. We all want the Philadelphia teams to win, but not at the expense of somebody getting badly injured, as in Michael Irvin's case.

As I recall, the longer Michael Irvin stayed on the ground and it became obvious this was more serious than initially thought, the crowd's cheering subsided. At this point, they realized that the injury could be more serious.

Bill Campbell

Philadelphia Sportscasting Legend

You have been a broadcaster for decades and have literally seen it all. When would you say the Philadelphia fans began to acquire their tough reputation? Is that something that happened over time?

I think the fans are used to so many losing seasons. Look at the records over the years of the Phillies, Eagles and teams who were never able to win a championship. Although some teams crashed through to win a championship, the fans got used to so much defeat and took on the aura of heartbreak so often that it just became a normal routine.

Over the years, have you observed any fan base as criticized and maligned as the Philadelphia fans?

You could say that about almost anywhere. I've been around it long enough, and I really think it's that way all over the country. The only place that might be an exception is Los Angeles. One thing they do is leave early before the game is decided. If you walk into Dodger Stadium in the seventh inning, the park is half-empty. Why that is, I don't know. It's Hollywood, and they're very blasé and have so many other things to think about.

Do you feel that Philadelphia fans are more passionate now or in previous eras?

I think they're more passionate now because teams like the Phillies keep winning. They have their division titles and all these consecutive sellouts. People react to victory and defeat, and I think you'll find that's true no matter where you go.

It has been estimated that two million fans showed up for the Phillies' World Series parade in 2008. The Flyers' 1974 parade is recognized by many as one of the largest ever in sports. Due to the fact that the Eagles have gone so long without a title, could that parade possibly dwarf those other ones?

I broadcasted the last game the Eagles won in 1960. We just had a celebration and I have a watch the Eagles gave me. As far as the parade, it probably wouldn't be of gigantic proportions. I think the people would be overcome and overjoyed, but I think the Phillies' parade in 2008 is probably as big as you're going to see around here, and the Eagles would be very close.

Merrill Reese

Eagles Play-by-Play Radio Announcer: 1977-present

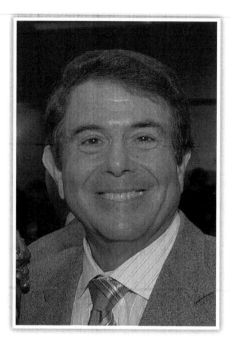

The Eagles haven't won a championship since 1960, but year after year, Lincoln Financial Field is packed and there is still an Eagles waiting list for season tickets. Why do you think that the expectations are still high despite never having a parade down Broad Street?

Because Eagles football is their greatest passion. The Phillies are wonderful and they've had a great stretch, and as much as people have enjoyed their run, I still believe that this is first and foremost a pro football town. They have been raised with it and it has gone on for generations. People just love their Eagles. Every year, hopes spring up and fans ride this team for as long as they possibly can. They either taste success once every 30 years or they just get ready for the next year, but they just love this football team.

Was there one moment in particular during an Eagles game where you applauded Eagles fans for their exemplary behavior?

Oh, there's been a lot of times. These are great fans. I really believe they are great fans. You have your incidents where you have unruly fans who create some problems, but I don't think that's the bulk of our fans. I think the bulk of our fans are the people who love this team, and love and appreciate the sport. From the ovation they give this team, how they become the 12th man on defense in key points in the game, the way they welcome back stars. The first time Donovan McNabb and Brian Dawkins came back, they respond appropriately. I think they're great.

You can hear the E-A-G-L-E-S chant almost anywhere during the late summer through winter. Have you seen a fan base in any other market who will so readily cheer for their football team at other sporting events or at other venues?

No. I think there is a lot of passion in Pittsburgh, and obviously the Giants fans are rabid. There's no doubt about that. I think Green Bay is amazing, too. It's a small town and the Packers are basically all they have. But to me, there's still something where the passion is greater here in Philadelphia than any place else.

It has become widely known and commonplace for Eagles fans to sync up the television broadcast to your voice. How does this make you feel, and what does it say about your connection to the Philadelphia fan?

It means a lot to me. It's the highest compliment you can receive as a broadcaster, but I love the fans. I feel connected to them, they feel connected to me, and the fact that I'm getting through to them is great. It makes me feel wonderful, but it goes both ways. I feel like I'm reaching out to them. I can feel what they feel. I grew up here, I've been living this for my entire life, and I feel what they feel. I think very often that when I say something, it hits home because that's what they're thinking. We've had the same background, we've been through the high hopes, the pain, the bitter disappointments, we've been through this together. So basically, I feel that in some senses, I'm one of them. I've just been fortunate enough to have this wonderful vantage point and great job, but their emotions run right through my veins.

As the longtime voice of the Eagles, have you witnessed Eagles fans evolve over the years with respect to their passion or patience?

I don't think they've changed. I think their passion is just as great. I think they voice their disappointments just as quickly. I think perhaps as the years have gone by, they've become more and more knowledgeable as to the strategy and technical aspects of the game because we have so many shows today where the fans get to see game tape broken down and plays of the offensive line. People have seen this more now than ever before, so they're more sophisticated right now than they were 20 years ago. Now they know the requirements of the linebackers in a 30 defense as opposed to a defense that features a four-man front. I think they're a lot more sophisticated in their knowledge, but their emotions are still just as taxed.

Bill Clement

Former Flyer, Two-time Stanley Cup Champion; TV Analyst; Actor; Author

On the Philadelphia fans:

Sports is almost like religion for Philadelphians. They become attached to their sports teams as much as any fans in the world. In some regards, Philadelphia fans are a lot like European soccer fans. I think Philadelphians in general wear their hearts on their sleeves. What you see is what you get. They don't beat around the bush, they're pretty straight forward, and I think that can be misinterpreted as rough and mean-spirited. It's really just an extension of their emotions the way I look at it.

I think Philadelphia fans aren't afraid to voice their appreciation, lack of appreciation, anger, love, emotion. Whatever it is, Philadelphia fans are going to show it. There's nothing middle-edged about Philadelphians. They're straight ahead, tough, and like it or not, this is how we feel. And if we don't like you, we're going to tell you.

It meshed with our team perfectly. We were the same way. There was nothing polite about how we approached what we did, nor were we apologetic for the way we did it. Philadelphia sports fans are the same way, so it was a perfect match.

211

Steve Coates ("Coatesy")

Philadelphia Flyers Broadcaster: 1980–present

Although the franchise has been close many times, it has been well over 30 years since the Flyers skated around the ice with Lord Stanley's Cup. What does it say about the fans that they keep coming to the arena with such belief in their team?

Well, it says a lot, first of all, about the dedication of the Philadelphia Flyers fans. But, in saying that, you also have to have something to cheer for! And that's where we have to recognize the success of the organization as a whole since its inception as part of the National Hockey League in 1967.

For example, you mention the two Stanley Cups in your question. But a number that really stands out, which illustrates the success of the Flyers, is that only the Montreal Canadiens have a better winning percentage than the Philadelphia Flyers in regular season play. Also, there is only one team, again the Montreal Canadiens, who have been to more Stanley Cup finals since 1967. These facts and achievements are a tribute to Mr. Ed Snider, whose philosophy has been to put a quality product on the ice, at all times, and have a chance to win every year.

So, the combination of the Flyers hockey club as one of the elite franchises of the NHL and the commitment and dedication of the Flyers fans, make for a perfect marriage.

Where do Flyers fans rank among NHL fans in terms of: a) knowledge of the game? b) sheer passion?

The passion of the Flyers fans is what drives the bus. In other words, that passion leads the fans to continually educate themselves both in the game of hockey as well as about their team. In saying that, their knowledge of the game is synonymous with their passion, which tells you why Philadelphia has become such a great hockey town!

It's pretty easy to get fired up in the atmosphere at the Wells Fargo Center. Do you think a strong home ice advantage can actually alter the outcome of a game?

Absolutely! You spend the whole season attempting to finish as high as possible in the standings to achieve a better opportunity for success in the playoffs. One of those opportunities is home ice advantage, which allows you to begin the series at home as well as having the opportunity to have the seventh game at home in your own building! I have always felt that the fans are the seventh person on the ice. And don't think for a second that the players don't recognize having that feeling of support in their own building, the Wells Fargo Center.

I have to add something to this, to be very honest. The game has changed over the last thirty years, where intimidation used to be a big part of having home ice. The Broad Street Bullies wrote the book on intimidation, and it was actually nicknamed "The Philly Flu," as some visiting players would discover a way to not play in the Spectrum.

Also, the game has changed because of the players being bigger, stronger and faster, which has made for a very entertaining brand of hockey. A form of intimidation is still there, despite less fighting, and physical play is a large part of the equation. Combined with the fans being as rabid as ever, this leads to the conclusion that home ice in the Wells Fargo Center is huge!

Jim Jackson

Flyers/Phillies Play-by-Play Announcer

Over the course of a season, you're in every city that has hockey or Major League Baseball. What is different about the Philadelphia fans?

The one thing that I notice more than anything is how in tune they are with the game. In hockey, you can hear the boo or the cheer before the call is made, where in other places you don't. And in Philadelphia, there's an emotion behind the passion that you don't hear in many other towns. In some places, such as Boston, New York, and Chicago to some degree, you hear that passion.

In baseball, Phillies fans live and die with every game, 162 times a year. I do feed off of it when things are going well. I'd rather have it that way, there's no apathy in Philadelphia. I think it helps keep players intense. There are some athletes who aren't made for Philadelphia because they don't like that pressure. It's like John Kruk said, if you can't play here, you don't rise to the occasion.

Let's elaborate on the point about the boo or cheer before the call is made. You're saying that's an example of how well fans in Philly know the sports?

They learned the game from (late Flyers announcer) Gene Hart back in the 70s. They've taught their kids and we've gone through another generation, so now the crowd, they know what's going on, they watch every play. I've had many people tell me, when you're winning here, there's not any better.

After many years as a Flyers announcer, you joined the Phillies broadcast team as well. How do the fans of the two teams compare?

It's tough to compare, being that baseball is the long season, the marathon, whereas hockey is such an intense game. It can get physical, nasty out there. But in both venues, they (the fans) are intense. They're there to cheer when they feel they're getting supreme effort from their guys, and remind the players when they perceive they're not getting 100 percent effort. That cuts right across all the sports lines. Philadelphia sports fans anticipate—demand—top effort from their teams. If you don't, you're going to hear about it.

Lou Nolan

Voice of the Flyers (Wells Fargo Center)

What's the craziest example of fan behavior you have witnessed in all your years as the Flyers PA Announcer?

There is one incident that stands out for the craziest example of fan behavior at a Flyers Game. It was actually initiated by Toronto bad boy Tie Domi when he sprayed fans behind the penalty box with water during a game on March 29th, 2001.

One fan, Chris Falcone, leaned on the plexiglass from the second row and it snapped. He fell into the penalty box and Domi immediately pulled his jacket over his head, just as he would do with a jersey, and got in a few licks before linesman Kevin Collins broke it up.

Far and away number one.

What was the toughest announcement you've ever had to make behind the microphone during a Flyers game?

My most difficult announcements encompassed an entire Flyers game. On Thursday, November 14th, 1985, there was a memorial service at center ice conducted by

Gene Hart, to remember Flyers goaltender Pelle Lindbergh, who had been killed in a horrific automobile crash. Although I didn't conduct the memorial, the announcements that night (despite a Flyers win against the Edmonton Oilers), were my most difficult.

Next (in order of difficulty) have always been moments of silence for police, firefighters, and military personnel, along with honoring our true heroes.

But most of all, that night in November will never be forgotten.

Describe the Flyers fans' role in keeping George Bush's speech on the Jumbotron after 9/11 in during the preseason game vs. the Rangers:

Plans were for the President's speech to be broadcast at intermission and then switch to the TVs in the concourse for its conclusion. It didn't work out that way.

During the second intermission of the game, George W. Bush's speech began. When the teams came out for the final period, I announced that the speech would

215

be shifted to the concourse, and the fans voiced their displeasure with very loud boos and *"U-S-A"* chants. Prior to the third period puck drop, a decision was made to switch back to the ArenaVision Jumbotron. The players went to their benches or just sat on the ice. It went on for some time.

When it concluded, another decision was made to suspend play and call the game a tie. That's when something special happened. I made the announcement, and the teams met at center ice and shook hands as is done at the conclusion of a Stanley Cup series. I would think it may be the only time that has happened. It was extraordinary.

After winning the previous two Stanley Cups in 1974 and 1975, the Flyers were swept by the Canadiens in the 1976 Stanley Cup. The fourth and final game was at the Spectrum. In an act of appreciation, the Flyers' fans stood up and cheered as time was expiring. In 2010 however, the fans' reaction after Patrick Kane's Stanley Cup-winning goal was not so positive. Where do you think the fan's negative reaction was directed and do you think it was justified?

The fans' reaction to the Flyers being swept by Montreal after two consecutive Stanley Cups and being beaten by an overtime goal by Chicago in 2010 is different for a couple of reasons in my estimation.

The reactions can be attributed directly to the difference in the fan base and how each arrived at that point in time. For instance, a final game shootout victory to just get in the playoffs in 2010.

Fans in the Spectrum were, for the most part, a true family. They had been attending games, learning the sport, and knew that they would see the people in their section and row every game night. The fans had been rewarded twice in the previous years with championships. When they came to Game 4, rather than reacting poorly with booing, I believe they really wanted to say *thanks* to the Flyers for all they had given them.

On the other side of things, fans in the 2010 Stanley Cup Finals at the (then called) Wachovia Center had not had a championship in decades. They probably did not feel the family closeness to others in their sections and row (normal season ticket turnover, and as most of us felt, there was a real chance to win).

When games for the Cup go into overtime, there is always a finality to them. They are not like a 4-1 or 3-2 game with a great last period or last minute. They just stop. Add to that the uncertainty of the goal and the way most fans viewed it—with Patrick Kane whooping and hollering the length of the ice to celebrate, and the enemy being presented with the Cup on our ice—the fans were wanting to show Chicago how they felt.

Perhaps the fact that I have been through two Cups, and that announcers hope to be professional, I was very disappointed but not able to verbalize that to the fans.

Tim Saunders

Flyers Radio Play-by-Play Announcer: 1997–present

You've been broadcasting Flyers games for 15 years. How has the reality compared to your expectations when you came here?

It took me a little while to get used to it here. Everyone had warned me that it was a negative fan base. I do think they're hard on their teams if their teams don't give effort all the time, but I don't see anything wrong with demanding that.

How knowledgeable are Flyers fans?

It's funny that when we go around the league and in our league there clearly are cities that are hockey cities as well as those that are not traditional hockey markets. And you can tell just by the feel in the building how in tune the fan base is to the game. In Philadelphia, they know what's happening as it's happening. If you go into some non-traditional hockey markets, your call might have to reflect a certain amount of explaining, but that sure as heck isn't here.

Larry Andersen (L.A.)

Phillies Pitcher: 1983-1986; 1993-1994; Radio Color Analyst: 1998-present

You've gone on record that you have educated some of today's Phillies players about how to handle the Philadelphia fans, what to expect from them and what to do to win them over. What is some of the advice you've given them?

When you first get here, the best thing you can do is play hard. That's the bottom line. I look back at 1993, and we had a bunch of characters which I think the fans took to, but I think, as much as anything, they took to the way we played the game. We played hard. We partied off the field, but once we crossed the line, we played the game right, and I think Phillies fans recognized that. Freddy Garcia hits a ball and runs into the dugout a few years back and they crushed him. They booed the heck out of him. If they see guys not hustling, they will let you know, and they should. They absolutely should.

Speaking of 1993, you were a player on that squad, which was arguably the most beloved Philadelphia sports team of all-time. Besides the fact that the team almost won the World Series, why else do you think the fans in Philadelphia related to you guys so well?

The personalities. I believe just about anybody in the Tri-State area could relate to one person or another on that team, which isn't a good thing necessarily (laughs), but everybody could relate to somebody. I think the personality of that team was huge in the city. We were blue collar type players I guess, if you will.

Have you noticed any difference in Phillies fans between your playing and broadcasting days? Has your relationship with the fans remained the same?

I think they're the same, but there are just more of them now. There's obviously a nicer ballpark. You look at the sellout streak of late. I think any city responds to a team that's winning, but it's also guys playing hard and playing the game right. People here are educated fans. They follow the game. They follow each play. Guys have been here a week, walk down the street and people know who they are.

It's part of their life here. You're gonna get booed here when you don't play well, and I expected it. When fans boo a player here, they shouldn't take it personally, they just don't like what they're seeing. They're not happy with it, but I think it's part of it.

As far as my relationship with the fans now, well....I don't get booed as much! (laughs).

In 1985, your Phillies teammate Mike Schmidt said some unflattering words about the Philadelphia fans to the press that made its way back to Philly. Anticipating the reaction the crowd was about to display upon returning home to Philadelphia, he came out on the field wearing a wig, and the crowd gave him a standing ovation. Some people might not know this, but that was your wig. How did that come about? Did he ask you to borrow it? Was it your suggestion?

That was my idea. He made some comments, but it was early in the season. And they waited until the Phils were in a downfall trend at that time, and then they brought the article out. We were on the road, and I think they put it out the day before we got home from Montreal. And he was like *'I'm just gonna get killed.'* He knew it.

My biggest thing with Schmitty was that he never allowed himself to be vulnerable, and the fans here wanna see vulnerability. They don't want the superstar untouchable player. They want down-to-earth players who can screw up and accept it. They wanna see that human element in a player here. They just don't wanna see the player, they wanna see the person, and it was tough to see Schmitty because he was introverted, and he had a hard time enjoying what he was doing.

In fact, when Harry (Kalas) and I were working a game in Florida and Schmitty came over to the game and we had him up in the booth, Harry asked him what was the one thing he regretted more than anything else, and he said *'I wish I would have had more fun.'* Here's a guy at the top of his game, the highest paid player at the time, arguably the greatest third baseman and player in Phillies history, and he couldn't let himself go. He always put so much pressure on himself. So the wig was just one of those things where it was like *'Go out there. Let them see that you're normal,'* and when he did it, he went out there and got a standing ovation. That probably pointed out more to me than anything about being a person first in this city. Play the game right, but be a stand up person, be a human person, be vulnerable. Allow yourself to make mistakes and admit it, and I think that's huge. From that point on, I really think it made a big difference with him and the fans. He was relieved more than anything, and I knew he appreciated it, and it helped him immensely with the fans. Look at Mitch (Williams). People wanted to blame Mitch for everything in the (1993) World Series. Mitch stood up and said *'I screwed up.'* It was at that point to me where the fans said *'He's ok.'* He didn't lose the game. Everybody helped lose the game. You can go back and look at all kinds of things.

Because of what I do and because I live here, I think a lot of it just sounds like BS, but I honestly, deep-within mean it when I say I think it's the greatest place to play sports in the country. I know New York is great, but there's eight billion people there. I'd say Boston, Philly and Chicago, with Boston and Philly being very, very similar. I played in Boston, and fans might be worse in Boston than they are here. We got in the playoffs in 1990, I came into a game for Roger Clemens, and I went 2-0 on (Mark) McGwire. I gave up three runs that whole month, went 2-0 on McGwire, and you would have thought I did what Mitch did! They said you don't hear it when you're out there...the hell you don't! I'm deaf in one ear and I still heard it! I don't think they would do that in Philly, I really don't. They're both two great sports cities with tremendous fans, but I can't imagine a better place to play than Philly.

Scott Franzke

Phillies Play-by-Play Radio Broadcaster: 2006-present

Questions by Matt Babiarz

As a former Texas Rangers announcer, what differences exist between Rangers fans and Phillies fans? Are there any similarities between the fans from those vastly different locations?

When I was there, it was more of a thing to do until football season started. But since I've been gone, they've obviously gotten a lot better, so I think their fans are a little more into it. In Philadelphia, they're more serious about wanting to win. Each year that I've been here, the expectations get a little bit higher, and that adds to it in a couple of ways. Not only are the expectations higher, but the frustration level gets higher when things are not as good. When things aren't going well, I think the fans get a little more riled up than they might in some other places. For me, it's been really cool to be in a place that it matters. As an announcer, especially coming from my situation, you're just trying to get a job as a full-time announcer somewhere. That might be in Texas, Houston, Kansas City, Boston, or New York, but you're gonna take it and go there. For me to come here and see how much it mattered to people was a very cool thing, right from the beginning.

As far as similarities go, I think all fans are at an event to enjoy the game. Philly fans might have sort of a reputation, but they still appreciate a good play, whether it's for us or the other team. I feel confident that I can talk a certain way about an opposing play and not be frowned upon. It's not like you're in that guy's corner over your guy's corner, it's just that you appreciate a good play. If they truly love the game, I think you can appreciate that kind of thing almost everywhere.

Which team's fans would you describe as being the least "Philly-like"?

That's a tough one. The thing that stands out about Phillies fans is that they travel. They go to every ballpark we go to. We don't see that with other clubs. I don't think anybody is quite like that. Boston has had fans that are passionate and travel here, the Mets used to have it, the Yankees have fans everywhere, but I've never seen a group as passionate as Phillies fans about seeing their team home and away and turning out all across the country.

When you visit other cities and interact with other team's announcers or players, is the Philly fan ever a topic of discussion? Do you think people from outside the Delaware Valley "get" the Philly fan, or do you find yourself trying to explain the phenomenon?

There are certain stereotypes that get played up, but I think that's a little bit of pandering going on there with the audience. It's a pretty easy thing to do the whole "Boo Santa Claus" thing. That's a pretty easy shot. I think some announcers might fall back into that. I guess it's really not too much of a difference to talk about the fans in LA, and we talk about the fact that fans don't show up before the third (inning) and they don't stay past the seventh. That still kind of holds true. We're not booing Santa Claus every day, but their fans are still showing up in the third. But there is a certain perception out there about Philly fans that they're rough, but we've gone to a lot of places, and you talk to other people who watch games in the stands, and they'll say how other fans are vocal and not welcoming. Everywhere we go there's the same thing going on in other parks. My wife can certainly attest to that from seeing games and being in certain parks, and some are worse than others. LA has had some very public problems with their security over the last few years. I think a lot of the fans that were out there for the NLCS in 2008 and 2009 saw some stuff that they would say rivals the more ugly side of being a fan.

Gary ("Sarge") Matthews

Phillies Outfielder: 1981-1983, 1983 NLCS MVP; Phillies Television and Radio Color Analyst: 2007-present

You had pretty big shoes to fill taking the place of Greg Luzinski in 1981 right after the Phillies won their first World Series the previous year. Can you recall one particular moment during your playing days in Philly when you realized you won the fans over?

The same as it would be with anyone...you get booed. You have to realize, they had seen Greg out there for a long, long time. So unless you were a player who came in and was hot right away, it wasn't gonna work. But the fact is, they gravitate to your game, and my game was different from Greg's. He was a power hitter and hit a lot of home runs. My game was more all-around if you will. But the fact is, they couldn't have won it without Greg playing here. He was a good player.

There wasn't one particular moment when I won the fans over, but I do know there was a respect factor. I played here from 1981 to 1983, and hit third in the lineup most of the time. Maybe after the NLCS in 1983 because the Phillies had never beaten the Los Angeles Dodgers in the playoffs. As a matter of fact, the Dodgers had knocked them out twice before from being in the World Series. In that particular year of '83, they beat us 11 out of 12 times, but we ended up having the last laugh because we beat them to get into the World Series.

You're a native Californian and broke into the major leagues with the San Francisco Giants. How would you describe the passion of the fans on the west coast compared to fans in an east coast city like Philadelphia?

You can't compare them. Let's face it: there's so much to do on the west coast with the weather, boating. If their team's playing bad, why go spend $300 or $400 bucks there when you can get a bottle of wine in wine country? Here in Philly, they're more into their sports as opposed to people on the west coast.

You've spent a lot of time in the Cubs organization as a player/ coach and with the Phillies as a player/broadcaster. Do find any similarities between the two fan bases?

No, because with the Cubs, they've never won or tasted any joy of success. In Philly, they're a little bit spoiled because they have tasted it, and they relish it and become a part of it everywhere they go. With

the Cubs, they have a saying *"Wait Till Next Year."* That's why they always call it the friendly confines. You can have a hot dog and a beer, and they'd say *'Look at the Cubs, or listen to them lose.'* Loyalty wise, they might be the same. Cubs fans might actually be more loyal, because they want to still be there the day they do win, instead of saying *'Hey, I'm not a Cubs fans now,'* they're saying *'I hope they win in my time.'* I have a friend who's in his seventies now, and his father told him on his deathbed to *'Stop being a Cubs fan. They will never win in your lifetime,'* and he ended up dying.

You joined the Phillies near the end of their glory era in 1981 and played here through 1983. You rejoined the team as a broadcaster right at the beginning of the team's other greatest era in 2007. Have you noticed a change in the fan base as opposed to when you were playing?

No, they're just as ornery as ever, but they're very respectful because it is a blue collar city and they respect you for your effort. But most of the fans are pretty hard all over: New York fans, Boston fans, Yankees fans. It's just on the west coast where they're a little more subdued.

It's really the same in broadcasting. They didn't particularly care for me right away because they had to get used to a new voice. They were used to Harry's voice, they were used to good ol' Larry's (Andersen's) voice, but it takes time for the fans to get used to people. My buddies over at Nick's Roast Beef told me *'Hey Gary, we didn't know if you were gonna make it with us after that first year. Now, it's like you're part of us now.'* It's because they're fans, they're passionate, and they want to understand. Some of the radio guys that were actually ripping me said they were only doing it because some of the other people were doing it, and after they listened to what I was saying, they apologized.

Anybody broadcasting here can't tell you what it's like to face pitches that are 100 or 102 (mph) They can't tell you what it's like to be out there with 50,000 people and drop a fly ball or ground ball. It's a different kind of feeling you have as opposed to describing it. I've lived that. I've lived being at the stadium, taking over for a favorite player, going through the boos. But in my particular instance, it made me a stronger person, as opposed to wanting to jump ship. That's why I can go down into the clubhouse and say *'Man, J Roll, what the hell were you trying to do to that ball?'* or *'What were you thinking on that?'* If Wheels were to do that, they would turn around and say *'Excuse me?'* With me, they have to come up with the right answer. I'm not intimidated. I can go up to someone and say, *'Hey man, I'm Gary Matthews,'* and they'll say *'Hey, didn't you just get through playing?'* and I'll say *'No, no, no. That was my son. I'm the one who can hit!'* (laughs).

Tom McCarthy

Phillies Television Play-by-Play Broadcaster: 2001-2005; 2008-present

Replacing Harry Kalas had to be one of the most difficult jobs in Philly sports history. Did you receive much constructive (or otherwise) criticism from the Philly fans? Can you also describe the support you received during that first season?

I probably received criticism only because of the difference in styles. For so many years, Harry was a minimalist, and made the big call better than anybody even to this day. I don't think anybody can make a big call sound as good as he did. But I think a lot of that (criticism) was folks just getting used to a different sound. Now I was here for five years working radio with Harry, went to the Mets for two years and then came back. When I came back, he was one of the first people to call and was very pleased that I was coming back to do television, and when he retired, I would take over for him. Scott (Franzke) and I are very different than Harry was. We chat, which is different. But no matter where I went, whether it was Rutgers, Princeton football or basketball or the Mets, there were always fans who would give criticism because they weren't used to your sound, but it wasn't anything I've never heard before. The positives certainly outweighed the negatives.

You have been a broadcaster for both the Phillies and Mets. What are the differences and similarities between Phillies fans and Mets fans?

Honestly, I think they're very similar. There are more similarities than there are differences. I think the biggest difference is, if you're rooting for the Mets, you're rooting against anybody who plays the Mets, like the Phillies or the Braves, and you're also rooting against the Yankees, so you have a double passion there. With the Phillies, you don't have the A's anymore. I think the Phillies are more passionate about their seasons, whereas I think sometimes Mets fans and New York fans as a whole can easily look to the Jets and Giants and Knicks, Rangers or Devils. They have so many other teams that they can focus on if the season is not going well. For Phillies fans, they're thinking about the Eagles, and they're probably thinking about the Flyers and somewhat about the Sixers, but they're still focused on the Phillies and what's happening, particularly in this day and age, and I think that might be a little different too. But I think New York and Philadelphia fans are very similar in their passion and love for their specific teams.

Is there a moment from your career when a Philadelphia fan (or fans) did something that meant a lot to you personally?

The (Phillies 2008 World Series) parade. I mean that was something that, I don't know even if we win another championship again, if we'll ever see it. It was mind blowing how amazing that was. It was like nothing I ever could have imagined. Everywhere you went, there was just red. It was a sea of people in a sea of red. To me, that was one of the proudest moments where, if I was a fan of the Phillies, and obviously we were, I would be overwhelmed with pride for how the city reacted to that world championship. If I were a player, that would drive me to win another championship just to see that again, because it was remarkable. It really was. Just going around the corners onto Broad (Street), it was

crazy. It was like nothing any of us had ever seen before. Wheels and Harry probably saw it with 1980, but I can't imagine '80 being as overwhelming as this was.

There is unjust criticism of the Philly fan, and I do think it's unjust. If you go to any city, you're gonna have specific things happen that you're going to look at and say *'Oh that city's scarred.'* Do you think that Los Angeles doesn't have this? Do you think San Francisco has had specific occurrences where fans maybe go overboard? They all do. I think there are people in every society and every city that do stupid things. It's just the way it is. It's not specific to Philadelphia, it's not specific to New York, it's not specific to Dallas, Texas, it happens. Just think about the cars being overturned when a specific hockey team doesn't win the Stanley Cup in Canada. I think there's so much more to be proud of being a Philly fan than there is negative.

Special thanks to Matt Babiarz

Gregg Murphy

Phillies Field Reporter/Comcast SportsNet Anchor

A big part of your job is reporting from the stands during Phillies home games. Can you cite any specific examples of things you have seen or heard that represent the toughness, fairness, and/or energy and loyalty of the Philadelphia fans?

Honestly, I see a little bit of that every night. When you're walking around the stadium like I do, you talk to dozens and dozens of people, and the conversations are always intelligent because Philly sports fans understand the game probably better than any other city. I really believe that. We're not talking about *'Hey, I think this guys gonna hit a home run.'* It's more along the lines of *'With a 3-1 count, why is he running on that pitch?'* It never ceases to amaze me. Whether it's a man, a woman, teenager or whomever that comes up to me, they're passionate about the game and they're knowledgeable about it. It's a blast for me. I can't tell you how many times a current or former Phillies player comments that the Philadelphia fans are so knowledgeable and passionate. If you play here as an opponent, you can't help but be impressed by how the fans are. I don't think it's a knock when someone says that Phillies fans are rampant or passionate. I think it's a compliment from the people who are playing the game.

Being stationed among the fans during games, to what degree have you seen the much-publicized "negative" side of the Philadelphia fans? How common is the "bad" Philly fan among the crowds you interact with?

My feeling is that there are knuckleheads everywhere, and there are knuckleheads in Philadelphia. There's no doubt about that. People that, for whatever reason, decide they want to insert themselves into the storyline: whether it's getting into a fight in the stands, or verbally abusing someone wearing a different jersey. That kind of stuff happens. Anyone who says it doesn't would be kidding themselves. I've always said that it doesn't just happen in Philadelphia, it happens everywhere. For whatever reason, some sports fans think they need to act that way, whether it's for credibility or toughness, or whatever.

I've seen fans go over the top in Philadelphia, but I've also seen it in Milwaukee, Minnesota, San Francisco, Chicago, you name it. So the reputation of Philly sports fans being an arrogant and out of control bunch, is false. It's absolutely incorrect. For the most part, they're just great sports fans that are enjoying themselves.

During the Phillies road trip to Milwaukee in 2012, I had an usher say to me *'I heard everybody in Philadelphia is awful, but everybody I'm meeting is terrific.'* I probably heard that three times that year when we've been in opposing ballparks and Phillies fans are there because they travel so well. I've had opposing ushers and security guards in ballparks come up to me and tell me just how great the Philadelphia fans are. As a Philadelphian, I beam with pride because I'm taking it upon myself to educate the rest of the sports world that Philadelphia fans are fantastic. They're not this group of arrogant loudmouths that prefer violence. It really angers me when the national media, or some beat writer in San Diego or St. Louis goes on television or writes some of the things they do about Philadelphia. It's the laziest form of journalism, and they're only perpetuating those myths about Santa Claus and all that other nonsense. Most of them have never even set foot in Philadelphia or seen a game here. I would challenge any of them to come from another city, wear the jersey of an opposing team and sit at a game to see if they get treated that way. I'll guarantee you they won't. It drives me absolutely crazy.

Special thanks to Matt Babiarz

Chris Wheeler (Wheels)

Phillies Broadcaster: 1977-present

Questions by Matt Babiarz

You've been a Phillies announcer since 1977. In what ways have Phillies fans changed over that period of time?

I think they stayed the same because they still have the same passion. They want to win. It's a part of our identity. It's in our DNA here passed from generation to generation. It's important. It's not entertainment. We also got really good again, it's Citizens Bank Park. It's like a big party here when you look out on Ashburn Alley and see all the young faces. It's fun! It wasn't an *"in"* thing to go to Phillies games back then. It's date night when you come here now. It's a nice place to meet your friends. The tailgating has become a football type of tailgating here. I think the ballpark atmosphere and the combination of the team winning just changed everything. People don't come here pissed off anymore like they did at the Vet. A lot of nights they came in to see whose butt they could get on that night. I don't think they come in Citizens Bank Park that way, pick out one or two or three guys and

say *'they stink,'* and *'we're gonna run them out of town.'* I don't get that anymore, and I think we used to get that. And I say that lovingly. It's just the way they were, and they weren't very good. There were plenty of guys to pick on. They did a great job with the new park, and they put a good team together at the right time.

In your time with the Phillies, which players do you think were given the most latitude by the notoriously tough Philly fans? Conversely, which players did you feel could not even catch a break from the fans?

Well for starters, they've never liked the pretty boys, they like the "dirtball" look. They liked John Kruk, but they didn't like Von Hayes. Put aside the whole "Five-for-one" trade—he was this big, tall good looking guy. They don't like the cool guys. Cole Hamels has gone through that here. I would hear it all the time. Fans thought he was soft because he was this southern Californian guy, and I would say *'you're so wrong. He's a tough competitive guy, but he just doesn't look the part.'* But guys who looked the part like Schmitty (Mike Schmidt) came off as "too cool" and "aloof." They loved Tug (McGraw) because he had all that emotion, as well as Jay Johnstone. Bake McBride could play him up a tree, but the fans used to tell me Johnstone was a better player than he was. Gimme a break. It wasn't even close. If you come in, and you're really good looking and cool, the fans are really gonna test you.

Pat Burrell was one of those guys who they made earn it. He was a good looking guy, he had all this hype, was the number one pick, but they don't care. They were gonna make him show them, in my opinion, they tried to crack him, and he didn't crack, so they liked him at the end. He could have said *'Ah, they stink. I don't wanna play here.'* But he always said *'I wanna play here. I don't ever wanna leave here. I love Philadelphia.'* The more they booed him, the more he said he wanted to stay, as opposed to some guys I've been around over the years where the more they booed him, the more they wanted to get the heck out of here. He hit .209 in 2003, but they couldn't crack him. There was something about Burrell to where they tried and tried and tried and booed and booed and booed,

and he would just get in there and strike out again, but he would never speak out against the fans or Philadelphia saying *'they're too tough,'* or *'they're too tough on us.'* When you look back, he never, ever said that publicly, so after a while they begrudgingly respected him. And even though they kind of booed him, they would put up with him.

When I was a little kid, I will never forget the way they used to boo Del Ennis, and he was from here! I guess because he was the big slugger and all that, not because he was a big, good-looking guy or anything. I just think it's part of playing.

I've always said that you start in New England, you end south of Wilmington, and it's a different market. You start in New England, down to New York and Philadelphia, and it's not a game. People wake up, and their identities sometimes are connected to what their team just did. They have a good or bad day because of what happened the day or night before. That doesn't happen with the Dodgers, Giants, Cardinals, or Cubs. I've been there hundreds of times, and it doesn't happen. The Phillies were out in Los Angeles in 1983 when the Sixers beat the Lakers four straight in the finals. Those people got up and went to the beach the next day. It was no big deal. *'Oh, congratulations. Nice going.'* Out here, it's *'This guy stinks. It's his fault. The coach stinks!'*

That's one thing I've always noticed. I've tried to explain it to guys when they used to come here, and they don't understand. When the Phillies were struggling In 1993, the players would ask me *'Why are they bringing up the 1964 Phillies?'* I said *'You don't understand what it was like here in 1964. I do.'* I lived through the whole thing. It's scars that never leave with something like that.

Was there ever a time when you felt Phillies fans were portrayed especially unfairly by either the national media or the media from another city?

Yeah. The snowballs at Santa Claus thing....back then nobody even knew what happened. So they keep bringing that up all the time. Was it good that the fans threw batteries at J.D. Drew? No. It becomes urban legend now, though. I think it's hard to get rid of a stigma now that it's built up over time. Have they earned some of it? Yeah. Visiting players who come in will tell you they're tough. The home players will tell you at times they're really demanding, tough, foul-mouthed, and all those things. Are they the worst? No! I just think there's a lot of passion here and people really care. As soon as an incident happens, then it sounds like were the only place where this crap happens. But how do you get rid of it? It's not going away.

233

Matt Cord

Sixers PA Announcer; Senior Correspondent for Sixers.com; On-Air Personality, 93.3 WMMR

Were you primarily a Sixers fan growing up? And if so, does this contribute to the passion you show towards the team?

I've always been a passionate sports fan of all four Philly sports teams, but I was a huge Dr. J fan. I remember his speech at JFK Stadium at the parade in '83. I went to his last home game in 1987 and still have the *'Dr. J's Last House Call'* t-shirt from that game at the Spectrum. The fact that I get to interview him and other superstars now is just mind- boggling. It's pretty intense.

One of the reasons fans identify with you through your work as the PA announcer for the Sixers is how you get the crowd going whenever a Sixers player scores ("Iguodala, 'dala, 'dala... "). However, when the other team scores, your tone is borderline somber/sarcastic, which really reflects the emotions of the crowd. Is this something instinctual or did this develop over time?

I used to do the Philadelphia Wings games from 1993 to 2000,

which overlapped the Sixers games. When I first started working the Wings games and a team like Buffalo scored, I would announce (in a lower and non-enthusiastic tone) *'Buffalo goal.'* So at one of my first Sixers games which I think was against Toronto, Vince Carter scored, and I did the same thing as I did when I was with the Wings: *'Vince Carter,'* in the same tone. The guy next to me goes *'Buffalo goal,'* and it was like the Wings all over again and it just stuck.

I was told in my second year around 1999 that I couldn't do that anymore. The league told me I had to be louder, so I told (former Sixers owner) Pat Croce, and he told me not to worry about it and he would pay the fine if it came to that. I never heard anything else after that.

Do you feel your presence on the airwaves as a local disc jockey helped with your connection to the Philadelphia fan?

Without a doubt. Our listeners are the Philadelphia fans. You go to a local concert, it's like going to an Eagles or Flyers game. It's a very similar fan base. They're passionate about sports and music.

(Perhaps) In the last decade, the Sixers' fan base has seemed to lag a little behind that of the other Philly pro sports teams. Can this become a great pro hoops town again?

No question. Just look at Allen Iverson in 2001. I think it's never been done before, but I think the Sixers were on 35 or 40 straight covers of the Daily News during that playoff run. That never happened with the Phillies or the Eagles. This is a basketball town and we have a lot to choose from, especially when you have six Division I college basketball teams. This town can definitely get back to that again. When a pro team kicks it into high gear like the Sixers did in 2001, this town went crazy.

We introduced both Dr. J and Allen Iverson during the 2012 NBA Playoffs. It's almost blasphemy to say this, but the ovation Iverson received was way louder than Dr. J's. The days of Doc were before hip hop, and A.I. really crossed over to that hip hop market, which was huge. For a large part of the 80s, I don't think this town was that passionate. It was getting there, but it's not like it is now. The Flyers would sell out, but the Phillies were empty. It has a lot to do with the product, too. The Eagles got better and the Phillies got much better. We even have two full-time sports radio stations now.

Tom McGinnis

Sixers Radio Play-by-Play Announcer: 1995-present

The Sixers are a team that has had more downs than ups during your broadcasting tenure with the team. However, much like the Philly fans, you are so passionate about the game. Do you think that's one of the reasons why you fit in so well here?

Your point about fitting in may have some validity based on a shared passion for basketball and Philadelphia sports in general. Our fans want effort and performance. We all have developed a pretty good sense of when that's on full display. I hope I fit in, because I love my job and our whole area.

Describe the role of the Philly fans during that magical 2000-2001 Sixers season:

In the spring of 2001, the NBA Playoffs at the (First Union) Center were a big part of the team's success. The atmosphere was electric, I mean a buzz was percolating well before tip-off. You could feel the vibe. I'm sure it helped our guys, especially at the defensive end.

In the past, you have the ability to get the fans excited on a dunk by Andre Iguodala in a preseason game. Can you imagine how they would react to your call if the Sixers ever became NBA Champions again?

For Sixers fans and for our city, the night the season ends with one of the 76ers players holding the trophy will be the culmination of a long-awaited return to the top of the basketball world. Lord willing, my call of those final few seconds will be a proud stamp to signal the wait is over!

Marc Zumoff

76ers Television Play-by-Play Announcer: 1994-present

Questions by Earl Myers

Game 3 of the first round series against the Orlando Magic in 1999 was a special night for Sixers fans. What do you remember most about the impact they had on that game?

I will tell you that in all the games I've done in my career, that one was my favorite. Our crowd, without being physically nasty, was bloodthirsty. They really got a nice warm-up, because Orlando was a three seed, the Sixers were a six seed, and they split the first two games in Orlando. So there was this tremendous buildup, not to mention the fact this was the first Sixers playoff game in that building, and the first one in Philly in eight years. The players fed off the fans' energy from the very beginning. There was one scenario where the players were jousting in front of the Orlando bench to the point where Matt Geiger and Chuck Daly were going at each other. And the crazier it got on the court, the crazier the fans got—to the point where you couldn't even hear yourself think.

Then, Allen Iverson, who always fed off the fans with the cupped ear and everything else, goes out and sets an NBA record with 10 steals. He was literally covering the floor by himself. To see somebody do this with the energy and passion that he played with, he couldn't have done this in a vacuum or before a crowd that was indifferent or just merely happy, he would had to have done it in front of a crowd that was in a frenzy. That's how they were that night and he performed accordingly. The greater he played, the louder they got. The louder they got, the more inspired he was. It was an outrageous performance by both Iverson and the fans.

You've been the Sixers television play-by-play announcer since 1994 and have 29 years with the broadcast team overall. How does the basketball knowledge of Sixers fans compare to that of fans in other NBA cities?

The Philly fans are more knowledgeable. The roots of the game in Philadelphia run deeper when you consider a lot of the NBA cities quite frankly don't have the basketball history that Philadelphia does. And I'm not talking just about college, I'm talking professionally: teams like the SPHAs, who go back to the 20s and the 30s. We're an eastern city, and the game was invented not that far from here, the first college basketball games were played not that far from here, and the Philadelphia Warriors was an original NBA franchise.

Not to mention back in the 50s, when college basketball was not that big of a deal nationally, the Palestra was the mecca. So you had a fan base that knows the tradition of the game, and that knowledge has been passed down from generation to generation. In my experience, if I interact with the crowd or perceive how they're watching the game, you can just feel and hear that Philadelphia basketball fans really do have an intrinsic idea as to what's going on in a basketball game.

The Sixers have only had one perennial all-star in the last two decades, and the knock on the team at times over the last few years is that they have a bunch of nice players, but no true super-star. How do you think the arrival of a player of Andrew Bynum's caliber will add to the luster of the Sixers as well as ignite their fanbase? (At the time of the interview, there was great optimism about Bynum's arrival. Halfway through the 2012-13 NBA season, he has yet to suit up for the team)

In terms of selling tickets, Andrew Bynum's arrival gives you a single identifiable face. In many sports, but particularly in the NBA, the addition of one franchise-type player can really change things for a team on the floor. It's pretty obvious he has all the ingredients to be a very good player: 20 points, 10 rebounds, he blocks, he's a seven footer. He's something that is highly valued in today's NBA in that he's a low post, back to basket player. From an offensive standpoint, you want to be able to present the other team's defense with somebody who makes you think about a double team. When you do that, it clearly opens up a lot of possibilities on the offensive end. On and off the floor, you clearly can't underestimate the addition of a guy like Bynum.

I see more excitement for this Sixers team than at any point since Iverson left. And it's simply because the fact that they now have that identifiable face that puts a face on the franchise. From that perspective, the way they presented him at his news conference shows that, as an organization, the Sixers know the benefits of having a guy of that profile. They didn't just have your normal garden variety news conference at the arena. They rented a high profile facility, attracted several hundred fans in the middle of a work week, and created a lot of excitement. So right there, you can really see the value of adding a guy like that.

I think the nature of basketball is that you have to have a guy who is "the guy." I think in some aspect, it had previously taken some of the luster off the 76ers and the potential that's on the city in general. I certainly think it always helps the team, it helps pro basketball, and helps to enliven the fan base when you have a single identifiable figure they could point to and say *'Hey, let's go out and watch Wilt (Chamberlain) and the Sixers, let's go out and watch Dr. J and the Sixers, Charles Barkley and the Sixers, Allen Iverson and the Sixers.'*

Michael Barkann

Host: Comcast SportsNet; SportsRadio 94 WIP

You've spent time in Boston as well as Philadelphia during your sportscasting career. Can you explain the dynamics of those two fan bases?

Passion: both cities are the same. Sports knowledge: both cities are the same. Woe is me attitude: both cities are the same. Venom and nasty: Philadelphia has a clear edge.

If you were an athlete and had your choice of a team to play for based on the fans, would it be New York, Boston, or Philadelphia?

Philadelphia or Boston, with the edge going to Philadelphia. There are few superstar athletes who can live up to New York billing.

You cover all four of Philly's professional sports teams (and more) for both Comcast and WIP. Have you found any differences in expectations amongst fans of these teams?

Eagles fans have the highest expectations and standards (the Super Bowl). The Flyers fans are the most loyal.

Your own enthusiasm and passion never seems to wane, which must be a large ingredient in your success as a broadcaster in this city. How do you find that balance between being an ardent fan and being an objective journalist?

I think one can be both so long as one doesn't cheerlead. If the team plays poorly I say so. If the team plays well, I say so. There is an element of personal sensibility and if I feel a player crosses that line, I call him out on it. We all have our biases, but as long as they don't get in the way of objectivity (that is the goal, at least) then everything is ok.

It seems as though Philly fans are continually ripped—sometimes for decades—over particular incidents, while the national media seems to have a much more lenient standard for other cities. For example, Detroit isn't continually demonized for the Malice at the Palace incident and Chicago isn't eternally lambasted for their fans attacking an opponent's first base coach. Are we being too sensitive, or if not, why do you think there is a double standard that works against Philadelphia?

I think the double standard IS us. We can't object to that national perception, yet still perpetuate it at the same time. After all, there is a reason there was a jail at Veterans Stadium.

Ron Burke

Anchor/Reporter; Comcast SportsNet

Do you feel as though Philadelphia fans are fairly/unfairly judged?

Fairly/unfairly, I think is a misused term in this argument. I prefer "properly/improperly" judged as a measuring stick.

It may *seem* unfair because fans of other cities may appear to get passes, but understand the Philly rep is often worn as a badge of honor by local fans—until the national media get involved. I believe if it's earned, own it, so fairness is not involved in the equation, in my view.

I say the treatment Philadelphia fans receive from the national media is proper. What *is* improper, however, is the way the national media generally project the fans in other cities, and that is irrespective of what goes on in Philadelphia.

So, do I hear you saying that if the riots in Vancouver after the 2011 Stanley Cup Finals had happened here, the national coverage would've been different? Harsher?

Absolutely, because the reputation precedes the city, so the coverage would have taken into account the reputation. It's simply that Philadelphia would be treated as a repeat offender because of its history, and the media/society treat repeat offenders more harshly.

So when you say we should "own it," how do we do that?

Don't let the national media's words send you into a tailspin. They are only stating facts about the fans' history, so own it. Those episodes happened for a reason and they have crafted your image, for better or worse, so why not just own it? Don't run from it. But, one reason why fans take issue with how they are projected is because they have not won championships. Trophies do wonders for a fan base's psyche, and crushing losses take something away.

Ray Didinger

Comcast SportsNet; NFL Hall of Famer

Why does the national media seem to bring up the Santa Claus and Michael Irvin incidents whenever they get a chance to take a shot at Philly fans?

It is just lazy reporting. The national media has drawn this ugly portrait of the Philly fan and it seizes upon every opportunity to reinforce it. If there is any kind of misbehavior at a Philly sports event, they drag out the old rap sheet—Santa Claus, Michael Irvin, Judge Seamus—and say, *'Now we can add to the list...'* Unfortunately, the bad stuff did happen, we can't pretend that it didn't, but there has been bad behavior everywhere. The trouble is, Philly is the only place where the networks and pundits define it as somehow cultural. It is very unfortunate because the vast majority of Philly fans are good people, but they are painted with the same brush as the knuckleheads. I don't think it will ever change, sadly.

Sports has such a profound effect on the fans because they have such a vested interest in their teams. Before you embarked on your Hall of Fame career as a writer, you grew up rooting for the Eagles and Phillies. Is it true that the collapse of the 1964

Phillies had such a profound effect on you that you almost flunked out of college?

Pretty close. I enrolled at Temple in September, 1964, just as the Phillies were about to collapse. When they went into their losing streak, I was numb, physically and mentally. I couldn't concentrate in class because I was thinking about that night's game. Then I would watch the game and when it was over, I was too distraught to study. I couldn't sleep, I couldn't do much of anything. It was November before I snapped out of it and by then I was way, way behind. There also was the matter of adjusting to college level work and adjusting to having girls in class (I went to an all-boys Catholic high school) so it was like the perfect storm of distraction. My first semester grades were pretty ugly.

You have seen Eagles' fans adopt certain players—and not always those regarded as superstars—as their favorites over the years. Can you cite any examples, and why you think they had such great appeal to our fans?

I think Andre Waters was a good example. Not a superstar by any means, a player of average ability, but he was a tough, hard-nosed safety who played fearlessly for the Buddy Ryan teams. There were many better players on defense, such as Reggie White, Eric Allen and Seth Joyner, but the fans loved Waters because he was so aggressive and, yes, even a little dirty. He was seen as a blue-collar worker and there are a lot of Philly fans who fit that description as well.

You have admitted many times over the years that you can't be a "fan" as long as your broadcasting career continues. How hard is it for you to remove yourself from being a fan when you witness so many heartbreaking losses as well as thrilling wins for Philadelphia teams over the years?

It is not hard. I grew up as a fan of the Philly teams, a true diehard, but once I crossed the line and became a reporter that all changed. I had to cover the teams in the same objective fashion that city-side reporters cover City Hall. It is my job, it is my responsibility. I can't be a fan.

Howard Eskin

Broadcasting Legend; Talk Show Host: SportsRadio 94 WIP; FOX 29 (Philadelphia) Sports Anchor

Do you feel as though Philadelphia fans are the most maligned fans in the entire country?

If you want the simple answer, it's no. I don't think they're the most maligned, but we believe that because we're here, it's a personal thing, and fans are more sensitive when they hear themselves mentioned. They mention other cities. Cleveland threw beer bottles on the field one time, but we don't care about Cleveland. In New York, that's a joke up there, but they'll get criticized too. We only hear the negative about Philadelphia, but I don't think they're the most maligned. And honestly, sometimes they deserve to be criticized. Throwing batteries at J.D. Drew? That's enough already. They cheer when Michael Irvin could have been paralyzed lying on the football field. So they deserve to be maligned in those situations. When something happens, people are criticized, but we only hear it from one side here.

Do you feel that the fans have treated any of our athletes unfairly?

There's probably some but I can't remember any. I do think they fall in love with athletes too quickly. I was never a Bobby Abreu fan, because I didn't think he played for the team, I thought he played for himself. They fell in love until they realized that when he left, the Phillies became better. They didn't malign Allen Iverson, they weren't unfair to him and they didn't jump on him. They were overly positive, and this guy broke all the rules, was late for practices, was arrested, you could go right down the line, but they loved him. I think Philadelphia fans actually fall more in love with players.

Now, did they criticize Andre Iguodala unfairly? At times they did, and at times they've gone over the top. Can he shoot? No, not really well. Can he play good defense? Terrific defense. Is he a good player? Yes, but it wasn't his fault that he signed an $80-million dollar contract, but people criticized him because he signed an $80 million-dollar contract. If he signed for less than that, and was only the third best player on the team, he'd be terrific. So if I'd have to point to one recent player, it would be Iguodala.

What is your most memorable moment regarding Philadelphia fans?

When were they at their best? There's probably not one moment. They were really good in the 70s, when the Phillies were winning those division titles. They were terrific in '80, when they won the World Series. When the Sixers won the championship in the '82-83 season, and even when they lost the championship to the Lakers in the '00-01 season, they were good. When you give them a winner, they're really good. When the Eagles went to the Super Bowl in the 2004 season, they were unbelievable. There's just something about a football crowd with the noise and volume level at a game which is unmatched by any other sport.

Philadelphia's shortcomings in championship games and the playoffs are well-documented. Do you feel like the fans have a right to be so frustrated due to the endless disappointments?

Yes, they certainly have a right to be disappointed. The teams will always tell you that they have a chance, but a chance isn't good enough. Now sometimes, they do get a little crazy. Should the Eagles have won a Super Bowl? Yes, somewhere along the line, they should have won a Super Bowl, so I can understand their disappointment. Should the Phillies fans have been disappointed that the team didn't get to the playoffs for 14 years and didn't win a World Series between 1980 to 2008? Sure. The Flyers have created disappointment. There's certainly a lot of things to be disappointed about. That's why you're fans, because you want to see your team win a championship. And in Philadelphia, it's no longer acceptable to just be in the playoffs. It's unacceptable if you don't win a championship. Totally unacceptable.

In your own experience, are there more geniuses or dopes among the Philly fan base?

You want me to be honest? There's more dopes, and it's not even a question, but that's part of being a fan. You think you know everything, you think you've got all the answers, you think you've got it all figured out, and that's why they're fans. They don't have the connection, which is not their fault. They don't have the connections where they can talk to the people and understand more things. That's not to say that there's not a lot of geniuses, but if I had to take a poll, there would be more dopes. I don't know if it would be 60 percent of 70 percent of the fan base, but it's more than 50 percent, so that means there's more dopes than geniuses.

Marc Farzetta

SportsRadio 94 WIP; NBC TV (Football)

Your work with NBC often takes you to cities outside Philadelphia. Have you ever been surprised at just how far the negative stereotypes of Philly fans can reach?

I was out on the town once in San Diego and ended up making some friends. One of the guys was from Mexico, and asked where I was from; when I said Philadelphia, the first two things out of his mouth were *"Parking Wars"* and *'You guys booed Santa Claus.'*

On the other hand, the nice thing about travelling is you probably see Philly fans wherever you go, right?

I'm privy to a lot of things regarding the goals of the production (at NBC) and one of the things that always get pointed out is when we have a Steelers away game, or an Eagles away game, they show up in opponents' stadiums. The director and cameramen try to capture how much the Eagles and Steelers fans travel to watch their teams.

Mike Missanelli

Radio Host: 97.5 FM The Fanatic; Phillies Post-Game Television Analyst

You have always been one to go to bat for Philly sports fans in this town when someone in the national media takes a shot at them. You've had run-ins with Mike Golic and Colin Cowherd, as well as your now legendary tiff with Skip Bayless. You stumped Golic by pointing out Andy Reid's record against winning teams and Golic was completely unaware of the fact, as was Cowherd. Why do you think these guys never do their homework?

It's much easier for national journalists to rely on past perceptions of Philadelphia because that means they won't have to do any additional research. Perhaps it's not their fault. They have to know a lot about a lot, and maybe don't feel they have enough time. Nobody nationally can know more about someone else's local sports scene. Sports fans live their teams daily through every basketball bounced, puck dropped, ball pitched, and football thrown. In Philadelphia, perhaps the scrutiny is more intense. We watched EVERY snap Donovan McNabb took, so we would know his shortcoming

more than a national pundit's perception of how he played. We've viewed every one of Andy Reid's play calling and we know his success rate against the really good teams. My biggest problem with the national perception is that they think Philadelphia sports fans are stupid. I resent that, since we take our sports very seriously here.

In February 2002, the Philadelphia fans poured their collective boos upon Kobe Bryant in the NBA All-Star game. Afterward, you vehemently defended the Philadelphia fans, going toe to toe with ESPN's Michael Wilbon. It was very memorable as well as entertaining radio, and greatly appreciated by the Philadelphia fans. Whether it's justified or not, Philly fans have been historically dragged through the mud by the national media. What was it in particular about Wilbon's comments that set you off?

Michael Wilbon was the classic example of an arrogant national sports writer relying on old perceptions. Had Wilbon done ANY research, or talked to ANYONE from Philadelphia, he would have learned that Kobe Bryant went out of his way to disassociate himself from his home, the Philadelphia area, by making various critical comments over the years. No sports fan base would take kindly to that because all sports fans are prideful of their respective areas. So, when he was introduced at the All-Star game, this was a chance for the Philadelphia fan base to tell him—via boos—that we didn't appreciate his comments and that he probably should be thanking us for spawning him. He was coached here and played here to cultivate his craft. All it would have taken for Wilbon to learn that was an hour worth of study.

Do you feel like Philadelphia fans have a right to be demanding of their players?

I think that any fan base has a right to be demanding of their players. Sports is paid entertainment. Would we not have a right to demand that the opera be high quality if we are paying a nice price for a ticket to see that opera? In sports, not only do we pour in financial resources for our teams, we pay in emotional resources. So yes, we have a right to demand that the teams do right by us and work as hard as they can to deliver a successfully entertaining product.

Are Philadelphia fans the most passionate in the nation?

There is no question in my mind that Philadelphia fans are the most passionate in the nation. I worked in New York City for two years doing sports talk radio and NYC is bland compared to how fired up we get here. I'll leave that to a sociologist to figure out why.

Eytan Shander

Former Radio Host: SportsRadio 94 WIP/ 97.5 FM The Fanatic; Current Talk Show Host: NBC Sports Radio

As someone who gets to do talk shows with a national audience in addition to your previous experience talking to Philly fans on several stations during your time in the city, what major difference do you see?

I think the biggest difference is more numbers in Philadelphia are going to be willing to stand up stronger for their teams. In Philly, we are so focused on our four teams here, you don't have distractions from it. Not to say there's not history or passion in New York, but in Philadelphia, there's a sense with our sports that there's a small town mentality where all we have is our teams. We don't care about other things sports related as much. Other big cities like Dallas, Houston, Chicago, have other things on their priority list, whereas in Philly, Freddy Galvis is more of a concern than the NFL concussion lawsuit. If we were in Nashville or Columbus, Ohio or Memphis, or San Antonio, cities that don't have four (teams) across the board, we'd still be more ramped up about our own.

What's the view of Philly as a sports town from the national callers you talk to?

A lot of times I get people calling up and saying Philly isn't the worst place; the worst place is wherever they are.

Brian Startare

Sportsradio 94 WIP

How would you compare the Flyers' fan base to the other team's fan bases in Philadelphia?

The Flyers fan base is a very loyal fan base. Their season ticket numbers have been consistently high. I think every team in the city has a loyal following, but the Flyers never see a dip in attendance and are constantly putting forth a product to compete amongst the best in the NHL. Fans appreciate a commitment to strive for excellence. Now, if they could just win a Cup one of these days.

Now that you're in the broadcasting field, how do you balance your rooting interest in the teams you grew up supporting and being an objective professional?

Plain and simple, when I'm working, I feel as though I have no problem with objectivity. It's not difficult at all. Growing up, rooting for the teams that I now cover, in fact helps me stay more connected. I also enjoy our city and want all four to win, so when I'm off from work, I try to enjoy every minute of it.

10

PHILLY FANS ARE
DANGEROUS AND NEED TO BE TASED

The Phillies have emerged as one of the powers in Major League Baseball. They won the NL East from 2007-2012, the World Series in 2008 and made another appearance in the Fall Classic the following season. One would think that their fans would be thrilled to just enjoy their powerhouse of a team.

Oh no, this is Philly, where drunken hooligans run around the field waving towels, bringing action to a halt. In Philly, that also means that fans—and there are just a few civil ones...we think—got treated to the spectacle of this drunken bum getting tased by a cop who got tired of trying to chase him.

And, should anybody be surprised that those notoriously restrained Philadelphia cops used such excessive force.

Perhaps, it would have been more appropriate for the cop to have beaned him with a frozen snowball instead.

"How do you corral an obnoxious Phillies fan who suddenly decides to jog around the outfield in the eighth inning? Zap him like a bug."

-CORKY SIEMASZKO, NEW YORK DAILY NEWS 2010

RESPONSE: DENNIS BAKAY AND JOE VALLEE

DENNIS:

Philadelphia has become synonymous with booing, poor support of players, and at times even violence against players on opposing teams. You especially hear this from many national media types and bloggers in other markets.

Yes, I know we had the 700 Level at the Vet, where you couldn't even look at a Philly fan if you were wearing the team colors of the enemy. While chances are the worst that would happen was you paid a visit to Judge Seamus McCaffery, the same cannot be said for Dodger Stadium, where Phillies fans were threatened by Dodgers fans who happened to be gang members. Talk about showing your true colors.

Throughout this book, we have presented our case as to why Philadelphia is the collective whipping boy for the national media, who would have you believe the majority of the proud fans of this area go to the games simply to wreak havoc. They force this concept down the throats of listeners and viewers alike, and the end result is a skewed perception. However, that's not to say that a bad apple won't exist in every bunch, but this should not depict an entire fan base.

One of these bad apples was a 17-year-old named Steve Consalvi, who has the dubious distinction of being the first known fan to ever get tased on a baseball field—and it just so happened to be right here in our backyard. It turns out that Consalvi was harmless and just looking to fulfill his dream. However, the fact of the matter is that the police did what they felt was in the best interests of protecting the players on the field, and perhaps more importantly, the other more civilized fans in the stands. They had no idea that they were chasing after an everyday kid from a suburb 45 miles west of Philly with a motive of showing off for his dad. During the game, Consalvi told his father Wayne that he was going to run onto the field of play. *"This would be a once-in-a-lifetime experience,"* [1] he said to his dad. The elder Consalvi acknowledged to the press that he didn't approve of the stunt and warned him not to do it.

Our country was forever changed on September 11th, 2001, and no sporting event will ever be the same again. In today's world, any crazy thing is possible. It was totally reasonable for the cops to assume that anyone at any time can do the unthinkable at a public event, and Steve Consalvi was certainly no exception to this rule.

JOE:

Dennis, I have watched close to 4,000 Phillies games in my life. In my youth, I blew off plenty of homework assignments and stayed up late just to watch those God-awful 1988 and 1989 squads. I've been the team's batboy for some games, witnessed no-hitters, triple plays, All-Star games, World Series games, and everything in between.

That includes some crazy fan-related incidents that have occurred on the field. There was one guy who thought he was Daniel LaRusso about to take down some Cobra Kai (aka Phillies security), and one particular fan who just wanted to fist bump Pedro Feliz (who actually gave him the 'heads up' that he was about to get pummeled. Pretty funny in retrospect). From afar, the sight of a younger person virtually outrunning five guys on the field does become kind of comical after a few minutes. However, what is often lost here is the fact that this guy or girl could have been stone cold nuts. And although (for better or worse) we have some real characters here in this city, deplorable behavior transcends the City of Philadelphia by leaps and bounds.

Do you remember the fan that bloodied the Astros' Billy Spiers in Milwaukee? How about the fan that attacked Randy Myers of the Cubs before promptly getting dropped by Myers himself? And of course, there was that ugly incident where Royals' first base coach Tom Gamboa was jumped by a father and son duo in Chicago. Keep in mind that, with the exception of the Gamboa incident, all of the above mentioned took place before 9/11, a tragedy that singlehandedly frayed the nerves of everyone. My father and I were in attendance at Super Bowl XXXVI in New Orleans (the first post 9/11 Super Bowl), where there were terrorist threats made throughout the weekend—leaving us with a very unsettling feeling. Security checked us from head to toe upon entrance into the Superdome. Ironically, the fact that the stadium was domed didn't exactly make us feel more secure from the dangers of a possible attack, because we had no idea what was going on outside!

Not only do intolerable acts of fandom occur outside of Philadelphia, but they stretch beyond the four major American sports. A deranged German tennis fan with an unhealthy love for Steffi Graf stabbed Monica Seles back in 1993. Oddly enough, this actually knocked the Phillies off the cover of Sports Illustrated in the process.

Run-ins with fans can result in different outcomes, and this doesn't necessarily apply to just sports. Did you ever see the footage of The Rolling Stones' Keith Richards walloping a fan who looked like he was about to bum rush Mick Jagger? On the other side of this, I was at a Van Halen concert once when a fan rushed Eddie Van Halen, only to shake his hand. While security was throwing the guy off stage, Alex Van Halen motioned for them to bring the guy back so he could bow with the band at the end of their show. Go figure. And as far as Richards goes, he reportedly even bailed the guy out of jail, but that's beside the point.

Although an Oakland Athletics' fan was tased in the stands during a game by Oakland police[2] in 2009, it was not an on-field incident, but it still happened. Does anybody remember Scott James Ashley, who was tased by Pittsburgh cops at a Pirates game at PNC Park[3] after being arrested for abusive language and public drunkenness? Of course you didn't, because "stuff like that only happens in Philly."

Steve Consalvi could have been any 17-year-old from any city in the world, but it just so happened he was a Phillies fan. He certainly wasn't expecting Philadelphia police to treat him like Zach Galifianakis in *The Hangover*. Consalvi didn't have a gun or a knife. Hell, he wasn't even drinking or taking drugs. Like many of us at 17, he did something completely and utterly stupid. Only problem was, he did this in front of a sellout crowd of 45,000 people.

At first, it seemed the policeman's use of the taser on Consalvi was a bit much, considering there have been several reported deaths when a taser gun has been deployed. On the flip side, nobody knows who is playing with a full deck and who isn't these days. At the end of the day, Philly broke new ground again for an example of rabid fan behavior, and not in a good way. For the record, taser guns are still being used at ballparks, as a fan was chased down by a sheriff's deputy waving a taser gun at Safeco Field in Seattle during the summer of 2012 before he finally surrendered without incident. And if you REALLY want to get technical, yes, there have been streakers at Citizens Bank Park as well, but you KNOW they're not hiding anything...

From what I can recall, I've only seen security involved when a fan runs on the field, but never the police. Like many stupid fans before him, Consalvi probably figured he was just going to get tackled. After all, nobody had ever seen anything like a fan getting tased on a baseball field. And come to think of it, nobody has seen it since. I was at Roy Halladay's postseason no-hitter against the Reds, and nobody ran on the field to celebrate with him like that jackass who mobbed Johan Santana after he no-hit the Cardinals a few years later. Although there haven't been many incidents of this ilk at the Bank since the Consalvi tasing, there was the red spandex man who was 'tripped' by Braves' left fielder Matt Diaz a few months later. For the record, Diaz received an ovation from the crowd after "it" was apprehended by security. You have to also keep in mind that somebody was killed outside of McFadden's (the stadium pub) a year earlier in 2009 (although that reportedly stemmed from an argument- not a fan-related incident), so security was not going to take any chances.

All things considered, the general consensus is the police acted appropriately by taking extreme measures of caution to protect the players as well as the sellout crowd. Philadelphia Police Commissioner Charles Ramsey said so himself. A national poll supported this opinion, as well.

Still, the bottom line here is simple. The action taken by police to tase Steve Consalvi was unfortunate, yet a necessary evil. The incident occurred mostly as a result of the insecure, post-9/11 America we all live in. Sad, but true. No chance is worth taking anymore.

Another black eye for Philadelphia sports fans was not the result of 45,000 rowdy, uncontrollable fans in the stands; instead, there was just no better alternative to properly protect those other 44,999 fans. To really put things in perspective, think of it this way: in today's world, we may see Morganna (the Kissing Bandit) Roberts being stunned instead of doing the stunning.

When the dust settled, it turned out Steve Consalvi was just a kid rebelling and seeking attention. He was not a danger to society, or to the people in the ballpark that night. However, he chose a bad venue for his antics, and the cops made sure he found this out the hard way.

Much like Santa Claus found out at the "evil" hands of the Philadelphia fans that day at Franklin Field...over 40 years ago.

11

WIN, LOSE OR DRAW...
PHILLY FANS REACT VIOLENTLY

Luckily, Philadelphia teams never win enough championships to totally unleash their crazy, violent fans on the innocent bystanders and poor, unsuspecting businesses that happen to be in the way of these hooligans.

It is well documented that Philly fans are violent to any opposing player or fan during games, but they are even less magnanimous and peaceful in celebration. Philadelphia is the only city that had to have mounted police and German shepherds lining the Veterans Stadium turf as pitcher Tug McGraw was about to strike out Willie Wilson to end the 1980 World Series.

Yes, even the city of Philadelphia knew that their own fans were violent, and it has been fortunate that their teams have only won it all twice since that cold, fall day in 1980.

"All told, Philadelphia stadiums house the most monstrous collection of humanity outside of the federal penal system. 'Some of these people would boo the crack in the Liberty Bell,' baseball legend Pete Rose once said. More likely, these savages would have thrown the battery that cracked it."

-Adam Winer, GQ Magazine, March 2011

RESPONSE: RYAN DOWNS

Sports and violence often go hand in hand. Heck, depending on the sport, violence is— at least in some form—a part of the game. Just ask the New Orleans Saints. Beyond the field of play, however, violence seems to creep in at the biggest moments: when a championship is at stake.

In recent years in Philadelphia, the futility of our sports teams—especially in crunch time—*has* been well documented. Since 1983, our four sports teams have lost a combined nine times with the title on the line. One may ask how much more can fans in this city take.

Thus, the prevailing thought was that the city would go insane with the next championship, and the level of anticipation (and insanity) only increased with each subsequent setback.

Yet, despite all these instances—the thrill of rare victory or the agony of another crushing defeat—the Philadelphia fans have kept their collective composure. When carefully examined, you will be hard pressed to find any fan-related incident in the history of Philadelphia sports championships that extend beyond the realm of petty crimes and misdemeanors. The perception is not really even close to the reality.

After the Phillies won the World Series in 2008—ending a quarter century drought and alleviating decades of doubt, frustration, and irritation—there was plenty of emotion filling the streets, but most of it was positive. Sure, you had your collections of delinquents and idiots look-ing for any excuse to steal and destroy, but they were the exceptions to the rule. The pages read *"Philly riots at a minimum"* and incidents of *"requisite looting and vandalism."*

Nothing violent here: The greatest moment in Philly sports history in the last 30 years.

That's pretty much the extent of it.

Essentially, requisite looting and vandalism is layman's terms for basic idiocy that could have happened any other night for any other reason, here or in any other city.

Speaking of other cities, such examples of violence have occurred all over the map as a result of championship wins and losses. In the past ten years alone, you can point to a plethora of despicable situations which have taken place throughout the country and, in some cases, just outside of it.

Here is a brief overview of the stark contrast between Philadelphia and other places that have actually turned to violence—in both good times and bad:

DETROIT:

Widely credited with being the riot that put violent sports celebrations "on the map" in the U.S., the celebration of the 1984 Tigers' World Series victory resulted in countless arrests and injuries and reports of rape and murder in its aftermath. Police officers on horseback tried desperately to control the mayhem, which was littered with fires and overturned vehicles.

And as if that wasn't enough, the Motor City fans took to the streets again in 1990 following the Pistons second consecutive NBA title, and proceeded to shoot, stab, and loot at an alarming rate. The result: several dead, hundreds injured, and more than 100 arrests.

Even for a city largely defined as much for crime and violence as it is for automobiles, these incidents were dreadful and unforgettable, leaving a lasting imprint amongst the realm of violent sports incidents.

BOSTON:

Prior to the Bruins' championship in 2011, there had been a vicious, unfortunate consistency in Beantown over the last decade in sports. Each of their four major sports teams had won championships, and some of the collateral damage was horrific – and at times even fatal.

Following the 2004 Patriots' Super Bowl celebration, a young man was killed after being hit by a car. After the Red Sox won the 2004 American League Championship in an epic comeback against the rival Yankees, a college student was killed by a flying projectile during a violent outburst in which police resorted to using pepper guns. In 2008, another young man lost his life when he stopped breathing while in police custody during the Celtics championship celebration (although it was reported that he had a heart condition).

However, to the city's credit, these incidents were instrumental in motivating the city to increase preparation for the Bruins Stanley Cup victory in 2011. The result was far less incidents of violence and property damage and mercifully, no fatalities.

Yet, despite the fact that these unfortunate incidents were all publicized, Red Sox Nation and the citizens of Boston live on as darlings of the national sports media.

LOS ANGELES:

The City of Angels was hardly full of angels after the Lakers won the 2000 NBA title over the Indiana Pacers. Fans ran into the streets and started bonfires, which morphed into a full-blown riot, resulting in substantial property damage throughout the city.

In 2009, a riot ensued after the Lakers won yet another championship. Fans danced on parked cars and even turned a news van over. This once again resulted in significant property damage throughout the city. L.A. Times reporter Adam Rose was there to witness the unruly behavior.

"I was standing between LA Live and Staples Center within an hour of the Lakers' victory. I was walking the streets a little further east as the LAPD struggled to chase the last of the knuckleheads from downtown. What should have been a proud moment for the redeveloped area was anything but." [1]

The Los Angeles police had their fill and put the fans on notice in 2010. Again, the Lakers won the championship and—once again—the fans began to riot. According to Time Magazine reporter Madison Gray:

"Despite a heavy police presence, which was publicized yesterday by Mayor Antonio Villagairosa and police chief Charlie Beck, fans who were ecstatic over the Lakers' Game 7 victory over the Boston Celtics

met near the Staples Center, throwing bottles and debris at cops, and setting fire along arteries leading from the arena." [2]

In one case, a police officer had his nose broken by an object flying through the mayhem. A total of 10 people were injured and 50 arrested.

Throwing bottles at cops? Breaking their noses? Enough is enough. Poor Lakers fans, it must be tough to win all those championships.

VANCOUVER:

In 1994, all hell broke loose in Vancouver following a Game 7 Stanley Cup Finals loss to the New York Rangers. The fans took to the streets as if they were protesting atrocities by the government. The result was $1.1 million in damage to the downtown area, and a reported 200 injuries.

To make matters worse, things got even uglier in 2011 following another devastating Game 7 Finals loss, this time to the Bruins. This time it happened at home, and $5 million in damages was incurred. For a city widely known as a marijuana-toking, feel-good town full of hippies, the feeling wasn't so laid back on this night. A litany of violent acts turned disappointment into disaster, as fires, overturned cars, and burning police vehicles littered the city now most infamous for being violent sore losers.

There were a total of nearly 100 arrests and roughly 150 injuries reported in the angry outburst. Fans were not happy, and understandably so. But these types of actions are just reprehensible and unfortunate.

As you can plainly see, all of the aforementioned cities—and more— have had widespread reports of reprehensible fan-related violence. But you won't find any such incidents reported in Philadelphia. Sure, Philly fans may be involved in some scuffles, as is the case in many crowds at sporting events, but not to the extent that is often publicized.

The reality is that no matter how you slice it, there is collateral damage in every city after a championship. The stakes are high and so are the emotions. However, it is the extent of the damage that is the most telling. Considering Philadelphia has won one title over a quarter of a century, the sample size appears smaller, but it is the lack of attention given to some of these other heinous incidents that is a bit disheartening to the Philadelphia fan. Especially since our fans never did go insane after any of our heartbreaking championship losses.

The feeling in Philadelphia is that the national media should pay more attention to the people who died on the streets of Detroit and Boston, as well as the senseless violence in the streets of Los Angeles and Vancouver. The actions of other cities seem to get swept under the rug real quick. As mentioned, the City of Brotherly Love did not erupt into combustible, widespread violence and mayhem when the Phillies finally brought home that elusive championship in 2008. For all intents and purposes, the city rejoiced without incident—and that fact was not emphasized in the media. Not one bit.

In all actuality, this is the way things should operate. That said, if there was any major incident in Philadelphia after the 2008 World Series, it would have made the front page of every major newspaper and sports media publication known to man. It almost certainly would have dwarfed the publicity that came out of Boston, Detroit, L.A., or Vancouver. Contrary to popular belief, such violence—in both victory and defeat—is something much more prevalent outside of Philadelphia.

Almost two years after the Phillies won the World Series—in June 2010— the city of Philadelphia hosted a Stanley Cup celebration. The only problem was it did not break the Flyers 35-year Stanley Cup drought; instead, it ended the 49-year drought for the visiting Chicago Blackhawks. A soft and shocking goal allowed by Michael Leighton in sudden death overtime stunned Flyers fans into submission, ending a magical postseason run. The goal was so sudden and brutal that hardly anyone realized the game, and season, was over—except, of course, goal scorer Patrick Kane. And as if that wasn't enough misery for Flyers fans, here's a little more salt to throw into that wound: The Blackhawks selected Kane as the #1 overall pick in the 2007 NHL Draft (the Flyers drafted the injury-prone and recently jettisoned James van Riemsdyk at #2), despite the fact that the Flyers had the worst record in the league.

The impending celebration was agonizing for long-suffering Flyers fans, who were unfairly criticized for booing NHL Commissioner Gary Bettman—a widespread and rightful target of hockey fans everywhere. Beyond this though, the Philly fans treated the Blackhawks with respect and, more importantly, took to the streets without incident. This is more than can be said the following season (in a similar situation) when Western Canada was ignited.

Vancouver, as well as the other cities noted, had incidents far more violent and gruesome than anything that ever occurred in Philadelphia. But you'd never know that by paying attention to the talking heads in the national media.

Once upon a time in Philadelphia, we threw snowballs. Cold, wet balls of precipitation. No fires, no overturned police cars, no rapes or murders. Yet, somehow *we're* still the bad guys.

This is further proof that reputations ultimately burn brighter than flames.

CLOSING REMARKS

BY BRAD LIDGE

Whether or not the fans in Philadelphia know it, they have a reputation that extends far beyond the great city of Philadelphia. I grew up in Colorado and that is where I live, but don't think that just because Colorado is almost 2,000 miles west of Philadelphia that this reputation doesn't stretch there. It goes far beyond that—all around the cities of the west coast. So whenever I am home in Colorado, talking baseball with my friends, or with total strangers, people want to know more than just what it was like to throw the last pitch of the World Series in 2008. They want to know about the fans. When people ask me what I think about the Philadelphia fans, I have to laugh for a second and say the first thing that comes to my mind:

You wouldn't believe it if I told you.

Of course they want to hear details, so I give it to 'em.

I'll tell them about the time in 2008, during our first series at home against the Mets, when I saw a Mets fan come down by the bullpen and start ragging on us and talking too much smack to the Phillies' fans.

I tell them that what happened to that fan was not pretty, as he was decked with a punch, dropped to the ground and jumped on. The whole incident lasted fairly long and when it was over and he was finally helped up off the ground with a bloodied face by security guard, he was the one kicked out, not the Phillies fans.

When I tell my friends in Colorado that story, they invariably come back with a *"whoa"* and an incredulous look on their face. Now I tell them I surely don't condone violence but I also tell them that I have to admit, it was pretty awesome watching it unfold.

That incident was one of my first forays into the tastes of the passion, and the ravenous desire to defend their team that I had seen.

Here's some more questions, comments and so on I hear all the time from my friends in Colorado, followed by my answers:

Do they boo their own players all the time like I heard?

"OK, that is sometimes true, but I'll tell you what, when you get booed in Philly, you know you have it coming. Chances are you sucked that night, or that month, and it's not a surprise. Guess what else, if you get the job done then and there, even if you are having a bad year, they cheer the hell out of you and that's that. They want to win like everyone else's fans, they just want to win MORE. In most places, after a bad game, fans go home unhappy and then start their lives again, forgetting the game. Not so in Philly. These losses hurt them, sometimes worse than the players it seems."

So they are invested in the team more than other cities. That's just for show?

The answer is easy for that one:

"If you could have seen how many fans came up to me after 2008, with sincere tears in their eyes, telling me I had no idea what that meant to them and their families, the dads, and their grandparents, who they had watched every game with for as long as they could remember: If you could see the pride these fans had on Broad Street that fall, you'd know it's not for show, it's for real."

Ok, ok, they are passionate, I'll give 'em that, but it's like they are in their own world, not knowing about any other teams, they only know about their players.

"When I was a visiting player, closing for the Houston Astros, I would dare say that they knew my stats better than I did. How do I know that? Cause if I had one stat that wasn't pristine I would hear about it the second batting practice started, never mind when I was warming up in the bullpen."

What was that like?

"It wasn't fun. You had better be wearing a hard hat if you are a visiting player, cause you are gonna get shelled. They know your stats, they know just what to say, they know your family's names for goodness sakes. I know closers who normally get to the bullpen in the fifth inning or so, but when they come to Philly, you won't see them down there until the seventh. They don't want that kind of abuse for two extra innings."

So, when they are cheering you on, does that really help you out as a player?

"I think there is an energy that is working through those fans that is just stronger than other places. If you are pitching against the Phillies, all that energy is going against you, but when you are about to throw that last pitch of the World Series, that energy is coursing through your veins, you let it in and it feels like you are invincible. Yes, that energy exists in other stadiums, but just not as much of it."

Wow...that is amazing, I guess they are the most passionate fans. But they still boo their own players!

What can I say about the fans in Philly. They are simply into it more than other places. If I was them I'd be proud as hell of my reputation, cause it makes winning in that city the absolute pinnacle of sports.

Brad Lidge is one of only two Philadelphia Phillies pitchers to close out a World Series title.

ABOUT THE AUTHORS

Joe Vallee is one pretty patient guy. After all, this WAS the same kid who ditched his homework to stay up and watch the Phillies in the mid-1980's. For his patience, Joe was rewarded with a World Championship in 2008. During that time, Joe either bat boyed in some of those games or had a front row seat by way of his family's season tickets for most of them. Before you give him too much credit, this is the same guy who pushed his way to the front of the White House line to get a picture of him and Ronald Reagan because his head was down when the first picture was taken.

Joe is a graduate from Bishop Eustace Prep and Saint Joseph's University in the fields of English and Business. Joe hosted his own radio show, but after failing to secure an internship while in college at a certain station, Joe continued to work his way up in the family business at Vallee and Bowe Cadillac in Woodbury, New Jersey, before they closed its doors in 2006.

Joe has indeed had a crazy journey, picking up the pieces numerous times and landing several odd jobs to make ends meet (even painting houses in twenty degree weather!). In April 2008, he started Philly2Philly.com with Dennis Bakay. After a year of planning, the website launched in June 2009 and has reached over 2 million views. On the side, Joe is a musician, having released two albums with his bands while drumming in practically every venue in the Tri-State area for 13 years. He was a contestant on 97.5 FM the Fanatic's Dream Job, guest hosted 'The Artie Clear Show' with Artie Clear, and broadcasted podcasts for "The Daily" on the Apple i-Pad as well as video game commercials for Activision. His voice can also be heard on numerous KYW News Radio commercials.

Joe currently resides in Woodbury, New Jersey.

Dennis Bakay is a Montgomery County native, graduate of Temple University, and co-founder of Philly2Philly.com along with Joe Vallee.

Dennis is a true four-for-four Philly sports fan. He doesn't proudly admit that he was a bit of a "front runner" when he was younger. This was before he understood what Philly sports are all about. Being a Philly sports fan is a religion and a lifestyle for him. He still isn't over the Eagles' brutal defeat to the Tampa Bucs in the 2002 NFC Championship Game and the Phillies' 1-0 Game Five NLDS loss to the Cardinals in 2011.

Dennis points to 2004 as the most brutal year in Philly sports history-thanks to the Eagles' loss to the Panthers in the NFC Title Game, the Flyers' loss to the Lightning in the Eastern Conference Finals, St. Joe's losing to Oklahoma State in the Elite 8, Smarty Jones choking in the final leg of the Triple Crown, and yet another disappointing season by the Phillies during the Bowa-era.

Dennis is currently employed as a manufacturing engineer for a wire harness company in Norristown. He resides in Berks County with his wife Amanda and their furry son Martin, a 10-year-old Shiba-Inu / German Shepherd mix.

Ryan Downs is a lifelong Philadelphia sports fan. He was an employee of the Reading Phillies while in high school. Ryan has a bachelor's degree in English and a Master's degree in Business Administration from Saint Joseph's University. He has also served as a contributing sports writer to Philly2Philly.com.

A native of Reading, Ryan now lives in Blue Bell, Pennsylvania with his wife Maria, daughter Allison, and dog Sammie.

Matt Goldberg, the author of four previous books, is a dynamic writer and public speaker who writes and speaks with both clarity and hilarity. That is a rarity.

A natural humorist who was described by a best-selling author as "a genius of words and a genius of comedy," Matt is passionate about providing smiles and laughs and *just enough wisdom* as both an award-winning writer and speaker. At the same time, he has been known to take both his humor and his sports very seriously.

In the last two-plus years, Matt has published well over 200 eclectic sports columns for publications including *Philly2Philly.com*, *jewocity.com* and *Bleacher Report*. This creator of both *Bagels and Jocks* (a weekly column on the Jewish sports scene...yes, there is one) and *Wordapodia* (he has created and defined nearly 300 new "wordapods") also provided the voice of the national media editor for this book.

A lifelong Philly sports fan, Matt resides in Cherry Hill, NJ with his wife and son. For more information about his books and columns, and for custom writing and speaking requests, visit www.tipofthegoldberg.com, or contact via matt@tipofthegoldberg.com.

Billy Vargus is best known for his work as a sports anchor in the Philadelphia area, most recently for Fox 29, where he did his thing for 12 years. Known to many viewers simply as "Billy V," he was nominated for Emmy Awards 9 times, and won the Emmy for "Best Sports Anchor" in the Mid-Atlantic region in 2008 and 2009.

After graduating from Temple University, Billy V. worked for several different radio stations in Philly before turning to television as a news writer at Channel 3 (formally KYW-TV). He made his on-air debut less than a year later at WHYY-TV, covering sports in Philly and Delaware, as well as moonlighting as a fill-in anchor for Channel 10 (now NBC10 Philadelphia).

After a stint at WWOR-TV in New York and Channel 4 in Buffalo, Billy V. returned to Philly in 1997, anchoring, co-hosting the Philadelphia Eagles post-game shows and doing some sideline reporting for the Fox Network on NFL games.

For the past three years, Billy V. has been a full-time actor, producer and voice-over artist.

CHAPTER QUOTE REFERENCES

Ch. 1

"Philly fans' rogue image got boost when Santa booed in 1968 - NFL - ESPN." *ESPN: The Worldwide Leader In Sports*. Associated Press, 31 Jan. 2005. Web. 29 Sept. 2012.

<http://sports.espn.go.com/espn/wire?section=nfl&id=1980880>.

Ch. 2

Levy, Dan. "Andy Reid: Fans and Media in Philly Have Already Fired Him, but Will the Eagles? | Bleacher Report." *Bleacher Report | Entertaining sports news, photos and slideshows*. N.p., 29 Nov. 2011. Web. 29 Sept. 2012

Ch. 3

Kapadia, Sheil. "Deion Sanders rips Eagles fans." *Philly.com: News from the Philadelphia Inquirer, Philadelphia Daily News and Philly Sports*. N.p., 28 Nov. 2008. Web. 29 Sept. 2012.

Ch. 4

Stewart, Wayne. "Wacky Quotes." *The Gigantic Book of Baseball Quotations*. New York, NY: Skyhorse Pub, 2007. 560. Print.

Ch. 5

Johnson, Bailey. "Flyers fans pick wrong time to boo (during anti-cancer PSA) - Sports Blog - CBS News." *Breaking News Headlines: Business,*

Entertainment & World News - CBS News. CBS Interactive Inc., 13 Oct. 2011. Web. 29 Sept. 2012.

<http://www.cbsnews.com/8301-31751_162-20119831-10391697. html>.

Ch. 6

DeMarco, Tony. "Joe Maddon: Talking Schmidt's, Rolling Rock and Coors Light - National MLB | Examiner.com." *Welcome to Examiner. com | Examiner.com.* N.p., 26 Oct. 2008. Web. 11 Oct. 2012.

Ch. 7

Macnow, Glen, and Big D. Graham. *The Great Book of Philadelphia Sports Lists.* Philadelphia, PA: Running Press, 2006. 34. Print.

Ch. 8

"Mike Schmidt Quotes." *Baseball Almanac.* Baseball Almanac, Inc., 1974. Web. 29 Sept. 2012.

Ch. 9

"CNN/SI - NFL Football - Irvin injury brings out worst in Philly fans - Thursday October 14, 1999 07:21 PM." *Breaking news, real-time scores and daily analysis from Sports Illustrated SI.com.* Associated Press, 14 Oct. 1999. Web. 29 Sept. 2012.

Ch. 10

Siemaszko, Corky. "VIDEO: Phillies fan Tasered after running across field: 17-yr.-old hit with stun gun - New York Daily News." *Featured Articles From The New York Daily News.* N.p., 4 May 2010. Web. 29 Sept. 2012.

Ch. 11

Winer, Adam. "The Worst Sports Fans in America: Lists: GQ." *GQ Magazine Online: Look Sharp, Live Smart: GQ.* N.p., Apr. 2011. Web. 29 Sept. 2012.

REFERENCES

Ch. 1

1. "Joe Kuharich Record, Statistics, and Category Ranks - Pro-Football-Reference.com." *Pro-Football-Reference.com - Pro Football Statistics and History*. N.p., n.d. Web. 29 Sept. 2012.

Ch. 2

1. "Umenyiora, Giants sack Eagles 16-3 - NFL- NBC Sports." *Sports News Headlines - NFL, NBA, NHL, MLB, PGA, NASCAR - Scores, Game Highlights, Schedules & Team Rosters - NBC Sports*. Associated Press, 1 Oct. 2007. Web. 29 Sept. 2012. <http://nbcsports.msnbc.com/id/21072362/>.

2. "Jeffrey Lurie's press conference: Transcript." *Comcast SportsNet Philadelphia*. Comcast Sportsnet Philly L.P., 3 Jan. 2012. Web. 29 Sept. 2012.

<http://www.csnphilly.com/blog/eagles-talk/post/Jeffrey-Luries-press-conference-Transcri?blockID=624176>

3. Perez, A.J. "Philadelphia Eagles fans point the finger at Andy Reid - NFL News | FOX Sports on MSN." *FOX Sports on MSN l Sports News, Scores, Schedules, Videos and Fantasy Games*. N.p., 28 Nov. 2011. Web. 29 Sept. 2012.

<http://msn.foxsports.com/nfl/story/Andy-Reid-Philadelphia-Eagles-New-England-Patriots-takes-the-blame-112711>.

4. "NFL Network's Mike Mayock Says Dominique Rodgers Chromartie Is As Gifted As Any Cornerback He Has Ever Seen In His Life | m.975thefanatic.com." *m.975thefanatic.com.* WPEN, 3 Aug. 2012.

http://m.975thefanatic.com/2012/08/nfl-networks-mike-mayock-says-dominique-rodgers-chromartie-is-as-gifted-as-any-cornerback-he-has-ever-seen-in-his-life/. Web. 29 Sept. 2012.

5. Swartz, Cody. "How Does Andy Reid Do Against Playoff Teams?" *Rant Sports — Sports News, Rumors, Videos and More.* Rant Media Network, LLC., 18 Jan. 2012. Web. 29 Sept. 2012.

<http://www.rantsports.com/philadelphia-eagles/2012/01/18/how-does-andy-reid-do-against-playoff-teams/>.

6. Pasceri, Ron. "Philadelphia Eagles: Andy Reid's Struggles in Winning Time | Bleacher Report." *Bleacher Report | Entertaining sports news, photos and slideshows.* Bleacher Report, Inc., 9 Feb. 2012. Web. 29 Sept. 2012.

7. [a][b] McLane, Jeff. "On the Eagles defense, does size matter? - Philly.com." *Featured Articles from Philly.com.* Philadelphia Media Network, Inc., 22 Jan. 2012. Web. 29 Sept. 2012.

<http://articles.philly.com/2012-01-22/sports/30652962_1_eagles-fans-howie-roseman-eagles-defense>.

8. [a][b][c] "6/1/11: Colin Cowherd Joins Mikey Miss To Talk About Andy Reid, Donovan McNabb And Perception Of Philadelphia - News // All | 97.5 The Fanatic." *Philadelphia's First FM Sports Station | 97.5 The Fanatic.* WPEN, 6 June 2011. Web. 9 Oct. 2012.

9. Aronson, Arielle. "It Is What It Is » Boomer Esiason on D&C: Eagles have 'a bunch of lunatics'." *It Is What It Is.* N.p., 28 Nov. 2011. Web. 29 Sept. 2012.

<http://itiswhatitis.weei.com/sports/newengland/football/patriots/2011/11/28/boomer-esiason-on-dc-eagles-have-a-bunch-of-lunatics/>.

10. Smith, Michael D. "Andy Reid on Peyton report: I have final say, and Vick is our guy | ProFootballTalk." *ProFootballTalk.* N.p., 23 Mar. 2012. Web. 29 Sept. 2012.

<http://profootballtalk.nbcsports.com/2012/03/23/andy-reid-on-peyton-report-i-have-final-say-and-vick-is-our-guy/>.

11. Neal. "14 Reasons Why Philadelphia Has The Worst Fans In Sports «." *COEDMagazine – College Lifestyle | Sexy Girls | Funny Photos | Beer Culture | Sports | Celebrities*. Coed Media Group, 11 Jan. 2012. Web. 29 Sept. 2012.

<http://coedmagazine.com/2012/01/11/philadelphia-worst-sports-fans/>.

Ch. 3

1. Kapadia, Sheil. "Hopkins rips McNabb (again)." *Philly.com: News from the Philadelphia Inquirer, Philadelphia Daily News and Philly Sports*. Philadelphia Media Network, 12 Nov. 2008. Web. 9 Oct. 2012.

<http://www.philly.com/philly/blogs/moving_the_chains/Hopkins_critical_of_McNabb_again.html>

2. Kapadia, Sheil. "Deion Sanders rips Eagles fans." *Philly.com: News from the Philadelphia Inquirer, Philadelphia Daily News and Philly Sports*. N.p., 28 Nov. 2008. Web. 29 Sept. 2012.

3. Wilbon, Michael. "Michael Wilbon - Washington Redskins' trade for Donovan McNabb is a perfect fit." *Washington Post: Breaking News, World, US, DC News & Analysis*. N.p., 5 Apr. 2010. Web. 9 Oct. 2012.

<http://www.washingtonpost.com/wp-dyn/content/article/2010/04/04/AR2010040403463.html>.

4. Hill, Jemele. "Donovan McNabb deserves cheers from Eagles fans, a win in return to Philly - ESPN." *ESPN: The Worldwide Leader In Sports*. ESPN.com, 29 Sept. 2010. Web. 29 Sept. 2012. <http://sports.espn.go.com/espn/commentary/news/story?id=5629567>

5. Mosley, Matt. "McNabb makes himself at home in Philly - NFC East Blog - ESPN." *ESPN: The Worldwide Leader In Sports*. ESPN, 10 Oct. 2010. Web. 9 Oct. 2012.

6. [a] "Mike Shanahan says Donovan McNabb not in shape for 2-minute drill - ESPN." *ESPN: The Worldwide Leader In Sports*. Associated Press, 2 Nov. 2010. Web. 29 Sept. 2012.

7. Maese, Rick. "Redskins Insider - Donovan McNabb: 'I respect Mike's decision as a head coach, but I strongly disagree with it.'." *Blogs & Columns, Blog Directory - The Washington Post*. The Washington Post, 17 Dec. 2010. Web. 9 Oct. 2012.

<http://voices.washingtonpost.com/redskinsinsider/donovan-mcnabb-i-respect-mikes.html>.

8. Preston, Dave. "McNabb: RG III might not fit with Redskins (VIDEO) - WTOP.com." *WTOP.com - Washington, DC News, Traffic & Weather - A CBS Affiliate - WTOP.com*. WTOP., 29 Mar. 2012. Web. 12 Oct. 2012.

<http://www.wtop.com/41/2807392/McNabb-RG-III-might-not-fit-with-Redskins-VIDEO>.

9. [a][b][c] Smith, Michael D. "McNabb: I'm the most unfairly criticized quarterback in NFL history | ProFootballTalk." *ProFootballTalk*. NBC Universal, 30 Mar. 2012. Web. 29 Sept. 2012.

<http://profootballtalk.nbcsports.com/2012/03/30/mcnabb-im-the-most-unfairly-criticized-quarterback-in-nfl-history/>

Ch. 4

1. "Booing." *Wikipedia, the free encyclopedia*. Wikimedia Foundation, Inc.. 22 Jan 2004. Web. 24 August 2012. <http://en.wikipedia.org/wiki/Booing>

2. Burke, Don. "Can't Stop The Bleeding » Billy Wagner's Fond Memories Of Philly." *Can't Stop The Bleeding*. Newark Star-Ledger, 26 Feb. 2006. Web. 29 Sept. 2012.

<http://www.cantstopthebleeding.com/billy-wagners-fond-memories-of-philly>.

3. Macnow, Glen, and Big D. Graham. *The Great Book of Philadelphia Sports Lists*. Philadelphia, PA: Running Press, 2006. 33. Print.

4. Miller, Randy. *Harry the K: The Remarkable Life of Harry Kalas*. Philadelphia, PA: Running Press, 2010. 262. Print.

5. Zolecki, Todd. "Eaton plans to pitch somewhere in '09 | MLB.com: News." *The Official Site of Major League Baseball | MLB.com: Homepage*. 13 Feb. 2009. Web. 29 Sept. 2012.

6. Murphy, David. "Phillies Notebook: Could Hamels handle pressure of World Series Game 7? - Philly.com." *Featured Articles from Philly.com.* Philadelphia Media Network, Inc., 2 Nov. 2009. Web. 29 Sept. 2012.

7. "Iguodala: Lou Williams 'can't guard anybody'." *Comcast SportsNet Philadelphia.* Comcast Sportsnet Philly L.P., 4 Apr. 2012. Web. 29 Sept. 2012.

8. Mooney, Michael J. "The full story of Terrell Owens's time with the Allen Wranglers of the Indoor Football League - Grantland." *Sports and Pop Culture from Bill Simmons and our rotating cast of writers - Grantland.* N.p., 21 June 2012. Web. 29 Sept. 2012.

9. Kilgore, Adam. "Jayson Werth: I'm motivated by Phillies fans - Nationals Journal - The Washington Post." *Washington Post: Breaking News, World, US, DC News & Analysis.* N.p., 7 May 2012. Web. 29 Sept. 2012.

<http://www.washingtonpost.com/blogs/nationals-journal/post/jayson-werth-im-motivated-by-phillies-fans/2012/05/07/gIQALdil8T_blog.html>.

10. Farmer, Sam. "Troy Aikman as an Eagle? - Los Angeles Times." *Featured Articles From The Los Angeles Times.* N.p., 1 Nov. 2009. Web. 29 Sept. 2012.

<http://articles.latimes.com/2009/nov/01/sports/sp-nfl-sunday1>.

11. Finger, John. "Philly Villains: No. 18 Chipper Jones." *Comcast SportsNet Philadelphia.* Comcast Sportsnet Philly L.P. , 29 Jan. 2012. Web. 29 Sept. 2012. <http://www.csnphilly.com/blog/villains/post/philly-villains-no-18-chipper-jones?blockID=631974>.

Ch. 5

1. Jason (AKA- Sportress of Blogitude). "Flyers fans boo 'Hockey Fights Cancer' PSA featuring rival players | Yardbarker.com." *Yardbarker: Sports Rumors, Gossip, Blogs, News, Discussion.* Sportress of Blogitude, 13 Oct. 2011. Web. 29 Sept. 2012.

<http://www.yardbarker.com/nhl/articles/msn/philadelphia_flyers_fans_boo_anti_cancer_ad_featuring_rival_players_during_game/7391497?GT1=39002>.

2. Johnson, Bailey. "Flyers fans pick wrong time to boo (during anti-cancer PSA) - Sports Blog - CBS News." *Breaking News Headlines:*

Business, Entertainment & World News - CBS News. CBS Interactive Inc., 13 Oct. 2011. Web. 29 Sept. 2012.

<http://www.cbsnews.com/8301-31751_162-20119831-10391697.html>.

3. Wyshynski, Greg. "Flyers fans boo rivals; alas, it's during an anticancer commercial - Puck Daddy - NHL Blog - Yahoo! Sports." *Yahoo! Sports - Sports News, Scores, Rumors, Fantasy Games, and more*. N.p., 12 Oct. 2011. Web. 29 Sept. 2012.

We'll Give You That

1. Weir, Tom. "Phillies fan charged with intentionally vomiting on cop's kid." *USA TODAY: Latest World and US News - USATODAY.com*. N.p., 16 Apr. 2010. Web. 29 Sept. 2012. <http://content.USAtoday.com/communities/gameon/post/2010/04/phillies-fan-charged-with-intentionally-vomiting-on-cops-kid/1#.UCiMJZ2PWD9>.

Ch. 6

1. Gloster, Rob. "Phillies Pass Yankees, Red Sox to Become No. 1 MLB Team in Fan Loyalty - Bloomberg." *Bloomberg - Business, Financial & Economic News, Stock Quotes*. BLOOMBERG L.P., 21 Mar. 2011. Web. 29 Sept. 2012.

<http://www.bloomberg.com/news/2011-03-21/phillies-pass-yankees-red-sox-to-become-no-1-mlb-team-in-fan-loyalty.html>.

Ch. 7

1. "Pat Burrell." *Wikipedia, the free encyclopedia*. Wikimedia Foundation, Inc.. 22 Jan 2004. Web. 26 September 2012. <http://en.wikipedia.org/wiki/Pat_Burrell#2007>

2. [a] Vallee, Joe. "Phillies' New Wall Of Famer John Kruk epitomized the Philadelphia Athlete | Philly2Philly.com." *Philly2Philly. com | Everyday Philly For Everyday People*. Game Time Media, LLC, 16 Aug. 2011. Web. 11 Oct. 2012. <http://www.philly2philly.com/sports/sports_articles/2011/8/16/57604/phillies_new_wall_famer_john_kruk_epitomized_the_philadelphia>.

3. "Philadelphia Phillies' Cole Hamels signs $144 million contract extension -ESPN." *ESPN: The Worldwide Leader In Sports*. ESPN.com, 27 June 2012. Web. 29 Sept. 2012. <http://espn.go.com/mlb/story/_/id/8197964/philadelphia-phillies-cole-hamels-signs-144-million-contract-extension>.

Ch. 8

1. "Mike Schmidt Quotes." *Baseball Almanac*. Baseball Almanac, Inc., 9 Mar. 1989. Web. 29 Sept. 2012.

2. "Mike Schmidt Quotes." *Baseball Almanac*. Baseball Almanac, Inc., Web. 29 Sept. 2012.

3. "Mike Schmidt Quotes." *Baseball Almanac*. Baseball Almanac, Inc., 26 May. 1990.. Web. 29 Sept. 2012.

Ch. 10

1. Gay, Jason. "Steve Consalvi, Tasered in Philadelphia During Phillies-Mets Game, Would Have Electrified New York - WSJ.com." *Business News & Financial News - The Wall Street Journal - Wsj.com*. Dow Jones & Company, Inc., 5 May 2010. Web. 29 Sept. 2012.

<http://online.wsj.com/article/SB100014240527487038667045752242 70138328614.html>.

2. "Disruptive fan Tasered at Oakland Athletics game | abc7news.com." *ABC Owned Television Stations*. ABC Inc., KGO-TV/DT San Francisco, CA, 6 Aug. 2009. Web. 29 Sept. 2012. <http://abclocal.go.com/kgo/ story?section=news/local/east_bay&id=6952731>.

3. "Report: Pittsburgh Pirates fan clubbed and tasered by police at PNC Park - MLB News | FOX Sports on MSN." *FOX Sports on MSN | Sports News, Scores, Schedules, Videos and Fantasy Games*. Fox Sports Interactive Media, LLC., 12 Apr. 2011. Web. 29 Sept. 2012.

Ch. 11

1. Rose, Adam. "Lakers riot: Walking through downtown Los Angeles after the NBA championship - latimes.com." *Blogs - latimes.com*. N.p., 15 June 2009. Web. 29 Sept. 2012. <http://latimesblogs.latimes.com/ sports_blog/2009/06/lakers-celebrations.html>.

2. Gray, Madison. "L.A. Riots Sparked After Lakers Win | NewsFeed | TIME.com." *NewsFeed | Breaking news and updates from Time.com. News pictures, video, Twitter trends. | TIME.com*. N.p., 18 June 2010. Web. 29 Sept. 2012.

Made in the USA
San Bernardino, CA
02 January 2014